THE
INVESTING
OASIS

THE
INVESTING
OASIS

Contrarian Treasure in the
Capital Markets Desert

J.T. Mason

WILEY

Published by John Wiley & Sons, Inc., Hoboken, New Jersey.
Published simultaneously in Canada.

For general information on our other products and services or for technical support, please contact our Customer Care Department within the United States at (800) 762-2974, outside the United States at (317) 572-3993 or fax (317) 572-4002.

Wiley also publishes its books in a variety of electronic formats. Some content that appears in print may not be available in electronic formats. For more information about Wiley products, visit our web site atwww.wiley.com.

Library of Congress Cataloging-in-Publication Data

Names: Mason, J. T. (Jay T.), author.
Title: The investing oasis : contrarian treasure in the capital markets
    desert / J. T. Mason.
Description: Hoboken, New Jersey : Wiley, [2023] | Includes index.
Identifiers: LCCN 2022008582 (print) | LCCN 2022008583 (ebook) | ISBN
    9781119871088 (cloth) | ISBN 9781119871101 (adobe pdf) | ISBN
    9781119871095 (epub)
Subjects: LCSH: Investments. | Portfolio management.
Classification: LCC HG4521 .M347 2022 (print) | LCC HG4521 (ebook) | DDC
    332.6–dc23/eng/20220329
LC record available at https://lccn.loc.gov/2022008582
LC ebook record available at https://lccn.loc.gov/2022008583

Cover Design: Paul McCarthy
Cover Art: Sky: © Getty Images | Romanovskyy
Desert: © Shutterstock | USTAS7777777
Photo: John C. Watson / IMPS

*As her favorite "investment guy," my mother supported my career by willingly moving
her funds between institutions with each progressive step. Yet, even into
her failing years, she extended trust to allow me to manage her wealth in her better
interests. Through good and bad markets, if she ever worried, I never
heard about it.*

The Investing Oasis *is dedicated to Mollie, who taught me that "integrity" is
"Doing the right thing, particularly when no one's watching."*

In loving embrace

Marjorie (Mollie) Edith Mason
July 14, 1917 – November 15, 2015
Source: Author

Duru Indi

My Transformative Guide

J A S M I N E   H O N G

I must also thank the other members of Team 2.2: Jasmine and her Duru Indi.

Both have been integral in this journey. Their patience and wisdom have both inspired and conspired to render me a better man. Love to you both.

Table of Contents

About the Author

Jay T. Mason, CFA®, CFP® is an independent Portfolio Manager registered with Fieldhouse Capital Management in Vancouver, Canada. He has 25+ years of progressive asset management experience with several major Canadian investment management firms. In 2012, he took a sabbatical to re-evaluate his role in an industry deserving of greater innovation. Through the combination of new technology, business experience, and following his convictions, the Oasis Growth Fund was launched.

> *"If you don't live for something,*
> *you'll die for nothing."*

—unknown

List of Abbreviations

ACB	adjusted cost base
ADR	American Depository Receipt
AIF	alternative investment funds
AML	anti-money laundering
ATM	at-the-money
BPS	bear put spread
CC	covered call
CBCD	central bank digital currency
CRRCFF	correlation coefficient
DAO	distributive autonomous organization
DIY	do-it-yourself
DCA	dollar-cost averaging
D/E	debt-to-equity ratio
DRIP	dividend reinvestment plan
EBITDA	earnings before interest, taxes, depreciation, and amortization
ESG	environmental, social, and governance
ETF	exchange-traded fund
FMV	fair market value
FOMO	fear of missing out
FORTH	fill outside of regular trading hours
FOSS	fear of a sinking ship
GICS	global industry classification standard
GTC	good 'til canceled
HNW	high-net-worth
IPO	initial public offering
IPS	investment policy statement
ITM	in-the-money
KYC	know your client
MACD	moving average convergence divergence
M&A	mergers and acquisitions
MER	management expense ratio
NFT	non-fungible token
OCC	Options Clearing Corporation
OGF	Oasis Growth Fund

OTM	out-of-the-money
P/E	price/earnings ratio
PFOF	payment-for-order-flow
PRI	principles for responsible investing
QARP	quality at a reasonable price
R&D	research and development
REIT	real estate investment trust
RMP	risk management plan
ROE	return on equity
RoR	rate of return
RSI	Relative Strength Index
RTH	regular trading hours
SaaS	software-as-a-service
SD	standard deviation
SDG	sustainable investment goal
SL	stop-loss order
SP	strike price
SPAC	special purpose acquisition corporation
SRI	socially responsible investments
TR	turnover ratio
TSL	trailing stop-loss order
VIX	CBOE volatility index
VP	value proposition

Introduction

"Investing is not just the study of finance.
It's the study of how people behave with money."
—Morgan Housel,
The Psychology of Money[1]

Gazing up at the nighttime sky in the heart of the desert is nothing short of awe-inspiring. Across the horizon in all directions, stars brilliantly taunt our imagination. Despite that scientists estimate there are about 200×10^{24} stars in the universe (two hundred thousand million million millon), Dorrit Hoffleit of Yale University used mathematical modeling to determine that the naked eye can only see about 9,096 stars on a cloudless night without the impingement of city lights.[2] Don't bother counting, but like the desert nomads for centuries, just a few of the salient stars and constellations were required to accurately aid their navigation across the formless deserts. The night sky has always been nature's most trustworthy GPS.

While metaphorically comparing a nomad's journey across a barren desert to investing in the capital markets may seem obtuse, there are many relevant lessons to be derived:

- That any long-term quest, let alone one that lasts a lifetime, requires planning, a road map, and the right resources.
- That hidden in the sand dunes are life-sustaining wells of investing opportunities and treasures to be discovered. But how far afield to stray before the dangers outweigh the rewards?
- That learning to read nature's subtle signs could improve an investor's fate.

---

[1]Housel, M. (2020). *The Psychology of Money*. Petersfield, Hampshire: Harriman House Ltd.
[2]King, B. (2014). 9,096 Stars in the Sky—Is that All? https://skyandtelescope.org/astronomy-blogs/how-many-stars-night-sky-09172014/ (Accessed 11 December 2021).

- That, to best navigate across unknown, hostile territory, success is more often aligned with following true North Star behaviors.
- That time spent exploring, overcoming challenges, and self-reflecting can lead to unexpected rewards.

Before launching into the pragmatics of investing, however, consider redefining your mission. Matching self-awareness with ambitions is a key to finding success in life, no matter the pursuit. By understanding the capital markets universe better and where your limits are, the journey will be clearer and easier.

Investors are awakening. "Do-it-yourself" (DIY) investing has come of age. Across all sociodemographic cohorts, investors globally are stepping up to test their mettle in the markets. Unrelenting advances in technology, access to refined data, analytics, and commission-free trading now offer unlimited opportunities for retail investors to enrich themselves. All in the comfort of the home.

According to a survey conducted by the Ontario Securities Commission, 60% of retail investors are men. Yet investing is more urgent for women because of pay inequities in the workplace, a subversion of their productive careers to look after family matters, and a longer life expectancy. The DIY movement affords women the possibility to pursue an investing agenda on their terms.

Whether supplementing day jobs (or lost jobs) with trading wins or fearing to miss out on next-gen IPOs or even being seduced by gamified trading platforms, the reasons for participation are varied. An unexpected outcome from the 2020–2021 pandemic was an increase in social investing activism. Most notably, in early 2021, a titanic struggle ensued between a cabal of retail investors coordinated through the social investing sub-Reddit site "WallStreetBets." To everyone's surprise, in the spring of 2020, the "Davids" were able to strike enough merciless blows against the "Goliaths," forcing several billionaire vulture capitalist firms to the brink of bankruptcy. Melvin Capital, for one, was forced to borrow $3B from fellow venture capitalists just to keep the firm solvent.

The power of investing is democracy in action. And with growing numbers, the network of retail investors is taking on real power. Every trade can be a vote for change. The Fourth Industrial Revolution (digital) is on our doorstep: AR/VR, EV, 3D printing, 5G/6G phones, IoT devices, AI and robotics, the genome project, autonomous vehicles, drone deliveries, SpaceX, and the renewable energy revolution are some of the many ways an investor can choose to participate. Further, in the interest toward building a more sustainable world, environmental, social, and governance (ESG) standards are now more relevant factors of analysis in making better investment decisions.

At this stage, are you prepared to make serious investment decisions that will influence the future of this planet? Ultimately, the best reasons to embrace mindful investing should be to assure a viable personal financial future while supporting businesses seeking to create a better world.

With more than 1 million retail accounts being opened monthly, the capital markets are undergoing a renaissance offering:

- Easier access to unlimited research and low-cost trading platforms.
- The growth of social investing communities.
- Unlimited investment choices, including the fractionalization of assets and IPOs.
- No time-wasting bureaucracy.
- Zero trading fees and no professional fees.
- Access to global exchanges and after-markets trading.

So, like the start to any grand adventure, market-beating fantasies are easily conjured.

Yet, according to Dalbar,[3] the leading US independent investment behavior research firm, over a period of 30 years ending 12/31/2018, the average investor lagged the passive S&P 500 index by a margin of 1.51%, annually. Even with a commission-free advantage, this underperformance has remained chronic for decades.

Like it or not, short-term trading is a zero-sum game. For every winner, there will be a loser. And despite holding many strategic advantages relative to the pros, retail investors are generally underprepared to tackle the capital markets head-on. While there are many unique ways an investment journey can get bogged down, the more common themes are:

No plan – Without a plan, weak convictions and poor diversification get exposed during market corrections, often inducing needless sacrificial selling. It's how an investor acts during difficult times that will define their ultimate success.

No limits – Making good decisions requires building perspective. Without accountability or guidelines, only an investor's conscience will keep them on a good trajectory. Too many choices without trading discipline can lead to buying on breakouts and selling on breakdowns. Prioritizing principles over profits could lead to better outcomes.

Attention deficit disorder – Following too many pundits, a short attention span, and easy access to trading technology can entice a long-term investor into higher-risk decisions. Accelerated trading

---

[3]Dalbar QAIB 2020 Report (Quantitative Analysis of Investor Behavior).

essentially converts solid, long-term investments into short-term gambles, while also increasing the costs.

Emotions – Passion is the greatest destroyer of wealth. It can seduce us into action against all common sense. At the extremes, greed is just the alter ego of fear (FOMO). Reactive trading never ends well. However, the "behavior gap"[4] can be dramatically reduced and even eliminated without having to overtly change an investor's behavior.

The Rise of AI – Machine learning algorithms are now responsible for 70% of all trades. Per second, any one algorithm will perform thousands of transactions. Humans can deploy about one per minute. Equally, as emotive creatures, we are prone to making cognitive errors that serve to feed price inefficiencies to these AI programs. Learning to trade proactively can help individual investors minimize the disadvantages.

> *"Strategy without tactics is the slowest route to victory.*
> *Tactics without strategy is the noise before defeat."*
> —Sun Tzu, *The Art of War*

Running headlong into trading stocks, though, is not for the faint of heart. In the capital markets desert, the signs are subtle, dangers abound, and the treasures are hidden. An investment warrior needs to keep their wits about them and to have the right resources to ensure a successful journey.

Unfortunately, there are no havens. While the day-to-day markets are notoriously fickle and sometimes downright frightening, these are the least of an investor's worries. The greater dangers lie within. In between an investor and every trading decision lies their emotions. Greed and fear are in a constant duel, yet both are compounded when intertwined with unduly risky assets and the combustion of leverage.

In an environment of such high stress and competition, to win more consistently requires a more conscious effort. There are no signposts to warn of the dangers. Staying safely on the path requires discipline. Every trade is a negotiation. Both investors won't be right.

---

[4]The behavior gap is the difference between investment returns when an investor makes rational decisions and those generated under the influence of our emotions.

*"A funny thing about the stock market is that
every time one person buys, another sells,
and both think they are astute."*
—William Feather (1889–1981),
publisher and author

Admittedly, the markets are rigged, but not for the conspiracy reasons proffered by social media. Given the test of time, they have overcome every calamity humankind could ever invent and yet, they continue to rise. This is a deeply underappreciated characteristic about investing. Too many live in fear of the markets because they listen to the unwise and the fearmongers, or they just don't yet know enough about themselves. The beauty of the capital markets desert is seeing beyond the sunset and believing that the sunrise will once again arrive. So goes life, so go the markets.

And along this investing journey are scattered many of the secrets to investing success. Some are obvious but little practiced, while others are overlooked due to inexperience or need of education. A patient, mindful contrarian, however, will likely unearth more of these treasures.

Through *The Investing Oasis*, the investor will learn just as much as necessary to competently carry out their desired mission. The pathway to these choices will be laid out soon enough.

The Investing Oasis is a master plan as deployed by the author in a fund called the Oasis Growth Fund (OGF),* an actively managed, equal-weight, North American hedge fund (see Chapter 26).

This guide is organized into the following sections:

- A foundation/discovery process
- Four tiers of purposeful portfolio management techniques
- A summary

Together, they introduce progressively more constructive ways to augment performance, mitigate volatility, diminish risks, reduce mistakes, and control costs. The essential focus is to improve the DIY investing experience.

Let the journey begin.

The Looking Glass

Warts and all, there is no one else to blame. The market is the market. Self-reflection and self-improvement should be integral to every investor's mission.
Focus on improving the process and oneself. The results will come.

---

*The Oasis Growth Fund is one of a trust series powered by Fieldhouse Pro Funds Inc. in Yaletown, British Columbia, Canada.

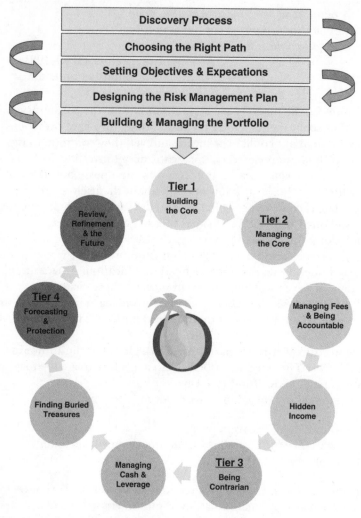

Figure I.1   Overview of the stages of purposeful portfolio management.

Figure I.1 is an overview of the multiple processes and steps involved in designing and managing an effective growth portfolio.

The founding principle practiced throughout *The Investing Oasis* is "integrity": "walking the talk." All concepts shared are principled, purposeful, and practiced professionally by the author. This guide is written logically and pragmatically to provide an easy-to-follow "road map," integrated along with a behavioral compass to guide investors toward making better risk-measured, capital markets decisions. Together, these provide a guiding hand to methodically build and manage a portfolio, yet with flexibility for investors to explore. Research ideas, suggested tools, investing insights, and trading tips are all woven together with proven portfolio management techniques.

Authoring *The Investing Oasis* has been a personal undertaking analogous to the hero's journey that most investors face. Navigating the capital markets is hard enough, let alone doing it solo.

The Investing Oasis brings to light many valuable wealth-creating processes:

- Crafting a holistic, four-tiered portfolio.
- Adoption of select professional practices.
- Deployment of proactive trading techniques and behaviors.
- Learning to seize alpha-generating opportunities as they arise.
- Reduction of undue risk exposures.
- Diminishment of costly behaviors.
- Learning to skew the "desertscape" to your favor.
- Learning to read the market weathervane.
- "Storm-proofing" a portfolio for market turbulence.
- Setting up portfolio protection techniques.
- Learning the benefits of being a better capital markets actor.

Traveling solo is always a chance to get to know oneself better. We grow by being open to alternative routes, learning new skills, broadening our horizons, and even coming to terms with our limitations. Yet it is only during times of challenge and stress that we truly discover ourselves. The stock market is one of the few arenas of open conflict that accepts all players, equally. Yet too many investors enter the fray too casually without regard for the intensity of conflict to be expected or the negotiation skills required. Following *The Investing Oasis* road map and guidance should improve the odds of a successful journey.

After a progressive career spanning 25 years at several major wealth management firms, I have codified the knowledge and skills of my own journey into *The Investing Oasis*.

Who Might Benefit?

At heart, this investing blueprint should appeal to active, risk-tolerant investors willing to do research, willing to deploy contrarian tactics, and seeking rewards that exceed a passive, low-cost indexing strategy. Those who might benefit most are:

- **New investors** seeking to begin their journey on the right foot.
- **Practiced investors** open to recalibrating and refining their investment plan.
- **Investment Advisors** promoting prudent practices to clients already "dabbling" in the markets.

To create an effective learning process, the chapters are written sequentially and progressively. Each is constructed with a clear objective, a presentation of the challenges, followed by pragmatic solutions and methodologies as deployed in the Oasis Growth Fund, followed by a summary.

Those who prioritize risk-taking and quick returns are less likely to benefit from this guide.

Beneficial Education:
- The Securities Industry Essentials Exam[5] offered by FINRA in the US, or
- The Canadian Securities Course[6] offered by the Canadian Securities Institute
- *In Pursuit of the Perfect Portfolio* by Professors Andrew W. Lo and Stephen R. Foerster.
- Interviews with 10 academic scions in search of the perfect portfolio.
- *The Intelligent Investor* by Ben Graham.
- Chapter 27 offers a list of educational materials which are quoted or resourced throughout this guide.

> *"If you were given six hours to chop down a tree,*
> *Take four hours to sharpen your axe."*
> —Albert Einstein (1879–1955)

---

[5]https://www.finra.org/registration-exams-ce/qualification-exams/securities-industry-essentials-exam
[6]https://www.csi.ca/student/en_ca/courses/csi/csc_enrol.xhtml?gclid=Cj0KEQjw8-LnBRCyxtfMl-Cbu48BEiQA6eUMGqqaonl83q40IOMkamRs4wT2dClYQzay8xEH_I2OIdUaAlag8P8HAQ

For DIY Investors

> *"Your lifetime performance as an investor will mostly be determined by what you do during wild times."*
>
> —Morgan Housel,
> *The Psychology of Money*[7]

The Most Competitive Arena on Earth

Before engaging in any major competition, whether sports, investing, or war, it is critical to understand your own skills and weaknesses and know how they match up with the competition. In the markets, since real money is at stake, success requires becoming a truly aware warrior. Winning consistently does not happen by chance. Success comes from being open-minded and resilient and learning to exploit weaknesses. In entering the most competitive arena on earth, one must also learn to skew the playing field to their favor. Sun Tzu's *The Art of War* offers many lessons that can be transposed to the investing arena.

> *"If ignorant both of your enemy and yourself,*
> *you are certain to be in peril."*
>
> —Sun Tzu, *The Art of War*

Investing Is Simple, but Not Easy

The strong appeals of DIY investing are found in the anonymity and freedom to deploy unconstrained tactics and strategies. However, quick rewards are rarely gained without eventually realizing the risks. Discerning which risks are worth taking and those to avoid is part of the art of investing. The greatest enemies of an investor lie at opposite ends of the emotional spectrum: an inflated ego and self-doubt. A few easy wins or a few miscalculations can quickly influence our self-confidence, both to our detriment. Investing requires a delicate balance. To become a greater warrior requires self-awareness, confidence, and the skills to recognize and manage risks, as well as the will and courage to seize opportunities. Approaching the markets with humility and respect will take an investor further than trading hot stocks.

---

[7]Housel, M. (2020). *The Psychology of Money*. Petersfield, Hampshire: Harriman House Ltd.

To earn greater rewards more consistently does not require taking undue risks with uncertain payouts. It requires making smarter decisions with the right tools, at the right time, on terms of your choosing. On any long journey there are many ways to arrive at a destination, yet only very few will be truly effective. Once a better path is known, the status quo will should pale.

Choosing a Mission

Becoming a more effective investor will depend upon your ambition. As a road map, *The Investing Oasis* provides guidance across familiar terrain and other paths less well-known, with a particular focus on avoiding traps and dangers.

As per Table I.1, there are four tiers, each equating to a potentially more productive mission. Ideally, an investor will master each tier before progressing to the next. However, not all investors may desire to deploy such a comprehensive suite of techniques. Each succeeding level will demand more time and effort. Increasingly complex tactics will require greater skills and capital markets savvy to beneficially negotiate the capital markets. We must be mindful not to exceed our level of competency. Being overly ambitious or impatient will come at a cost.

Tier 1 focuses on building and managing a purposeful portfolio of growth stocks. The three subsequent tiers offer added income, growth, and protection strategies, respectively. As an investor masters each tier, their confidence and convictions should grow, leading them to the next level. By design, Tier 1 is the most involved to establish, and yet, requires the least amount of time and energy to manage. Even successfully deploying the protection techniques of Tier 4 does not mean the mission is accomplished, it just means that an investor is now better prepared to handle the inevitable uncertainties that accompany any adventure into the unknown.

Table I.1   Four mission tiers.

| | Mission: To Outperform the . . . | | | |
| | Status Quo | Avg Investor | Avg Pro | Market |
	Tier 1	Tier 2	Tier 3	Tier 4
Build a Core Growth Portfolio	✓	✓	✓	✓
Core Management and Income from Covered Calls		✓	✓	✓
Managing Cash, Debt and Adding Stealth Growth			✓	✓
Adding Portfolio Protection				✓

"The real voyage of discovery consists not in seeking new landscapes but in having new eyes."

—Marcel Proust,
twentieth-century French novelist,
critic, and essayist

A Helping Hand

No one should be more motivated to manage and care for your wealth than you. Whether investing $50K or $10M, this guide has been mindfully crafted for driven and discerning investors. We guide readers to build and manage more professionally a four-tiered portfolio, depending on the mission chosen. The guide highlights strategies, tactics, and tips to introduce ways to create value, whether improving performance, diminishing volatility, reducing costs, or eliminating undue risks and mistakes:

- **INVESTOR TIPS** – Investing ideas that can create value.
- **TRUE NORTH BEHAVIORS** – Behavioral adjustments that can improve decisions.
- **WISDOMS** – Sensible principles and values.
- *AT THE OASIS* – How the author deploys tactics or handle a situation.
- **INVESTOR CAUTIONS** – Be forewarned.

Included, as well, are URLs to definitions, resources, and articles for educational and reference purposes. This guide is intended for the investor who sincerely wants to improve their long-term investing journey.

If this introduction resonates, likely we share common beliefs:

- Stocks allow investors to share ownership with some of the greatest intellects on earth.
- In the short term, the markets are emotional. In the long term, they are highly predictable.
- A diversified portfolio of North American stocks is a proxy for the global economy.
- Consistently profitable businesses with healthy balance sheets and visionary leaders make better investments.
- Not all corporations are sustainable. Pursuing prudent ESG standards starts at the top.
- Every trade should incrementally enhance portfolio performance, reduce volatility, or diminish undue risks.
- Contrarian practices render better results than following the crowd.
- Risk management should be proactive and woven into every decision.
- Quality stocks will survive even the worst of market purges.

- Discipline, patience, and courage will influence results more than tactical trading.
- As strategic weapons, cash and debt reserves should be deployed discerningly.

Counter Uncertainty with Stability

As in any of life's achievements, success requires effort, and is best accomplished one step at a time. *The Investing Oasis* is not a get-rich-quick scheme. The entire process is broken down into increments to introduce constructive ways to create value along the route. Better capital markets decisions will happen more consistently by staying focused on the path and learning to deploy thoughtful capital markets decisions. Control over anything but your own decisions is an illusion.

Becoming a better investor also requires learning how to make less bad decisions and practicing restraint. To achieve and retain success, accountability is a necessary part of personal growth, as is remaining humble when success periodically shines upon you.

Overall, investing is simple, but it requires mindful efforts. Whether we invest or not, the markets will continue to rise. Markets represent the progress of society. They reflect the accretive value of goods and services offered by publicly traded companies. An investor's biggest contribution of value to their portfolio is to use rigorous standards to find great companies, then deploy discipline to buy stocks at reasonable prices. The biggest mistakes come from second-guessing those decisions and following the crowd. When it comes to investing, being "market smart" means having a plan, deploying your strategy with discipline, and then patiently reaping the rewards.

> *"When setting out on a journey,*
>   *do not seek advice from those who have never left home."*
>
> —Rumi,
> thirteenth-century Persian poet

Walking the Talk

Like hiring an experienced adventure guide, *The Investing Oasis* promises to steward an investor effectively and safely across the harsh investment terrain to a desired destination. Having already experienced this journey many times, everything shared genuinely reflects how I professionally manage the Oasis Growth Fund.

"Life is like a desert.
  You only regret the oasis you let pass."

—Arab proverb

Setting a Social Contract

The Investing Oasis intends to challenge each follower to become a better investor and, along the way, to become a better self. As an investor progresses toward their chosen destination, hopefully every stride will have counted. This guide is designed to help investors manage their money better, but it also hopes to raise awareness to becoming a better global citizen.

Since the capital markets are a direct reflection of the world writ large, how we invest matters just as much as how we consume. Socially responsible investing is a process that takes into consideration both an investment's financial return and its social, environmental, and ethical impacts. This places the onus on the investor to choose among corporations that are striving to do better. On the other hand, ESG is an evaluation and ranking of each stock based upon their collective social, environmental, and governance data. Together, an investment strategy mindful of socially responsible investment (SRI) factors and ESG standards can render influence on this precious planet. Although *The Investing Oasis* is just one investing style, the lessons embedded are timeless and can help an investor become a more mindful capital markets actor, as well as a more successful investor.

CAVEATS

- The philosophies of *The Investing Oasis* are the antithesis of day trading. No apologies.
- There is no free lunch. Winning consistently comes from a convergence of intelligent, mindful, and disciplined decisions. Luck may occasionally be in play, but should be the icing, not the cake.
- This guide does not reveal which stocks to buy. Its tenets rely on common sense and focuses on self-development to make better decisions.
- It avoids the five DIY vices: quick wins, all-or-none trades, market timing, speculation, and undisciplined leveraging.
- In a universe of unlimited investing techniques, it combines a series of individually proven methodologies into one coordinated game plan.
- The focus is on building an effective portfolio of stocks. An investor should only invest in stocks if it is appropriate for their circumstances.

Each reader's asset mix decision is personal (i.e. stocks, fixed income, cash, real estate, and alternative investments).

- Every reader will interpret the information and recommendations uniquely. As such, there is no perfect way to deploy a portfolio. Outcomes will vary; however, the majority of readers should expect improvements from the status quo.
- I only invest in stocks because I buy to hold them for the long term. Historically, stocks have consistently outperformed fixed income securities (i.e. bonds) over 10+ years. However, fixed income securities could be beneficial to support an investor's lower degree of risk tolerance or when a pending obligation has a specific time horizon, for which a specific term and assuredness of capital would be paramount.
- The only advice offered in *The Investing Oasis* is to seek professional advice when a personal situation requires perspective, skills, or tools beyond the reader's capacity.

In Respect of Your Advisor

Before moving forward, it's possible that a professional may already be keeping you on track. This guide is not intended to disrupt a trusted relationship. Instead, if acting upon ideas presented in this guide, it could even enhance this rapport.

By becoming a more engaged investor, it might help to better appreciate the challenges facing an Advisor as they manage some, or the bulk, of your wealth. Being on the firing line of the capital markets and making critical decisions should reinforce the benefits of building a prudent portfolio.

Managing some of your own capital, however, is also not intended to be in competition with the Advisor. Though there could be overlaps in investment choices, the strategies deployed likely should steer in different directions. As in most long-distance treks, there are merits to exploring alternative routes to arrive at the eventual destination.

"The fears we don't face become our limits."

—Robin Sharma,
Canadian author of *The Monk Who Sold His Ferrari*

For Financial Planners, Advisors, and Family Offices

With respect to investment matters, this guide assumes that the financial professional has dutifully established themself as their client's primary service provider. Yet, despite pledging their trust, many clients still tend to "dabble" in the markets. While they may relish the thrill of participation, without a plan, unstructured investing could be a costly form of self-education.

With the markets already being ill-defined and uncertain, an investor pursuing day-trading tactics may unwittingly convert high-probability, high-quality assets into speculation. In other words, by relying on a relatively monolithic plan with the blunt tool of day trading, they add to the riskiness of the marketplace and to their wealth. Since the behavior gap is a very persistent problem, investors could improve upon the status quo with modest effort.

This guide has been purposefully crafted to complement and enhance a professional's value proposition. While mentoring requires patient stewardship, the process of building a client's investing acumen may be unduly cumbersome for the professional, along with their other duties and responsibilities. As such, the educational approach delivered by *The Investing Oasis* is intended to be a valued extension of the professional's hand.

From the perspective of a fellow experienced professional, *The Investing Oasis* offers a structured plan combined with insights, education, investing tips, and refined portfolio management techniques. We even outline ways to avoid unnecessary risks and identify where self-inflicted behaviors and mistakes could become problematic. Generally, investors are guided to act within their levels of competency and risk tolerance. The primary goal of this guide is to improve the odds of a more successful DIY journey.

As written, the desert metaphor implies a journey fraught with perpetual dangers and temptations where only the occasional oasis may offer respite.

As one such refuge, *The Investing Oasis* provides the foundation and guidance from which an investor can launch the next leg of their journey. To the financial professional, *The Investing Oasis* offers four potential benefits:

- **Better-educated clients make for more productive meetings.** This guide is designed as an educational support tool to enhance capital markets decisions and discussions rendering more effective meetings.
- **Appreciation.** Going DIY could save on professional fees, yet poor execution may quickly squander this advantage. With clients undertaking front-line investment decisions, this guide could improve their capital markets savvy and render an appreciation of the challenges faced by the Advisor.
- **Extending a professional's marketing initiatives.** With easy access to discount platforms and questionable social media influences, many clients are already being exposed and attracted to the DIY concept. *The Investing Oasis* can help to distinguish the financial professional as caring beyond the direct services provided. DIY investing and professional services need not be mutually exclusive.

- **One full chapter is dedicated to improving the client-professional relationship.** The features and benefits of working with a financial professional are highlighted in Chapter 6, including how to measure their value proposition and how to improve this relationship. All good relationships require a healthy feedback loop.

Realistically, *The Investing Oasis* is not for every client. Yet, for those destined to DIY, or even as a timeless educational platform for their children, it can enhance and extend a professional's overall value proposition across generations. This guide is intended as an investment into both the long-term well-being of your clients and that of your practice. Engaged clients are likely to be more satisfied clients.

FOUNDATION

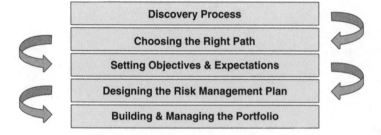

Figure I.2 Overview

Y ou are about to begin a journey into the relative unknown. The capital markets are all around us, yet they are nuanced and elusive to comprehend. Even if you've been investing for generations, the investment dunes shift with the wind, signposts disappear, and the risks are continually mutating. The market, at best, is uncertain and, at worst, can be downright vicious. Undertaking a lone trek through one of the most inhospitable environments on planet earth with a storm perpetually hovering on the horizon can be wealth-threatening and intimidating. Which path to take? In what to invest? In whom to trust? How to protect oneself? Questions abound.

Most investors could benefit from a respite at this oasis to review the road map and measure their options before relaunching the mission. Whether this is the very beginning, or a pause on your route, the time will be well invested.

Chapter 1

Eyes Wide Open

"Victorious warriors win first, then go to war.
Defeated warriors go to war, seeking to win."
—Sun Tzu (544–496 BCE), *The Art of War*

Objective:

Preparing for the investing trek ahead.

Hierarchy of Creating Value with Investing

Building a resilient portfolio capable of generating above-average returns requires taking a holistic approach with a focus on simplicity and common sense. Figure 1.1 is an adaptation inspired by Morgan Housel's "Hierarchy of Competency" in his book *The Psychology of Money*.[1] Through extensive research, he concluded investors should establish a foundation before attempting to tackle more complex layers of investing competency.

This adaptation has been evolved into a hierarchy of six areas where investors can actively create real value by heeding better practices. Since each investment is a series of micro-decisions leading up to a final negotiation in the capital markets arena, to get the most out of that next trade requires a thoughtful process. Time and experience usually improve our capital markets decision-making. However, the "behavior gap," a term coined by advisor, columnist, and author Carl Richards, is the chronic long-term underperformance realized by investors relative to the market due to erratic human decisions confounded by our emotions.

---

[1]Housel, M. (2020). *The Psychology of Money*. Petersfield, Hampshire: Harriman House Ltd.

Figure 1.1   Hierarchy of portfolio value creation. Adapted from https://www.fool .com/investing/general/2015/07/09/needs.aspx (Accessed 23 January 2019).

The pyramid in Figure 1.1 is in ascending order of relevance to the investing process. The relative size of each layer reveals the potential for investors to create value through improved personal decisions.

Being a consistently good investor requires having a plan, learning to distill valued information, using the right tools, deploying good judgment, and then holding to your convictions during the darkest hours. In escalating order of competency, here are the six areas where mindful actions can create real enhancements to building and managing a portfolio. Note that the top layer (Tax Planning) should be undertaken with a trusted professional.

- **The Asset Mix**

    Investing starts with determining the asset mix. According to research by Vanguard, the asset mix decision influences nearly 90% of a portfolio's returns and the degree of volatility. Historically, the more capital allocated to owning stocks, the higher the expected long-term returns. The trade-off is having to accept an increased range of short-term uncertainty. While the asset mix may not be top of mind, it's a starting point and everything else flows from there. Chapter 4 addresses setting an appropriate asset mix.

- **Good Capital Markets Behavior**

    Getting consistently reliable results has very little to do with picking a hot stock. Making the right allocation decisions requires research and perspective. Better decisions come from triangulation (using multiple sources to confirm a decision), patience, and having the confidence to stick to your plan. Poor capital markets behavior stems from spontaneous trading. The greatest improvements often come from simple behavioral changes. Chapters 2, 5, 14, and 20 outline ways to either improve capital markets behavior or to circumvent our behavior through proactive trading.

- **Portfolio Design and Management**

  Portfolio design should not be an afterthought. Chapters 11, 12, and 15 introduce effective methods to construct and manage a holistic portfolio with purpose.

- **Security Selection**

  A portfolio of winning stocks does not happen randomly. Choosing securities should be a thoughtful process centered around good investing principles. Historically, a portfolio of quality stocks has always been capable of withstanding the worst volatility. Yet this requires having confidence in the market and conviction in your security choices. Chapters 7–10 present 16 filters to help find quality growth stocks.

- **Trading**

  Deploying a trade is only one part of the investing process. Unfortunately, on average, high-volume trading tactics are relied upon too heavily to create wealth. As a retail investor's sole interface with the capital markets, trading requires our best, objective behavior to negotiate consistently good results. Those who rely primarily on trading instincts face three serious disadvantages:

  - Efficient algorithms dominate trading.
  - Certain trading sites allow "market makers" to intercept retail trades, potentially adding to trading costs. The claim is that they are improving the market liquidity. It's not fair, but it is legal.
  - Emotions and impatience frequently cloud our judgment. Achieving consistently successful trades requires purposeful and principled decisions. Trading "bots" can analyze reams of data in nanoseconds before pouncing on retail trading mistakes. The human brain can barely handle one trade per minute. That's hardly a fair fight.

"The more active you are as an investor, the worse you will do."
— Meir Statman,
author of *Behavioral Finance: The Second Generation*

Chapters 14, 15, and 20 introduce proactive and contrarian trading techniques to force the algorithms to meet you on your terms. When deploying trades, "less is more."

- **Costs**

  DIY investors are not exposed to the cost structure that professionals face. Therefore, they already have a built-in advantage.

"Portfolio Turnover" on the companion website[2] addresses how to measure and retain this strategic advantage.

Gaining the Upper Hand

According to Morgan Housel, investing without first having mastered good investor behavior could undermine the entire investing experience. Investors tend to spend too much time chasing stocks and generally mismanaging the rest of their value-creating opportunities. Coveted education and refined investment skills can be wholly unraveled without thoughtful planning, applying purposeful, risk-measured decisions, and a commitment to self-development.

For experienced investors, though, this doesn't mean starting over. If satisfied with the results to date, stay the course. But where the status quo is no longer acceptable, here are four fundamental ways that this guide can be useful:

1. **Purposeful Design** – Through step-by-step education and relevant examples, investors will learn to construct a well-founded portfolio and learn how to deploy more effective trades.
2. **Graduated Steps** – Four tiers of increasing challenge and value creation are presented, depending on which level of mission an investor desires to undertake. Each chapter progressively builds upon the knowledge and methods of the previous.
3. **Shared Methods** – I "walk the talk" and accurately share my portfolio management methods, tactics, and strategies.
4. **Increased Behavior Awareness** – *The Investing Oasis* identifies where adjustments in behavior could improve performance results, diminish risks, or introduce ways to circumvent the investing challenges altogether.

To emphasize the importance of practicing good capital markets behavior, Morgan Housel shares a compelling story in his book *The Psychology of Money*.[3]

A knowledgeable friend, who pursued an ultimately unsuccessful career on Wall Street, simply could not separate himself from his overconfidence and willingness to pose large, high-conviction investments that proved repeatedly to be misguided gambles.

By contrast, a woman of modest means lived simply and regularly invested into a passive portfolio of stocks. When she passed at

---

[2]www.theinvestingoasis.com
[3]https://www.collaborativefund.com/blog/the-psychology-of-money/ (accessed 15 February 2019).

age 100, she bequeathed an estate of $7 million to charity, the size of which shocked her family. By investing in quality stocks and by simply being prudent, she was able to generate long-term investment success far exceeding the average Wall Street hotshot.

Better Behavior Beats Brains

Deciphering and mastering the investment world isn't only about quant models and being a mathematical genius. Success comes more from understanding human behavior and, more specifically, learning how to profit when others are failing.

Some of the brainiest investors have failed to beat the markets. Just ask the principals of Long-Term Capital Management, whose brilliant team of PhDs had to be bailed out to the tune of $3.75B when their investment high-volume trading model failed them back in 1998. Or the TARP bailout (Troubled Asset Relief Program) offered by the Federal Government to the biggest and most elite US financial firms during the Great Financial Crisis of 2008–2009. So much for being smarter than the market. They only proved that they were more cunning than the government to capitalize their profits and socialize the losses.

Since the market is the sum of all good and bad investment decisions, on either side of a trade is a motivated investor with an opposing perspective.

Q: If these Ivy leaguers failed, how can the average retail investor expect to succeed?

As will be presented, long-term investing success requires the subtleness of understanding of human behaviors, deploying commonsense techniques, and practicing estraint more than insensitively relying on the law of large numbers through quantitative algorithms.

> *"An investor's most important quality is temperament, not intellect."*
> — Warren Buffett

Alternate Routes

When the time comes, how we react in a moment of crisis defines us. Our worst decisions usually occur when we fail to hold to our principles and stay on plan. Unfortunately, capitulation is just human nature. Studies have shown that the human psyche suffers more when losing money than the favorable sentiments generated when posting an equally winning trade. As paper losses mount, staying on course becomes a steeper and steeper challenge.

A core purpose of *The Investing Oasis* is to help frame the capital markets as a place of opportunity. A well-designed and managed portfolio should enable investors to learn that the fear derived from volatility is, instead, a signal of opportunity.

Invariably, it takes real courage to make tough decisions at critical times. How well do you know yourself?

Consumer, Dabbler, Gambler, Capitalist, or Investor?

Personal character predefines how we approach the markets and will lead to vastly differing results.

- An investment **Consumer**, by definition, defers most of their investment decisions to a professional Advisor/Broker. They would rather an expert manage their money than risk some or all of it in their own hands. They see their role as one of doing due diligence to hire the right people for the job. This guide could still be a useful education tool to enhance their relationship with an Advisor.
- An investment **Dabbler** tends to defer most of their portfolio to an experienced hand but periodically speculates based on the prevailing trends. This guide could help set reasonable guidelines to separate an investor's ad hoc investment choices from the core management duties of their Advisor.
- A **Gambler** is driven more by gut instinct than by following a road map. Using probabilities and intuition, they roam the markets for big wins. However, the use of gambling tactics in the capital markets is challenged.

  Winning and losing in a casino are mathematically determined probabilities. With the capital markets, the wins and losses can be unlimited, and the probabilities vary depending upon the prevailing circumstances. The dynamics of demand and supply and degrees of fear and greed (behaviors) introduce unquantifiable factors not present at casinos. In other words, with so many ill-defined parameters, it would be safer to gamble in casinos. But only for short periods of time. Gamble long enough and eventually the house wins.
- A **Capitalist** is an opportunist. "Carpe diem" would be their motto. When assets go on sale, they jump in, often with both feet. And as prices normalize, they liquidate and take their profits. Driven by a contrarian mindset, their principles rely heavily on research, instinct, and patience. They do get burned from time to time but justify that the cumulative gains warrant taking the occasional beating.
- A classic **Investor** typically does their own research and implements disciplined investment decisions. The emphasis is on building a

sustainable portfolio. By respecting stocks as viable businesses, they place their faith in competent and motivated corporate leadership. The motivation is to find quality stocks and construct a diversified portfolio. Historically, although dedicated investors are accountable for their decisions, they sometimes lack a road map or feedback to help refine their action plan.

The Investing Oasis offers the most value to committed investors desiring to explore their inner capitalist.

> *"Confusing speculation with investing will always be a mistake."*
> — Benjamin Graham,
> author of *The Intelligent Investor*

In DIY, there are unlimited investing options and no guardrails. Imagine just how much more effective this adventure would be with a road map and the right navigational tools. The first step should be to pick your method of travel.

Retail Investing – Three Alternatives

No matter the destination, an investor's character should be matched with an investing style. While no method is perfect, identifying how your personality may better align with one style or another could greatly influence the degree of personal satisfaction and eventual success:

    i. **Passive Portfolio Management**
   ii. **Day Trading**
  iii. **Active Portfolio Management**

i. Passive Portfolio Management: ETFs

"Be the Market, Not Beat the Market"

Investing in various exchange-traded funds (ETFs) is the lowest-cost and most straightforward method to creating a fully diversified portfolio. Performance and volatility characteristics will mimic the market. This might appeal more to passive investors who desire exposure to the markets but who place a higher priority on lifestyle rather than spending time researching, monitoring, and managing a portfolio of stocks. This more passive approach ensures returns equal to the markets, less the cost of the ETFs or mutual funds.

ii. Day Trading Stocks

Diametrically opposite to passive investing, day trading seeks to exploit investment opportunities using superior investment insights and proprietary trading skills. Day trading essentially objectifies stocks to capitalize on short-term price trends. Trades are often directed to unusually volatile stocks or leveraged ETFs. However, by trading on price increments and starting and ending each day in cash, this reflects a low-degree of risk tolerance. By deploying market-timing tactics on highly volatile securities, the actual risks taken are immeasurable.

Figure 1.2 emphasizes the difference in results generated by investing vs. gambling. In the short term, results generated by the two are nearly indiscernible. However, in the longer term, the dotted line demonstrates the inferior results for gambling relative to investing.

As noted in Figure 1.2, there is minimal difference between gambling and short-term investing in the short run. While the results of gambling can be favorable over a weekend, most gamblers should know that the odds favor the house over any extended period.

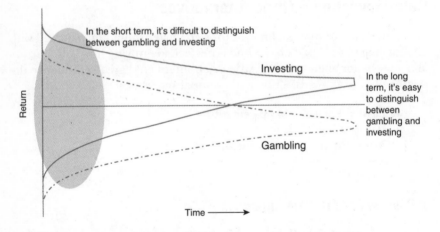

Figure 1.2 Investing vs. gambling.
Source: Reproduced with permission from an article titled "Decision-Making for Investors: Theory, Practice, and Pitfalls" by Michael J. Mauboussin during his tenure at Legg Mason. https://www.retailinvestor.org/pdf/decisionmaking.pdf

By choosing to trade quality stocks on short-term price trends, an investor introduces investing hardships:

- The volatility of a security is valued more than the fundamental business qualities.

- All wealth created through business activities deployed by the underlying management teams are never realized.
- Share price movements are highly random over the short term, introducing "luck" as an inordinately large determinant for success.
- Mistakes are inevitable with manually deployed, high-volume, reactive trades, which favor pre-programmed algorithms.
- Potential increased costs, either in the form of trading commissions or market maker profits.

Respectfully, some investors are just hard-wired to be day traders. Peace of mind requires that they be in control of their financial destiny. However, if a long-term investor desires to occasionally deploy day trades, see "Day Trading 2.0" at the companion website,[4] which presents our version of short-term trading with guidelines.

iii. Active Portfolio Management

Active portfolio management means deploying strategic and tactical decisions and may be better suited for those who believe:

- that the stock market is not perfectly efficient.
- that mispriced assets can be exploited for advantage.
- that the rewards generated are worth the time, effort, and anguish.
- in being fully accountable for their decisions.

The Investing Oasis breaks the process into multiple, value-creating steps:

- Identifying stalwart growth businesses (Tier 1).
- Buying targeted stocks at discounts from the market (Tier 1).
- Crafting a portfolio with broad economic exposure (Tier 1).
- Rebalancing the portfolio counter to market dynamics (Tier 1).
- Introducing supplementary income by selling covered calls (Tier 2).
- Leveraging growth by selling put contracts on devalued quality non-core stocks (Tier 3).
- Setting up portfolio protection (Tier 4).

Tier 1 focuses on learning how to pick quality stocks, implementing effective portfolio management techniques, and purposeful trading practices. Investors can then incrementally introduce wealth-accretive actions in Tiers 2, 3, and 4. Each tier will demand more time and effort, as well as increasing levels of competency.

---

[4]www.theinvestingoasis.com.

At the Oasis: Chapter 1

- No matter the stage of your journey, take time to assess and recalibrate your current path.
- Going DIY may save on fees but requires time, energy, and self-accountability.
- Choosing the right path, or combination, requires:
  - Self-awareness to know your weaknesses and level of competency.
  - Being open to learning.
  - Courage and gumption to take decisions at difficult times.
  - Resisting those shortcuts. Rare are the wins worth the eventual sacrifices.
- Go slowly and enjoy the journey.

"Knowing thyself is the beginning of all wisdom."

— Aristotle

Chapter 2

Choosing the Right Path

"The Financial Markets are a Zero-Sum game. For every buyer, there is a seller. If one investor beats the market, someone else must underperform. Collectively, we earn the market return before costs. The presence of exceptional investors dictates the need for subpar investors." [1]
—Brad M. Barber, *The Behavior of Individual Investors*

Objective:

Learning how simple behaviors can impact performance.

The Behavior Gap

What rate of return do you expect to achieve? For aspiring investors, Figure 2.1 could be a sobering chart.

The "behavior gap" is a term coined by Carl Richards[2] to explain the difference between total market returns and those achieved by the average investor. According to Dalbar, a leading US independent investor behavior analyst firm, the statistics are clear. Over the 20 years ending December 31, 2020, the average professionally managed North American equity fund underperformed the S&P 500 index annually by 1.01%.[3] Meanwhile, the

---

[1]Barber, B.M. (2011) "The Behavior of Individual Investors." Graduate School of Management, UCDavis.
[2]Carl Richards – https://behaviorgap.com.
[3]Soe, A. M., et al. (2019). SPIVA®U.S. Scorecard. https://www.spglobal.com/_assets/documents/corporate/us-spiva-report-11-march-2019.pdf (Page 13) (Accessed 9 March 2022).

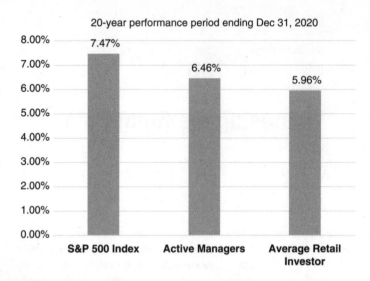

20-year performance period ending Dec 31, 2020

Figure 2.1   The behavior gap.

average North American investor underperformed the S&P 500 index annually by an average of 1.51%.[4] Although these performance differences may seem modest, they are consistent and, over time, they compound.

Q: What's behind these discrepancies?

Institutional Investors

For US institutional managers, management fees and operating expenses are the primary culprit. According to eVestment's report "The State of Institutional Fees" published in 2020, most of the 1.01% underperformance can be explained by management fees, the average being 0.63% (excluding incentive fees) for the three years ending December 31, 2019.[5] The challenge for institutional investors is learning how to generate enough alpha to overcome the fee drag.

---

[4]Dalbar QAIB 2020 Report (Quantitative Analysis of Investor Behavior).
[5]Laurelli, P. (2020). The State of Institutional Fees: What asset managers are marketing and what public plan investors are really paying across equity and fixed income strategies. eVestment Alliance, LLC. https://www.evestment.com/wp-content/uploads/2020/08/eVestment-State-of-Institutional-Fees-Report-August-2020.pdf (Accessed 3 September 2020).

Retail Investors

Retail investors may save on a complex of professional fees; however, chronic long-term underperformance is rooted primarily in undisciplined trading practices. This discrepancy is due to cognitive biases and emotions that distort the ability to correctly interpret and price investment risks.

Facts are facts. Except when our brain misinterprets them and fools us into making decisions that an otherwise objective person wouldn't make. In other words, our own brain can conspire against us.

A Cognitive Bias Example

Fresh from scoring a significant investment win in the Spring of 2015, Bill Ackman, CEO of Pershing Square, bought a truckload of Valeant Pharmaceutical at $200/share.[6] Upon striking an all-time high at $260 on August 4, 2015, within weeks, the shares suddenly plummeted to $90 due to an earnings miss and rumors of accounting malpractices. To some, including Bill, this appeared to be the bargain of a lifetime. A previously stratospheric share price increase from $10 to $250 had entranced investors. Naturally, this price discount was viewed by some as just a market overreaction.

Hidden in the numbers, unfortunately, were accounting fraud and malpractices through ownership in an "off-the-books" pharmacy. Deceptive practices had allowed Valeant to artificially inflate their revenues and therefore their share price. When finally revealed, investors couldn't get out fast enough.

Yet, instead of digging deeper into research, Bill averaged down on his investment. He not only bought more shares, but he also joined the Valeant Board and then went on a public crusade to try to convince the market otherwise.

Despite his market savvy and having privileged access to details and insights unavailable to the average investor, he rode this investment all the way down to $11 before eventually capitulating to sell his entire position. An otherwise astute investor eventually lost more than $3B in a series of ill-fated decisions. A fatal cognitive blind spot enticed him to buy at the peak and then capitulate at the low.

Examples of other uniquely bad investing decisions made by some of the most well-respected investors can be found in a book written by Michael Batnick: *Big Mistakes: The Best Investors and their Worst Investments.*[7]

---

[6]Prior to investing in Valeant, Pershing Square had held shares in Allergan, which was privatized by Activas, an Irish pharmaceutical firm, in a bidding war with Valeant Pharmaceuticals.

[7]Batnick, M. (1996). *Big Mistakes: The Best Investors and Their Worst Investments.* Hoboken, NJ: Bloomberg Press/Wiley.

For the rest of us, the leading example of poor capital markets behavior is usually framed around "market timing."

Market Timing – A Self-Fulfilling Prophecy

There is currently no agreed scientific definition for emotions. However, it is well known that negative emotions interfere with making clear-headed investment decisions, as do positive emotions.

Figure 2.2 compares a 15-year history of real investor fund flows relative to the performance of a hypothetical balanced fund (60% stocks/40% bonds) as presented by the wealth management firm PIMCO. This clearly reveals that capital flows track closely with our emotions. Net capital inflows increased during rising markets (volume bars above the zero net flow line) and net capital outflows dominated during declining markets (volume bars below). Despite average investors' best efforts to overcome those twin pillars of fear and greed, the graph doesn't lie.

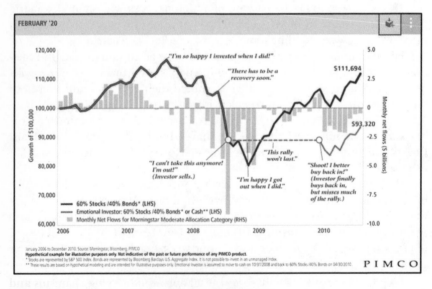

Figure 2.2   Investors are buying high and selling low.
Source: Image reproduced with permission from PIMCO, Canada Corp.

Beyond Our Control

The failure of market timing is well documented; reactionary trading practices are the go-to remedy to assuage market jitters.

Who could fault anyone for reacting poorly to heightened uncertainty? In the face of grave danger, we rely on our amygdala, the brain's "fight-or-flight" center.

Unfortunately, watching stock prices rise and fall should not register as life-or-death critical. Equally unfortunate is that our amygdala is too easily tricked into perceiving a state of self-preservation, thereby overriding all rational thoughts. In a 2005 article titled "Fear Conditioning: How the Brain Learns About Danger," Dr. Joanne Schauffhausen outlined that this false perception of life and death is a result of several coinciding factors:

- Watching undulating markets over countless hours hypersensitizes our brain to perceive volatility as being dangerous.
- Objectivity is lost because an investor feels personally responsible for their precious and limited capital.
- The hippocampus is our conditional fear center. It harbors painful memories of previous corrections.
- Signals from the hippocampus to the amygdala result in bursts of adrenaline and cortisol inciting immediate action.[8]

When triggered, it's too late. We lose objectivity. No amount of rational thought can overcome the fateful chemical cocktail released by the amygdala. The need for self-preservation blinds us into acting against our better interests. To avoid trading reactively, it first helps to understand how we are being triggered.

Professional Response

At this stage, professionals can usually arrest spontaneous trading impulses either with personal discipline developed through the market cycles or accountability mechanisms, such as regulatory oversight, the investment policy document, supervisory oversights, or team feedback.

Retail Response

For retail investors, it is the absence of all accountability mechanisms and easy access to technology that aids and abets reactive trading.

---

[8]Schauffhausen, J. (2005)."Fear Conditioning: How the Brain Learns About Danger," *Brain Connection*, https://brainconnection.brainhq.com /2005/08/26/fear-conditioning-how-the-brain-learns-about-danger/ (Accessed 15 March 2019).

If only the source of these dreaded fears were real, then acting in self-preservation would be appropriate. For those who attempt to deploy "market timing" as a wealth-saving defense, it becomes a self-fulfilling prophecy. Selling is often delayed until well after the downturn has commenced (denial). And only once the regret has waned are stocks repurchased, if ever, at higher prices.

North Star Compass

Market Timing Fantasy

Attempts at market timing achieve exactly what investors hope to avoid: locking in permanent losses while missing out on the juicy gains in the subsequent recovery. According to Statistics Canada, retail investors consistently get both the sell and the repurchase decisions wrong, by a long shot.[9]

Market timing requires four perfectly rational decisions during a period of heightened fear:

1. Picking a market top.
2. Choosing which stocks to sell.
3. Picking a market bottom.
4. Choosing which stocks to buy.

When markets are calm, the odds of making four concurrently favorable decisions are better in Vegas. Imagine those same odds when the markets get nasty.

Wisdom: Rationally, a market correction is no time to abandon one's convictions. So, when our gut shouts "sell," pause for thought. It is most likely a time to buy.

Except for contrarians, market timing is consistently a wealth-destroying activity. Without either finding ways to shield ourselves from the fear or learning to be contrarian, the behavior gap will persist.

"Volatility is not risk. Investing in a badly managed company is."
—Warren Buffett

---

[9]Shufelt, T. (2019). *"Investors Are Their Own Worst Enemies,"* Statistics Canada. March 27 (Accessed 27 September 2021).

Time in the Markets

Statistics don't lie. If an investor were to take a long-term buy-and-hold perspective, the 48-year graph of the S&P 500 Index in Figure 2.3 demonstrates that any rolling 15-year period, or longer, would have rendered positive results. Note that the rolling returns for each period are not symmetrical. This further reflects the long-term positive bias of the stock market.

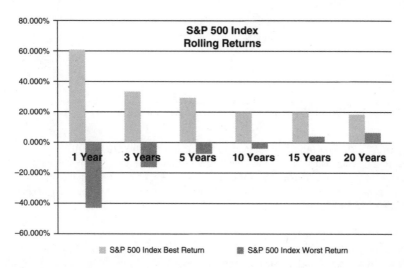

Figure 2.3 S&P 500 Index rolling returns (1973–2021).
Source: Graphic reprinted with permission from Dana Anspach, a certified financial planner, and founder and CEO of Sensible Money based in Phoenix, AZ. https://www.thebalance.com/rolling-index-returns-4061795.

On the other hand, Figure 2.4 identifies the impact of running away from the markets.

Despite holding a winning hand of quality stocks, investors who get spooked by the markets and capitulate, and then refrain from reinvesting for many weeks, will miss out on the market's most effortless returns. Figure 2.5 identifies that the best returns are often within days of the worst returns. Once the rout is on, staying invested, no matter the mental anguish, has historically paid off better than selling into a downturn and then trying to reinvest later.

Annualized price returns S&P 500 1996–2016
SOURCE:BLOOMBERG, IGIM

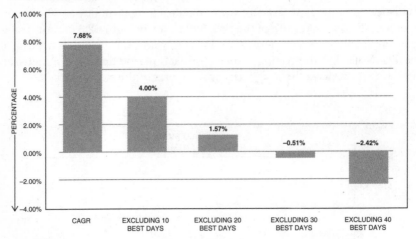

Figure 2.4   Annualized price returns for the S&P 500 Index (1996–2016).
Source: 2017 white paper produced by the Investor's Group, written by Stephen Rogers, investment strategist at the Investor's Group. https://www.ig.ca/content/dam/investors-group/more/wp-content/themes/ig_magazine/pdf/Whitepaper_Time-In-Not-Timing_EN.pdf (Accessed 15 April 2019).

Timing the market is futile:
The best and worst trading days happen close together

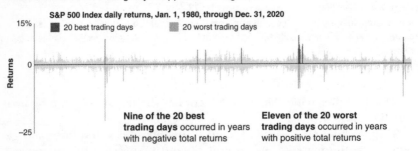

Figure 2.5   Timing the market is futile.
Source: Reproduced with permission. https://www.allodium.com/images/Educational/Vanguard-Market-Volatility-Slides-032020.pdf (Accessed 3 March 2021).

"For stocks, the best recipe for loss avoidance is time. The probability of losing money over one day is a little worse than a coin-flip (46%), but the probability declines over any 10-year window to just 6% in a study of the markets since 1929."[10]

—Savita Subramanian,
head of US Equity and Quantitative Strategy,
Bank of America Merrill Lynch

North Star Compass

Who Needs a Coach?

In the January 2020 edition of the *Advisor's Edge*, according to research firm Tulip and Natixis Global, 83% of Financial Advisors believe behavioral coaching to be important. Yet just 6% of their clients agreed.[11]

Since the behavior gap is well documented, either investors are in denial, or they are blissfully unaware.

Even "Successful People Have Coaches"[12]:

"At 31 Cristiano Ronaldo still sees the benefit of a coach to continue playing world class football. At 55 Barack Obama still needed coaches to continue to be the President of the United States until [his] last year. And at 62 Oprah Winfrey still relies on coaches to stay one of the most respected people in the Entertainment industry."

Who's your mentor?

---

[10]Ro, S. (2020). "How to Invest in Stocks if Record-High Prices and Volatility Make You Nervous: Morning Brief." https://ca.finance.yahoo.com/news/how-to-invest-in-stocks-record-high-prices-morning-brief-100013332.html (Accessed 8 September 2020).

[11]Shin, M. (2020). "ETFs and the Future of Investment Management." https://www.advisor.ca/news/etfs/etfs-and-the-future-of-investment-management/ (Accessed 27 September 2021).

[12]Macdonald, K. (2017). "Successful People Have Coaches." *Medium*, https://medium.com/@kieramacdonald/successful-people-have-coaches-d67dc2a1064 (Accessed 25 September 2021).

Capital Markets Behavior: What Works? What Doesn't?

Institutional Investors

Professionals are not smarter than retail investors, nor do they experience any less fear. However, they do follow checks and balances that reinforce better capital markets behavior. Key amongst them is that they work from a plan, are held accountable by a supervisor and the regulators, and benefit from a team environment.

Since professionals manage money holistically, their convictions are reinforced by using robust research and making decisions in alignment with a portfolio's risk and reward objectives. Positions are changed when no longer suitable to the whole. The focus is always on the long-term well-being of the portfolio. Panicked decisions end careers.

Retail Investors

Yet retail investors hold several advantages over the professionals:

- No regimen.
- No rules.
- No oversight.
- Flexibility to implement any trade, at any time, on any market.

However, these freedoms also render retail investors more vulnerable to mistakes. Spending time sitting in front of a computer screen watching price trends randomly gyrate is quite literally a fear-inducing activity: "False Evidence Appears Real." With the market perpetually in flux, investors are therefore kept in a constant state of vulnerability. Acting in self-preservation is the most powerful emotion in the human psyche. At times of heightened volatility, liquidation remains the go-to solution to safeguard one's wealth.

So, without solid convictions, or guidelines, or accountability to a higher authority, there is little to impede acting impetuously to perceived threats. When triggered by an adverse price movement, the next trade is not likely to be a best decision. Emotions fog our brain from correctly identifying and measuring the risks, or determining the most appropriate response to an opportunity or threat. In the presence of emotions, both good and bad, critical thinking is dimmed. Further, with a boost of cortisol or adrenaline, decisions always seem more urgent.

Ultimately, the two most consistent winners from volumes of reactive trades are the pre-programmed algorithms that feed on mispriced trading and the brokerage platforms that profit from increased trading volumes. All emotions outside of neutral, whether negative (guilt, self-pity, frustration, arrogance, anger, etc.) or positive (euphoria, passion, joy, etc.), can play a destructive role in wealth management.

And it only takes a few poorly executed trades to quickly undermine one's self-confidence.

Of course, professionals also experience the same emotions and temptations, but built-in checks and balances safeguard the portfolio from spontaneous, self-destructive trades.

Further complicating matters are the consumption of mood-altering substances like caffeine, alcohol, stimulants, depressants, or even external energies, such as loud music, a blaring TV, family noises, etc. While some investors thrive under such influences, for others, external intrusions could very well be detrimental to their wealth, if not their health.

North Star Compass

Less Is More

Babies are born with a limited sense of fear. Most of it is learned. And those fears are accumulated and kept alive in our hippocampus, an area of the brain that stores bad memories. It also recalls trading mistakes and the fears derived from watching trading patterns on stock screens. By spending too much time in front of a computer, we are literally training our brain to assess patterns that then trigger our amygdala into taking potentially self-destructive evasive actions.

"Don't do something. Just stand there."

—Jack Bogle,
founder of the Vanguard Group of Funds

Core Principle: A well-designed portfolio shouldn't require daily vigilance. We already know that markets are unpredictable. Sitting for prolonged periods to watch random movements in stock prices is equally stressful and tedious. Instead, buy quality. Then set proactive trade orders (see Chapters 14, 15, 16, 19, and 20). This allows the market to be the market and can bring some peace of mind that your portfolio is pre-programmed for opportunities or for protection.

Less computer time and more family time should not only improve portfolio performance but should also increase the joy factor. Investing should support your lifestyle, not become it.

Neutralizing the Environment

- Seek a place of calm for trading. Better decisions will happen in the warmth and comfort of your home (or a preferred place), surrounded by natural light, plants, and ethereal music.
- Reduce the distractions. Following multiple trading screens can seduce you into seeing patterns where there are none. The brain is easily fooled. Best long-term decisions are rarely made by watching stock price ticks.
- Put your phone on silent and close the door (if possible). Isolation should improve focus.
- Hold yourself accountable to spouse and others. If necessary, consider having a periodic discussion/review. Some accountability can be a good thing to keep an investor on the right path.

Neutralizing the Emotions

- Eat a proper breakfast and stay away from mood-altering substances that can unduly stimulate or deflate our normal range of emotions, coffee included. Consider switching to matcha tea.[13] Calmer minds deploy smarter decisions.
- Set trades in the pre-market and only check back later to avoid the daily opening market insanity. The first and last 30 minutes of trading can induce poor decisions.
- Take time-out breaks, particularly if deep energy emotions (anger) have been triggered. The emotional impact of a bad day on the markets can linger well after the trading session. Recognize that your family deserves your better self.
- There are five additional ways, in escalating order, to help reduce reactive trading:

    i. For every trade, like a pilot preparing for take-off, follow a decision-making sequence as outlined in Chapters 14 and 20. Unless you are a fighter pilot facing actual life-and-death consequences, all professionals follow guidelines before plying their trade(s).
    ii. Respect that a down day is best for buying and positive days are best for trimming. Being disciplined can add tangible value to a portfolio.
    iii. Limit your total screen time. Set a maximum number of trades per session or the time spent in front of the screen. Periodically step away to stretch and perform alternate activities to calm your

---

[13]Link, R. (2020). "7 Proven Ways Matcha Tea Improves Your Health." https://www.healthline.com/nutrition/7-benefits-of-matcha-tea.

energy. According to Dr. Adam J. Story, any one of drinking beet juice, squeezing a ball, or taking a brisk walk provide a nearly instant calming effect.[14]

iv. Meditate. Billionaire Ray Dalio claims that transcendental meditation has changed his life.[15]

v. Give yourself a reprieve. We all make mistakes, but the better traders learn from them. And thankfully, when you own quality, "Mr. Market" is very good about eventually repairing them.

*"Regret is an appalling waster of energy.
It's only good for wallowing in."*

—*Katherine Mansfield,*
author of *The Garden Party*

North Star Compass

Learning to Trust Is Cool

Fear, greed, and regret are low emotional vibrations that, without reprieve, can induce ill health.

There's a huge difference between market-induced fear (not real) and the fear elicited by a charging bear. One fear may induce you to run for your life, the other will save you from being eaten.

"Trust," on the other hand, is a high vibrational energy. Learn to practice this more. Being proactive with investment decisions is a good starting point. By pre-planning your trades, it allows an investor to "set and forget," thereby bringing greater peace of mind in uncertain markets. Holding high convictions in your stock choices and an undying faith that markets have always recovered are two other positive perspectives that can counter the negativity of being triggered by bouncing stocks.

The conviction that comes from making clear, constructive investment decisions will lead to a healthier, happier life.

All in the Family

Money should be valued as a living entity. Its well-being is as important as the health and welfare of your living family members. We spend a lifetime

---

[14]"How to Lower Your Blood Pressure Immediately." YouTube, uploaded by Adam J. Story, DC, April 24, 2021, https://www.youtube.com/watch?v=6VtmIfNkSiU (Accessed 7 October 2021).

[15]https://www.youtube.com/watch?v=wkoewqsV3lM.

guarding and managing the upbringing of vulnerable children, yet often deploy rather rambunctious decisions with our hard-earned capital. We should want the best outcome for all.

> *"Too many investors spend more time researching their annual vacation than doing due diligence on a promising stock to be held for a decade."*
>
> —Peter Lynch,
> ex-PM of the Magellan Fund

As investors, we need to respect that we are still only children of the capital markets. When we act badly, we get punished. The capital markets are very consistent in this regard. Being proactive steers critical decision-making to our slower, more mindful brain. In Daniel Kahneman's acclaimed 2011 book *Thinking Fast and Slow*, he outlines that relying on our subconscious brain (automatic processes) to render investing decisions is like allowing our inner child to drive the family car on a freeway. Never a good idea. Instead, we need to be in better touch with our outer adult.[16]

1. Think holistically.
2. Be mindful.
3. Act proactively.
4. Trust the corporate management teams.
5. Have faith in the market.

North Star Compass

Benefits of Mistakes

Daniel Coyle, in his book *The Talent Code*, describes how mistakes can be beneficial: **"Although effortless performance is desirable, it's really a terrible way to learn. Instead operating at the edges of your ability, where you make mistakes, will make you smarter."**[17]

When the brain struggles with new concepts, mistakes are a sign that we are forging new territory. Introducing new activities into our lives may slow down our synapses but the outcome should be personal growth.

Moral of the Story: A mistake is only a mistake if no lesson is heeded. If the result is repeated, either our behavior must change, or new methodologies need to be introduced.

---

[16]Kahneman, D. (1934). *Thinking, Fast and Slow*. New York: Farrar, Straus and Giroux, 2011.

[17]Coyle, D. (2009). *The Talent Code: Greatness Isn't Born. It's Grown. Here's How.* New York: Bantam Books, 2009.

Choosing a Path

Without consciously undertaking behavioral changes, a performance gap is most likely to persist. However, to lessen the performance gap, here are several alternatives, in reverse order of recommendation:

#3 – Hire an Advisor. Buffer those emotions by hiring an Advisor to stand between you and the markets. Peace of mind comes from knowing that a managed portfolio could reduce the behavior gap and let the Advisor bear those sleepless nights.

#2 – Don't Try to Beat the Market. Invest in low-cost, index ETFs. According to a study of the S&P 500 Index by Fisher Investments, between 1928 to 2017, markets advanced annually 75% of the time.[18] Simply investing in a low-cost, broad market ETF could potentially eliminate the behavior gap and remove the emotional and physical stresses that come with active trading.

#1 – Embrace the Contrarian Approach. With the knowledge and guidance embedded in the *The Investing Oasis*, an investor can generate tangible performance benefits by learning to overcome their "fight-or-flight" instincts and learning to take advantage of crowd behaviors. This guide introduces:

- A step-by-step blueprint for building and managing a more productive core portfolio.
- The choice to pursue up to three additional accretive tiers of portfolio management.
- How to deploy multiple contrarian investing methods.
- DCA and DRIP (dividend reinvestment) programs to seize the benefits of emotionless trading.
- How to weaponize cash and debt reserves.
- How to reap additional, complementary revenues by selling risk to speculators.
- How to profit from portfolio protection.
- Reducing mistakes, risk, and transaction costs through improved capital markets behavior.

Value-creating decisions require greater attention to details and patience to wait for the opportunities. It will also be more emotionally taxing than either path #2 or #3. Yet, following a master plan will build

---

[18]Fisher Investments (2018). "Historical Frequency of Positive Stock Returns." https://www.fisher401k.com/sites/default/files/2018-03/Historical_Frequency_of_Positive_Stock_Returns_K03171V.pdf (Accessed 10 September 2021).

confidence to trust yourself and the markets and reinforce that volatility brings opportunity. *The Investing Oasis* offers an abundance of ideas and solutions, all intended to make the journey a far more enriching experience.

Adopting a stable plan is the antidote for a volatile market.

Setting Expectations

For those willing to forge on, the ultimate goal should not just be to eliminate the behavior gap but to outperform the S&P 500, net of costs. That's a big ask. And one which even very few professionals have consistently been able to achieve. But then, the pros have the inherent burden of fees and operating expenses. This is a distinct strategic advantage for the retail investor. As well, the retail investor does not have to abide by the regulator or a corporate overseer. As such, they can deploy any of the value-creating portfolio management techniques presented in *The Investing Oasis*.

Whichever route is chosen, though, each has merit, and even a combination can be followed. Yet, the status quo really should no longer be acceptable. The best fit will depend on just how involved an investor wishes to be with the capital markets.

> *"The Three Cs of Life:*
> *Make a choice to take a chance, or your life will never change."*
> —Zig Ziglar,
> author of *See You at the Top*

Q: What to expect for long-term returns?

For years, the central banks of most major economies have traditionally targeted to keep inflation at 2%. Ideally, an investor should desire to generate as much greater than 2% as possible without introducing undue risks. The average annual returns for the S&P 500 Index have been ~8%.[19] So, that's a good starting point.

---

[19]Maverick, J.B. "What Is the Average Annual Return for the S&P 500?" https://www.investopedia.com/ask/answers/042415/what-average-annual-return-sp-500.asp (Accessed 25 September 2021).

However, even better annualized results could come from factors entirely within an investor's control. The Expected Performance Model in Figure 2.6 presents performance profile expectations if all four tiers are applied diligently:

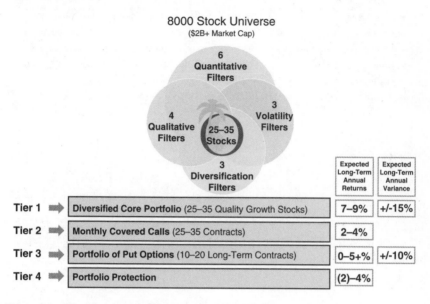

8000 Stock Universe
($2B+ Market Cap)

		Expected Long-Term Annual Returns	Expected Long-Term Annual Variance
Tier 1 ➡	Diversified Core Portfolio (25–35 Quality Growth Stocks)	7–9%	+/-15%
Tier 2 ➡	Monthly Covered Calls (25–35 Contracts)	2–4%	
Tier 3 ➡	Portfolio of Put Options (10–20 Long-Term Contracts)	0–5+%	+/-10%
Tier 4 ➡	Portfolio Protection	(2)–4%	

Figure 2.6   *The Investing Oasis* expected portfolio performance.

> *"It is within the gap between our desire and our behavior that one finds unhappiness."*
>
> —Dr. Stephen Maraboli,
> author of *Life, the Truth, and Being Free*

At the Oasis: Chapter 2

- The behavior gap can be reduced or eliminated, but it requires conscious effort.
- Focus on improving the process and oneself. The results will come.
- Professionals are not smarter. Better results are due to protocols, discipline, and oversight.
- Performance goals should include comparison to a benchmark. Accountability counts.
- With "Mr. Market," humans are the wild card. Practice being calm and proactive.

Oasis Core Investing Behaviors

- **Motivation** to build broader and deeper perspectives. An enriched mind makes better decisions.
- **Discipline** to not stray too far from the path. Reaching for undue risks rarely pays off.
- **Courage** to deploy actions in spite of our fears. Trust in the markets will take you further.
- **Patience** to wait for the results. Investing is a commitment to building a better future.
- **Humility** to appreciate that "winning" is an affirmation of the process, not the end destination.
- **Wisdom** to know that "success" is the journey taken one step at a time.

Chapter 3

Risk 101

"Risk comes from not knowing what you're doing."
—Warren Buffett

Objective:

Designing a risk management plan.

Building Perspectives

In the all-mighty pursuit of performance, risk management is most often an afterthought. Yet, as per any trek into the wilderness, risks abound, and are often well camouflaged. It takes a hunter's skill to recognize the types and potential amplitudes of the various capital market risks. How are each to be handled?

If you understand the differences between the following three categories of risk, you're already ahead of the crowd:

- Market Risk
- Stock-Specific Risk
- Behavioral Risk

Let's break these down.

Market Risk is volatility in the broad stock market impacting the value of individual stocks irrespective of the fundamentals of those stocks. When the gyrations are low to moderate, this is referred to as general market volatility. When a market discount reaches 10–20%, the event is known as a "correction." However, when the downdraft exceeds 20%, it becomes known as a "bear market." These will be further addressed in Tier 4.

Unfortunately, market risk is non-diversifiable. This means that investing in a greater number of stocks will not affect the outcome. All stocks tend to be impacted in a similar gross fashion. The only two ways to protect against the risk of such a market collapse are to proactively hedge a portfolio before the event (see Chapter 23) or to be holding fixed income assets (cash and/or bonds) (see Chapter 4).

Stock-Specific Risks are unique to a business or an industry. This is where diversification has merit:

- **Economic Sector Exposures** – Over the course of the business cycle, economic conditions in all 11 sectors of the global economy eventually incur challenges. Better to have a portfolio diversified across all of the economic sectors to provide resilience against periodic weak conditions in select sectors.
- **Industry Exposures** – Product innovations or obsolescence (e.g. technology), and changes in regulations and policies (e.g. health care) can undermine the fate of many established companies. With 69 different industry categories from which to choose, investors should be mindful to invest in businesses that represent different industries. In a portfolio of 25–35 stocks, why duplicate an industry? For example, at 27.5%, the technology industry is the largest component of the S&P 500, yet there are 13 technology sub-industries to consider before making final allocations. A well-diversified portfolio will limit its overlap.

Chapter 11 is devoted to consciously managing diversification across a greater range of unique risks.

Behavioral Risk is a discretionary decision where a security is traded without regard to its merit within the portfolio. In other words, relying on behavior and instincts by which to deploy trades introduces more uncertainty and stress into the investing process. Reducing or eliminating unnecessary trading can create tangible value in a portfolio. *The Investing Oasis* will introduce several behavioral controls and methods to circumvent trading temptations.

Isolating these three different categories of risk (market, stock-specific, and behavior) will make it easier to build a risk management plan. First, take a minute to scan Table 3.1. This is a history of all the market meltdowns (both corrections and bear markets) from the last 98 years (1928–2020). There were 54 events; essentially, one "calamity" every 20–24 months.

Table 3.1   89-year S&P history.

Peak Date	Trough Date	Peak Price	Trough Price	Percent Loss	Enduring Number of Days
5/14/1928	6/12/1928	20.44	18.34	−10.3	29
9/7/1929	11/13/1929	31.92	17.66	−44.7	67
4/10/1930	6/1/1932	25.92	4.4	−83.0	783
9/7/1932	2/27/1933	9.31	5.53	−40.6	173
7/18/1933	10/21/1933	12.2	8.57	−29.8	95
2/6/1934	3/14/1935	11.82	8.06	−31.8	401
4/6/1936	4/29/1936	15.51	13.53	−12.8	23
3/6/1937	3/31/1938	18.68	8.5	−54.5	390
11/9/1938	4/8/1939	13.79	10.18	−26.2	150
10/25/1939	6/10/1940	13.21	8.99	−31.9	229
11/9/1940	4/28/1942	11.4	7.47	−34.5	535
7/14/1943	11/29/1943	12.64	10.99	−13.1	138
2/5/1946	2/26/1946	18.7	16.81	−10.1	21
5/29/1946	10/9/1946	19.25	14.12	−26.6	133
2/11/1947	5/19/1947	16.14	13.77	−14.7	97
7/24/1947	2/14/1948	16.12	13.84	−14.1	205
6/15/1948	6/13/1949	17.06	13.55	−20.6	363
6/12/1950	7/17/1950	19.4	16.68	−14.0	35
1/5/1953	9/14/1953	26.66	22.71	−14.8	252
9/23/1955	10/11/1955	45.63	40.8	−10.6	18
8/2/1956	2/12/1957	49.74	42.39	−14.8	194
7/15/1957	10/22/1957	49.13	38.98	−20.7	99
8/3/1959	9/28/1960	60.71	52.48	−13.6	422
12/12/1961	6/26/1962	72.64	52.32	−28.0	196
8/22/1962	10/23/1962	59.78	53.49	−10.5	62
2/9/1966	10/7/1966	94.06	73.2	−22.2	240
9/25/1967	3/5/1968	97.59	87.72	−10.1	162
11/29/1968	5/26/1970	108.37	69.29	−36.1	543
4/28/1971	11/23/1971	104.77	90.16	−13.9	209
1/11/1973	10/3/1974	120.24	62.28	−48.2	630
11/7/1974	12/6/1974	75.21	65.01	−13.6	29
7/15/1975	9/16/1975	95.61	82.09	−14.1	63
9/21/1976	3/6/1978	107.83	86.9	−19.4	531
9/12/1978	11/14/1978	106.99	92.49	−13.6	63
10/5/1979	11/7/1979	111.27	99.87	−10.2	33

(Continued)

Table 3.1   (Continued)

Peak Date	Trough Date	Peak Price	Trough Price	Percent Loss	Enduring Number of Days
2/13/1980	3/27/1980	118.44	98.22	−17.1	43
11/28/1980	8/12/1982	140.52	102.42	−27.1	622
10/10/1983	7/24/1984	172.65	147.82	−14.4	288
8/25/1987	12/4/1987	336.77	223.92	−33.5	101
1/2/1990	1/30/1990	359.69	322.98	−10.2	28
7/16/1990	10/11/1990	368.95	295.46	−19.9	87
10/7/1997	10/27/1997	983.12	876.99	−10.8	20
7/17/1998	8/31/1998	1186.75	957.28	−19.3	45
7/16/1999	10/15/1999	1418.78	1247.41	−12.1	91
3/24/2000	10/9/2002	1527.46	776.76	−49.1	929
11/27/2002	3/11/2003	938.87	800.73	−14.7	104
10/9/2007	3/9/2009	1565.15	676.53	−56.8	517
4/23/2010	7/2/2010	1217.28	1022.58	−16.0	70
4/29/2011	10/3/2011	1363.61	1099.23	−19.4	157
5/21/2015	8/25/2015	2130.82	1867.61	−12.4	96
11/3/2015	2/11/2016	2109.79	1829.08	−13.3	100
1/26/2018	2/8/2018	2872.87	2581	−10.2	13
9/20/2018	12/24/2018	2930.75	2351.1	−19.8	95
2/19/2020	3/23/2020	3386.15	2237.4	−33.9	33

Source: Reproduced with permission of Yardeni.com.

Market Corrections (shaded lines) are discounts of 10–20%. They are short and are usually quickly overcome by the advancing market. Over 98 years, there were 33 corrections.

Bear Markets (unshaded lines) are declared when the market sells off by 20+%. They tend to endure longer (18–36 months) due to more macroeconomic issues that require companies to recalibrate their business models. Since 1928, the S&P 500 has experienced 21 bear markets.

Study Figure 3.1 (Bull vs. Bears). In the 24 years ending 2021, there were officially 3 bear markets and 10 market corrections (circles). Those 13 events match the long-term average of having a significant stock market discount happening every 20–24 months. Noteworthy is the increasing steepness of the three most recent bear markets.

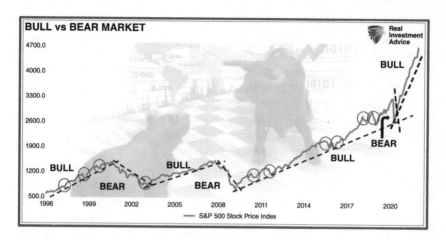

Figure 3.1   Bulls vs. Bears 1996–2021.
Source: Image reproduced with permission from Lance Roberts, Chief Investment Strategist for RIA Advisors, an investment advisory firm based in Houston, TX.

Despite that the markets have advanced annually three out of every four years,[1] too many portfolios suffer needlessly when the markets convulse. When the markets spike downward, to be shaken is understandable, but to act surprised would be disingenuous. Turbulence is the norm for the stock market, yet there are several ways to manage such uncertainty.

Q: Do you have a risk management plan?

A risk management plan can be improved by incorporating any, or all, the following four factors:

   i. **Proactive Decisions** – In the short run, the markets are entirely random. When they hit a saturation point, they collapse temporarily. This is not a matter of bad luck but rather bad planning. As depicted in Figure 3.1, there will be many more corrections and bear markets to come. Rather than fearing a potential market discount of 10–30%, with preparation each pullback could be embraced as an opportunity.

   ii. **Conscious Avoidance** – Once an investor knows their three risk parameters (Capacity, Tolerance, and Required Rate of Return – Chapter 4), they will then have a personal framework to limit their total risk exposure.

---

[1]Fisher Investments (2018). "Historical Frequency of Positive Stock Returns." https://www.fisher401k.com/sites/default/files/2018-03/Historical_Frequency_of_Positive_Stock_Returns_K03171V.pdf (Accessed 25 September 2021).

   iii. Portfolio Design – How a portfolio is designed can exacerbate or diminish the risks. With conscious design, a well-constructed portfolio should be more effective and efficient to manage. This is the essence of *The Investing Oasis.*

   iv. Better Behavior – Trading reactively and incurring undue mistakes aggravate portfolio uncertainty. The behavior gap is the proof. *The Investing Oasis* offers multiple ways to improve investor behaviors and even more ways to diminish making unnecessary mistakes. No need for both the markets and the investor to be unstable.

With our emotions lying at the root of most bad portfolio decisions, learning to build a healthier relationship with our fear could be invaluable.

Fear

While fear doesn't need to be defined, it should be better understood.

Fear robs the mind of thought. When danger is perceived, our body undertakes many physiological actions in deciding whether to take a "fight-or-flight" response. Yet, in the capital markets, our fears can be induced merely through the observation of undulating asset prices. Volatility is the number one fear-inducing component in the investing world. We either harness it or it will torment us. Unfortunately, too many investors allow themselves to be railroaded into a false narrative:

   A. Stay in the markets and be crushed; or
   B. Escape and relieve the tension by selling positions.

While "A" seems to be the worse of two evils, historically, it has only ever been a temporary inconvenience. The second choice leads to a self-fulfilling prophecy. By implementing "B," an investor assumes that they can outsmart the markets by liquidating, holding through the downturn, then repurchasing positions post-crash. This latter belief has far more sinister implications.

Rarely do investors who implement reactionary trades dare to step back into the market at the most opportunistic time (absolute market abyss). Capitulation trades happens because an investor feels vulnerable and lacks the conviction in their investment choices, or the market, to hold through the downturn.

To overcome fear-based decisions and be able to act contrary to our gut instinct, *The Investing Oasis* relies on several clear-minded portfolio management techniques:

- Populating a portfolio with quality assets.

- Using multiple degrees of diversification.
- Learning to trade proactively.
- Deploying hedging strategies.

Together, these methods and processes will instill greater confidence to not just withstand those volatility-induced fears but rather to learn to invest opportunistically when volatility strikes. In other words, learning to become a contrarian.

> *"Bargains do not exist in the absence of fear."*
> —Robert D. Arnott, CFA, Chairman of Research Affiliates,
> former editor of the CFA *Financial Analysts Journal*

Evolution in Risk Management

Much of current economic and financial theory is based on the assumptions that individuals act rationally and consider all available information in the decision-making process. However, this is not even close to how investors typically make investment decisions, nor how they construct their portfolios.

In the last 30 years, behavioral researchers have come to appreciate that investors are affected more by their psychographic state of mind (personality, values, attitudes, and interests) than by their demography (age, income, etc.) and almost not at all by the academic research. Therefore, behavior holds a greater influence on how investment decisions are formulated and how portfolios are designed, as well as how risk is addressed within a portfolio.

Risk management for retail investors more often takes the form of segregation between accounts rather than being governed holistically across the different accounts. In other words, investors tend to isolate risk between their different accounts and deploy independent trading decisions. While there is nothing wrong with a piecemeal approach, taking a more holistic risk approach could render a more effective risk management plan. This would suggest having a singular macro program by which to track your security positions across multiple accounts.

The plan that follows addresses risk management as if all accounts were to be managed holistically.

Risk Management Plan (RMP) Overview

With many corrections and bear markets still ahead, it could be beneficial to review your current portfolio in the context of this 16-Step Risk Management Plan. The ensuing plan is designed around four elements over which an investor has discretionary control:

1. Choices of investments
2. Portfolio design
3. Trading decisions
4. Personal behavior

Risk Management Plan (RMP) Overview

1. Establishing Risk Perspectives (Chapter 3)
2. Determining Risk Capacity (Chapter 4)
3. Assessing Risk Tolerance (Chapter 4)
4. Calculating a Required Rate of Return (Chapter 4)
5. Setting the Asset Mix (Chapter 4)
6. Filtering for Quality Stocks (Chapters 7, 8, 10)
7. Profiling for Stock Performance and Volatility Traits (Chapter 9)
8. Portfolio Diversification Techniques (Chapter 11)
9. Beware Those Temptations (Chapter 13)
10. Contrarian Rebalancing (Chapter 15)
11. Income and Protection with Covered Calls (Chapter 16)
12. Contrarian Cash and Leverage Management (Chapter 18)
13. "Storm" Forecasting (Chapter 21)
14. Prepping for the "Storm" (Chapter 22)
15. Portfolio Protection (Chapter 23)
16. Gold – The Ultimate Hedge (See "The Yin of Gold" at the companion website, www.theinvestingoasis.com)

RMP #1: Establishing Risk Perspectives

The term "risk" conjures different meaning to every investor. In *The Investing Oasis*, however, risk is defined as the real possibility to lose capital permanently under either of these two scenarios:

i. When a business becomes critically impaired (product obsolescence, management errors, C-suite turnover, legislative changes, lawsuits, fraud, etc.). Essentially, anything that hinders a business in a material way that could invoke a permanent decline in valuation is a real risk that could lead to unrecoverable losses.

ii. Impromptu trading in response to unexpected share price volatility. In other words, the surprise drop in a share price triggering an adverse emotional reaction to sell a security.

Professionals: Justified Trading

To the professional community, investing in the markets is not risky business. Volatility is necessary to perform their duties. Investing decisions are performed within the guidelines of an investment policy where the risks of individual securities are objectively measured and correlated within a portfolio.

Professionals need a solid reason for trading a stock. Without it, they usually leave well enough alone. Since short-term markets are nearly entirely random, false trading signals are a constant nuisance. Confidence and convictions are buoyed by investing in quality stocks and keeping a long-term perspective.

Yet, periodically, professionals will incur permanent losses. Real risks can appear in the portfolio due to material events imparted by the underlying corporate leadership. However, the decision to liquidate and move on is arrived at through logic, reasoning, and a clear conclusion. Although the price may have been a primary signal, research would have still been required to confirm the reasons to terminate a stock position.

Retail Investors: Behavior-Driven Trading

Yet why do even just small bouts of volatility tend to induce reactive trading? Unfortunately, it's in our DNA:

- **Perceived Vulnerability** – Retail investors represent themselves in the capital markets. Therefore, all portfolio decisions are deeply personal. Sharp discounts in stock prices are seen to be a threat to one's wealth, immediately triggering a fight-or-flight response.
- **Lack of Accountability** – Without an investment policy, a mentor, or a supervisor, there are no rules to inhibit an investor's decisions. Therefore, investment decisions rely heavily on the investor's experience and personal principles. Unfortunately, there are three major inhibitors between an investor and practicing best capital markets behavior:
  - **Ego** – Most investors believe they have a superior plan to beat the market. However, the first blind spot is the ego. Ego-driven decisions rely heavily on instincts and a personal worldview which obscures and dismisses the real risks. In other words, our ego will perceive that a stock trade holds greater promise and less risk than a more objective investor would otherwise determine.
  - **Memory** – Like flipping coins, each next stock trade is unrelated to prior transactions. Yet even well-intentioned logic can perceive

trends where none exist and fool us into deploying trades with negative consequences.

- **Emotions:**
  - **Euphoria** – Successful trades can induce a cocktail of neuro-transmitters: dopamine, serotonin, oxytocin, and endorphins. To be replicated as much as possible, they lead investors to over-trading and bigger bets. Cocaine produces a similar sensation.
  - **Revenge** – Anger over a prior decision can lead to highly inap-propriate follow-up trades.
  - **Regret** (also known as **"loss aversion"**) – Studies show that bad experiences weigh more heavily than the good. Lousy investment decisions can linger forever in our hippocampus and prevent an investor from reinvesting due to other similar bad experiences.

How our brain can fool us into false decisions is highlighted in the following excerpt titled "Why Monkeys Hate Losing Grapes and You Hate Losing Money."[2] This was a famous experiment where a group of monkeys were conditioned under two similar games. The experiment was conducted by Dr. Keith Chen, professor of Behavioral Economics at UCLA, and subse-quently cited in the book *SuperFreakonomics*.[3]

> *"In the first game, a monkey was shown one grape and, depending on a coin toss, either received just the one grape or a "bonus" grape as well. In the second game, the monkey was presented with two grapes to start. When the coin was flipped against him, the researcher took away one grape, and the monkey received the other.*
>
> *"In both games, on average, the monkeys got the same number of grapes. However, in the first game, the grape was framed as a poten-tial gain, whereas in the second game, it was framed as a possible loss. How did the monkeys react?*
>
> *"Once the monkeys figured out that the two-grape researcher sometimes withheld the second grape and that the one grape researcher sometimes added a bonus grape, the monkeys strongly preferred the one-grape researcher.*

---

[2]Philbrick, M., et. al. (2020). "Why Monkeys Hate Losing Grapes and You Hate Losing Money." https://advisoranalyst.com/2020/09/25/why-monkeys-hate-losing-grapes-and-you-hate-losing-money.html/ (Accessed 25 September 2020).

[3]Levitt, Stephen, and Dubner, Stephen J. (2009). *SuperFreakonomics*. New York: William Morrow.

"A rational monkey would not have cared, but these irrational monkeys suffered from what psychologists call loss aversion. They behaved as if the pain of losing a grape was greater than the pleasure of gaining one."

Unfortunately, true to our primate ancestry, the tendency is identical in humans. Losing money results in a greater emotional toll than winning by the same amount. As such, even minor price volatility can incite irrational fears, especially if we have preconditioned our memory to the perception of losing through countless hours of monitoring price changes on a trading screen.

Rational Conclusion

Becoming a seasoned investor means being self-aware that the blur of our ego or an overreactive hypothalamus can stand between us and our better interests. Yet once triggered, drawing an investor back from the brink of deploying a bad trade is unrealistic. Each one should be a lesson learned. If oft repeated, something must change.

A more assured approach, however, is to not allow the markets to incite us in the first place. See Chapter 5 on becoming more behaviorally consistent and Chapters 14 and 20 about proactive trading.

Winning with Market Corrections

Of course, deeper, more dramatic market moves can unsettle even the pros. But when tumult happens, have faith in the quality of assets and a plan which involves these ongoing contrarian and defensive activities:

- Buying core stocks on market weakness (see Chapter 14).
- Trimming core stocks on threshold targets (see Chapter 15).
- Setting a series of stop-loss and trailing stop-loss trade orders across the portfolio.
- Setting and harvesting gains from covered calls (see Chapter 16).
- Selling put contracts on discounted quality, non-core stocks (see Chapter 19).
- Deploying cash and debt opportunistically during wholesale market weakness (see Chapter 18).
- Setting and harvesting gains from portfolio protection (see Chapter 23).

Averaging down on quality stocks during a downturn should always be good advice. With these defensive and contrarian activities built into your plan, there should be less time spent reacting and more time spent preparing for the ensuing recovery opportunities. Once an investor accepts that volatility is the norm and that corrections and bear markets are inevitabilities, then a risk management plan should be more than just a liquidation strategy.

> *"If you have trouble imagining a 20% loss in the stock market, you shouldn't be in stocks."*
> —John C. Bogle, Vanguard Founder

Accountability Creates Value

Accountability for professionals is a tangible investing advantage, whether due to an investment policy document, their supervisor, the regulator, or their client.

Every portfolio decision must be thought out and justified. Stocks are bought and sold according to their performance and risk profiles. Risk mitigation is practiced at every step of the decision-making process. Professionals need to be mindful of the incremental risks being introduced into the portfolio and which marginal threats are to be diminished or removed. How a stock performs individually is not as important as how it fits within the portfolio. This helps to keep trading decisions holistic and objective.

Since most professionals invest for the longest of terms, day-to-day price volatility, or even stock market corrections, should rarely trigger ad hoc selling decisions. Professionals are expected to remain unimpassioned and guided by policy investment objectives.

Of course, this doesn't mean that the pros always pick winners and don't periodically act spontaneously. It just means that accountability to their clients, their employers, and the regulators demand them to follow a more disciplined path. This discipline inherently provides part of the performance advantage relative to retail investors.

Investors can choose whether to adopt some, all, or no accountability measures.

Chapter 4 will explore an investor's capacity to take on investment risks and setting limits to tolerate investment uncertainties.

> *"Decide whether or not the goal is worth the risks involved. If it is, then stop worrying."*
> —Amelia Earhart (1897–1937)

At the Oasis: Chapter 3

- Market volatility does not lead to permanent losses. More commonly, it is an investor's reaction that determines whether volatility becomes real risk.
- Watching markets too closely is most responsible for triggering undisciplined trades. Taking periodic breaks can benefit a portfolio.
- With quality stocks and learning to be proactive, most permanent losses can be eliminated.
- Risk tolerance limits are hard-wired; loss of sleep is a sign to reduce risk exposure.
- Don't be the monkey.

Chapter 4

Setting the Asset Mix

Objective:

Undertaking a holistic risk review.

Reviewing Personal Risk

When first meeting with a Financial Advisor, the primary order of business is to clarify a client's financial goals, constraints, and the risk parameters from which an appropriate asset mix (stocks, bonds, and cash) can be derived.

Every investor's risk profile should be reviewed according to:

- Financial capacity to accept risk.
- Psychological capacity to tolerate volatility.
- Calculating the minimum rate of return required to meet desired financial objectives.

RMP #2: Determining Financial Capacity

Investors deserve to know whether they can financially handle the worst market downturns without compromising their lifestyle. Assessing the breadth and depth of one's financial situation (assets, liabilities, income, and unique personal circumstances) reveals where, and to what degree, an investor might be vulnerable to a market downturn.

Use Table 4.1 to self-assess your degree of financial capacity. This becomes most important when an investor has a high degree of risk tolerance but may have constrained financial circumstances. On the other hand, where individuals have small obligations, large incomes, and good investments, their risk capacity may well exceed their psychological risk tolerance comfort. Ideally, an investor will learn that their financial capacity is sufficient to not impose any limitation on their asset mix decision.

For each of the 14 categories, pick the ranking (1–4) that approximately best applies to you. Each response is worth a score of 1, 2, 3, or 4 points. There are no right or wrong answers.

Table 4.1   Financial capacity test.

Financial Capacity Assessment Chart[1]				
	Scoring (Choose only one answer per category)			Personal
Category	1	2	3	4	Score
1 **Strength of Career**	Unemployed (not due to retirement)	Multiple part time jobs	Stable career or retired	Improving	
2 **Level of Family Income**	Receiving support from family/Gov't	$30–50K	$50–75K	$75K+	
3 **Cash Reserve**	None	One month reserve	6 months reserve	Strong surplus	
4 **Income Stability**	Highly variable	Regular part-time jobs	Stable	Growing	
5 **Consumption Level (relative to income)**	Overspend	Paycheck to paycheck	Live within means	Save a lot	
6 **Absolute Value of Investments**	$0–$100k	$100K–500K	$500K–1M	$1M+	
7 **Total Investments (relative to stage in life)**	Just starting	Behind	On target	Ahead	
8 **Home Ownership**	Subsidized by family/Gov't	Renting	Still have a mortgage	No mortgage	
9 **Level of Debts (mortgage, LOC, car, student loans)**	Overwhelmed	Serviced monthly	Accelerated payments	None	

Financial Capacity Assessment Chart

Category	Scoring (Choose only one answer per category)				Personal Score
	1	2	3	4	
10 **Time until Retirement**	10+ years	3–10 years	Just about to retire	Fully Retired	
11 **Number of Dependents (children, spouse, parents, etc.)**	Supporting 2 generations	3+	1–2	None	
12 **Personal Health and Wellness**	Long-term unwellness	Some complications	Normal	Exercise regularly	
13 **Family Health History**	History of family illness	Some unhealthiness	Normal	Excellent Family History	
14 **Expected Longevity (family history)**	Under 10 years	10–20	20–30	30+	
				Total =	

[1] This test is intended to provide a quick measure of personal vulnerability which could limit equity exposure. For a more accurate determination of your financial capacity, please consult a Financial Advisor.

Although this test is not comprehensive, it can provide a very tangible sense of an investor's capacity to own a portfolio of stocks. The score will range from 14 to 56; the higher the better.

- 42 to 56 – An investor's risk capacity should be relatively unaffected by market conditions. The asset mix decision should not be constrained by financial circumstances.
- 28 to 41 – An investor's risk capacity may be vulnerable. Consider limiting the percentage of equities held in the asset mix.
- <28 – An investor's risk capacity is vulnerable. When the stock market corrects, an investor could be forced to sell into the downturn to raise cash to handle other obligations. A low score likely indicates a need for a more conservative asset mix until other factors improve, though some equity exposure could still be acceptable.

Even if a score were to be less than 28, the financial risk capacity may be improved by any assets not included in the questionnaire above:

- Spouse also employed (dual incomes).
- Ownership in surplus non-liquid investments (e.g. rental/vacation properties, private investments).

- Expectations for a private pension.
- Potential for an inheritance.
- Reasonable coverage of life and disability insurance.

Once an investor has a clear sense of the strength of their personal financial situation, the next step is to determine their willingness to handle the psychological challenges of investing in risky assets.

RMP #3: Assessing Risk Tolerance

Risk tolerance is the psychological limit at which point an investor can no longer absorb investment losses before feeling the need to liquidate some investments to relieve the emotional stress. Despite that the breaking point is subjective and different for all investors, it can be reasonably assessed through scientifically designed questions. Below is a risk tolerance test created by the University of Missouri focusing on the character of a person and their disposition towards risk-taking. There are no right or wrong answers. Every individual will exhibit a different level of tolerance pursuant to their own financial circumstances, worldview, and life experiences. The test will generate one of five categories of risk tolerance.

University of Missouri Risk Tolerance Test[1]

Now align your test score with the following respective asset mixes in Table 4.2.

Despite the deployment of a sound scientific process, this determination may still need to be adjusted to reflect other factors not captured in

Table 4.2 Missouri risk tolerance key.

Score	Risk Tolerance	Asset Mix
33–47	High	Aggressive
29–32	Above-average	Growth
23–28	Moderate	Balanced
19–22	Below-average	Conservative
0–18	Low	Low

---

[1]Grable, J. E. and Lytton, R. H. (1999). Financial risk tolerance revisited: The development of a risk assessment instrument. *Financial Services Review*, 8, 163–181. https://missouri.qualtrics.com/jfe/form/SV_e5O9zdPbe1ND MWh (Accessed 25 September 2021)

the test. Table 4.3 is a sample list of factors that may encourage further single-point adjustments, either up or down.

Table 4.3 Intangible risk tolerance adjustments.

Reductions (Lower Risk Tolerance)	Augmentations (Higher Risk Tolerance)
• Employed but with occupational hazards	• Being self-employed
• Minimal financial education	• Naturally curious
• Lack of a mentor to provide guidance	• Preference to play competitive games
• Personal history of bad investments	• History of adventure travel
• Advanced age	
• Limited life expectancy (health concerns)	

Caveat: It is also possible that a reader's psychological discomforts may override their true capacity for risk-taking. In other words, despite a very normal and healthy financial situation, a psychological intolerance for uncertainty may dictate choosing a more conservative asset mix.

Note: Whatever conclusions might be drawn from a risk tolerance test, prior experience will be the best indicator of an investor's true tolerance for uncertainty. During the COVID-19 bear market in February/March/April 2020, did you sell, hold, or buy more stocks (indicative of having a low, moderate, or high risk tolerance, respectively)?
Note: Having a "high" risk tolerance does not imply a preference to invest in riskier assets. Instead, it suggests that market volatility does not unsettle your confidence to remain invested. Although the investment management industry has standardized risk tolerance categories (low, moderate, and high), risk tolerance is determined exclusively by the individual. A rule of thumb is that when investing concerns impact your sleep, consider unwinding some of your equity exposure.

North Star Compass

Risk Tolerance – A Migrating Target

- **Psychographics and Demographics** – Even though risk tolerance is firmly rooted in our personality, values, attitude, and interests, our perspective on risk tends to change with age, investment experience, and accumulation of wealth.
- **Beware the Bull** – Olympic gymnasts regularly perform near-death-defying routines. To them, such endeavors are risk-measured situations. With practice, their tolerance grows along with their confidence. Their perception of the risks undertaken diminishes, allowing them to perform even more sophisticated routines. The same is true for investors.

Continued

With time in the market, investors may grow more comfortable with higher volatility. However, just as gymnasts won't tolerate broken bones, neither should an investor accept permanent losses when their degree of risk tolerance is exceeded. Both must be mindful of their psychological limits. Therefore, during long bull markets, investors can be lulled into a state of complacency as their stock exposure rises. Individuals with lower risk tolerance can be seduced into a higher range of risk than originally understood. Periodic rebalancing helps to reduce volatility from a portfolio before that next market shock. However, if caught in a sell-off, only make the adjustments once the market has rebounded. And it will.

RMP #4: Calculating a Required Rate of Return

The next step is to calculate the rate of return required to fulfill an investor's financial objective(s). The Bank Rate Retirement Calculator[2] is one such tool.

Note: If you are already financially independent, then proceed to RMP #5: Setting the Asset Mix. Essentially, your asset mix would be entirely discretionary and constrained only by your risk tolerance.

Note: The maximum annual expected rate of return for an asset mix of 100% blue-chip stocks is 8%. This was the average annual return of the S&P 500 index over the last century. If the required rate of return (RoR) is greater than 8%, certain adjustments in the calculator could be considered:

    i. Save more annually.
    ii. Postpone the date of retirement.
    iii. Lower the expected retirement income and lifestyle.
    iv. Introduce leverage.
    v. Introduce assets with higher expected returns (see Figure 4.1).
    vi. A combination of i–v.

If your financial plan is behind schedule, spending time with a qualified professional could be valuable to explore these options.

---

[2]https://www.bankrate.com/retirement/calculators/retirement-plan-calculator/ (Accessed 25 September 2021).

RMP #5: Setting the Asset Mix

Asset Mix Refresher

Of all an investor's decisions, choosing the asset mix will hold the greatest influence on the long-term expected rewards and the degree of day-to-day volatility. While the asset mix is simply the proportion of a portfolio to be allocated between stocks, bonds (fixed income), and cash, it is the culmination of the above-noted risk discovery process of:

- Establishing financial goals.
- Determining your financial capacity to take on risk.
- Assessing your willingness to tolerate capital markets uncertainty (risk tolerance).

Q: So how does an investor determine the right asset mix?

Understanding the Reward/Risk Spectrum

In Figure 4.1, the asset categories are aligned according to their expected rewards vs. the expected degrees of uncertainty. The linear positive diagonal line, however, deceptively implies equally greater rewards relative to the increasing uncertainties. More realistically, investing above the zone of optimal investing (circled on the chart) introduces a greater number of uncertainties (speculative, political, foreign exchange, leverage, time limits, etc.), and each uncertainty also tends to have a higher range of variance without necessarily generating higher rewards. With each new risk, uncertainty is not additive; it multiplies.

Typically, the younger an investor, the higher the proportion of stocks that could be held (respecting their financial capacity for risk). A long time horizon allows for value creation by the underlying management teams, along with the compounding effect of reinvested capital. On the other hand, retiree portfolios are often steered toward a more balanced risk profile (60/40 stocks/bonds), matching up with income needs and averting concerns about outliving their capital. Yet even a retiree with an otherwise healthy risk capacity (i.e. adequate wealth, pensions, good health, and minimal financial obligations) may feel psychologically tolerant to invest more in the stock market than the bond market, especially if they have done so over their working life.

Analogous to a long investment journey, the zone of optimal investing is called the "Path." This is where the long-term returns relative to the degrees of uncertainty tend to be superior to all other asset categories.

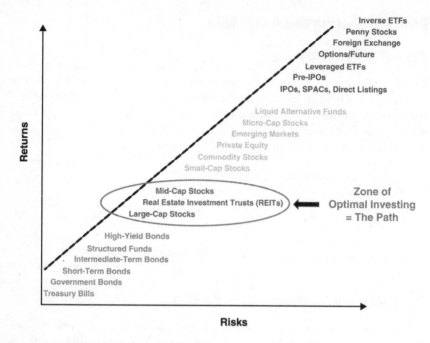

Figure 4.1   Return/risk spectrum.

According to 93 years of data provided by the New York University (1928 to 2020, inclusive),[3] the S&P 500 Index (representing 500 of the largest US companies) generated an average annual performance of 11.6%,[4] compared to 5.2% for US Government 20-year Treasury Bonds. In both cases, the calculations did not consider the reinvestment of dividends or interest.

But how did stocks and bonds perform relative to the amount of volatility experienced (also known as the "Sharpe ratio")?

Rewards per Unit of Volatility

From the same data, per unit of average annual volatility experienced over those 93 years, even though the S&P 500 volatility was higher, 19.5% vs.

---

[3]New York University "Historical Returns on Stocks, Bonds and Bills: 1928-2021." Published data (January 2022). https://pages.stern.nyu.edu/~adamodar/New_Home_Page/datafile/histretSP.html.

[4]Although these performance figures are historically accurate for the S&P 500 Index and 20-year US Treasury Bonds, the annual rates of return projected in *The Investing Oasis* are set more conservatively at 8% +/- 15%.

Table 4.4   93 years of market data from NYU.

	30-Year Average			93-Year Average		
	Returns	Volatility	Risk-Free Returns per Unit of Volatility (Sharpe ratio)	Returns	Volatility	Risk-Free Returns per Unit of Volatility (Sharpe ratio)
US Treasury Bonds	6.4%	7.7%	.28	5.2%	8.8%	.45
S&P 500	12.0%	19.5%	.44	11.6%	17.1%	.56

7.7% for US Treasury Bonds, when measured against the extra returns generated over the risk-free rate, investing in stocks also rendered superior results (.44 vs .28).[5]

Whether over 30 years or 93 years, stocks have generated superior results on both an absolute basis and relative per unit of volatility incurred. Since the investing horizon for most investors could be 30+ years, these numbers should be sobering and compelling when making an asset mix decision. And although higher returns could be earned in the higher reward/risk categories on the Return/Risk Spectrum chart (Figure 4.1), these will introduce additional risks that are not easily justified or rewarded even with patience.

Putting It All Together

In determining a personal asset mix, the three personal risk measures can now be considered in the following order of importance:

1. **Level of Personal Risk Tolerance** – How much equity exposure is acceptable before the degree of volatility disrupts your sleep. Prior market experience offers the most accurate assessment.
2. **Financial Risk Capacity** – How much wealth may be eroded without affecting your lifestyle. Measuring your capacity for risk is often simply qualitative: either you feel financially vulnerable, or you don't.
3. **The Required Rate of Return** – The minimum rate of return required to achieve your desired financial goals as derived from a financial calculator or projections made by an Advisor.

Note: If the required rate of return is less than 8%, an investor will have more discretion in their asset mix choice.

---

[5]The Sharpe ratio will be discussed further in Chapter 9.

The Asset Mix Decision

The asset mix is meant to be a long-term allocation to fulfill an investor's required rate of return while remaining within their capacity to handle financial losses, and which also shouldn't disturb their quality of sleep (risk tolerance). Table 4.5 displays six asset mix combinations, each with a decreasing percentage of fixed income (i.e. bonds). The projected average annual returns and volatility for each asset mix combination are derived from 30 years of historical returns (1988–2018) blended in combinations of bonds (20-Year Treasury Bond Index) and equities (comprised of the 66% S&P 500 and 34% TSX). Cash is addressed as follows:

- Cash intended for lifestyle interests should be kept outside a long-term portfolio.
- Cash held in a long-term portfolio is to be deployed opportunistically. Target = $0.

Included on the right column of each asset mix is a range of expected average annual returns. These projections are derived by combining a proportion of current annual bond yields and 30-year historical average equity returns across a range of the six asset mixes.

Disclaimer: *Past performance may not be indicative of immediate future results.*

Table 4.5   Asset mix projections.

Asset Mixes	Cash	Bonds	Stocks	Long-Term Historical Returns	Long-Term Historical Volatility	Worst 1-Year Return	Expected Average Annual Returns[1]
Income Only	0%	100%	0%	5%	5.4%	−5.3%	1–3%
Conservative	0%	75%	25%	5.9%	6.4%	−3.0%	2–4%
Balanced Conservative	0%	50%	50%	6.7%	9.3%	−11%	4–6%
Balanced	0%	40%	60%	7.0%	10.6%	−13%	5–7%
Balanced Growth	0%	25%	75%	7.4%	12.7%	−18%	6–8%
Growth	0%	0%	100%	7.9%	16.5%	−25%	7–9%
Aggressive Growth[2]							

[1] Each projection is a guesstimate based upon a weighted combination of the historical 30-year returns of a mix of equities (66% S&P 500 + 33% TSX) + the current 20-year US Treasury Bond Yield.
[2] An aggressive growth asset mix is not provided because it incorporates unnecessary risk-taking.

Asset Mix Hindsight

The asset mix is essentially a trade-off of performance vs. volatility. Investors must choose which regret will hopefully bother them the least, either:

- Taking the slower and more certain path but know that their journey will likely be prolonged due to lower returns; or
- Taking the route with more promise but be exposed to a higher degree of temporary, short-term uncertainty.

To help with this dilemma, Figures 4.2–4.5 demonstrate the differences in historical volatility and performance patterns between two polar-opposite asset mixes over 30 years (1990–2020)[7]: bonds (Figures 4.2 and 4.3) and stocks (Figures 4.4 and 4.5).

Investing 100% in Fixed Income

Figure 4.2 presents the individual yearly results for a portfolio comprised of 100% 20-year US Treasury bonds. The annual returns generated over 30 years was 6.43%, with only 4 negative years.

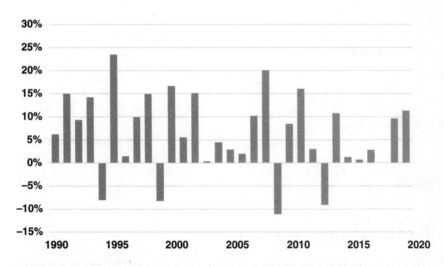

Figure 4.2   Annual returns history for a portfolio of 100% fixed income.

---

[7]Since results are based on index returns, there were no management fees or transaction fees included.

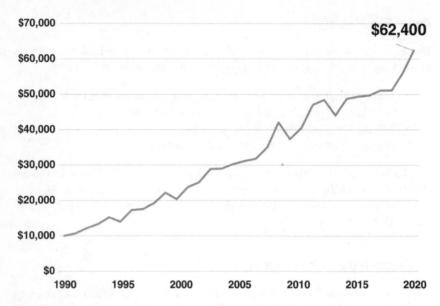

$62,400

Figure 4.3 Performance history for a portfolio of 100% fixed income.

The steady line in Figure 4.3 demonstrates the low degree of volatility as $10,000 invested in 1990 over 30 years grew to $62,400.

100% Invested in the S&P 500 Index

On the other hand, Figure 4.4 presents 30 years of annual results for a portfolio of stocks, represented by the S&P 500 Index. Even with 8 years out of 30 producing negative returns, including 4 greater than 10%, the average annual return was 11.5%.

Figure 4.5 demonstrates how an original deposit of $10,000 in 1990 would have grown to approximately $200,000 in 2020. Over a 30-year period, the asset mix decision to choose investing in stocks vs. bonds would have tripled an investor's wealth.

The Asset Mix Difference

These graphs tell a compelling story about how risk/reward decisions taken today can have significantly different outcomes 30 years hence. Same money. Same time. Different outcomes. The truth is, over any 30-year period in the last 100 years, the results have always favored a portfolio of

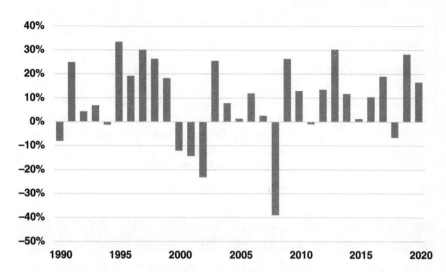

Figure 4.4   Annual returns history for a portfolio of stocks.

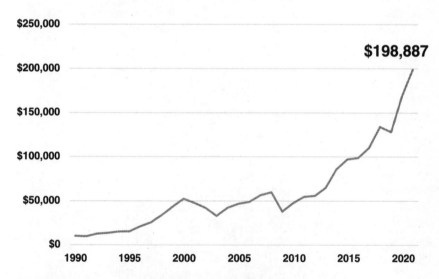

Figure 4.5   Performance history for a portfolio of 100% stocks.

equities over fixed income despite the greater range of volatility for stocks. With perfect 20/20 hindsight, an investor should now be able to choose the route that best matches their risk tolerance, and least regrets: growth, income, or somewhere in between.

At the Oasis

Investing for All Risk Types

Most investors should agree that investing in stocks is the way to build and maintain wealth over the long term. Yet even a conservative portfolio should still have some exposure to stocks. Once the asset mix has been determined, the portion to be allocated into stocks could be invested according to the mindful methodologies practiced in *The Investing Oasis*.

At the Oasis: Chapter 4

- The asset mix is the single strongest influence on volatility and long-term results.
- The asset mix decision is a commitment to your future self.
- Don't let today's volatility influence tomorrow's investments. Think quality and longer term.
- The asset mix will shift over time. In positive markets, trim stocks proactively. During corrections, use the cash reserve to reinstate the original stock exposure.

"Old Jeb here is our Risk-Free Money Manager.
He buries your money in the back yard."

Source: Cartoonstock.

Chapter 5

Firming Our "Backbone"

Objective:

Improving investment decisions by aligning

our intellect,

our principles,

and our gut instincts.

Keeping It Simple

The markets are already so very complex, and we further complicate our investment decisions by embracing countless hours of analysis and interpretation before ultimately pulling the trigger. Of course, best practices requires quantitative analysis and techniques; however, our decision-making could be vastly improved if we also tap into our qualitative skill sets: mindfulness, discipline, and courage. Better investment decisions will happen when we embrace these inner resources combined with simpler methodologies and smarter processes.

Occam's Razor:

"All things being equal, the simplest explanation is usually the correct one."

—Franciscan friar William
of Ockham (1285–1347), a scholastic
philosopher and theologian

This chapter focuses on the psychology behind making better, simpler decisions and how to stand by them. It starts by detailing how rational thinking, which overwhelmingly dominates the investment industry, only partially taps into our vast decision-making complex. An exploration of the tri-brain processes can help us to know just how to help ourselves, despite ourselves.

At the heart of the behavior gap is the need for self-preservation. Witnessing the collapse of a portfolio is always unnerving, even for the experienced. Predictably, at the first sign of trouble, the human psyche is hard-wired to jump to action. Despite that most of us should know better, we can be prone to self-induced panic.

Learning to overcome or avoid such spontaneous behavior is a core practice of *The Investing Oasis*.

Introducing the "Three Brains"

Investing requires copious amounts of decisions, at many levels. Yet, faced with identical circumstances, some investors seem better at making investment decisions than others, particularly under duress. Why?

Here is a quote taken from Marvin Oka,[1] a world authority in the field of behavior modeling:

> *"Unfortunately, our 'Three Brains' might not always be aligned on an issue:*
>
> - *My head has a narrative, 'I should . . .', 'My rules are . . .' or 'My logic says . . .'*
> - *'. . . but my heart really wants to do something else.'*
> - *Still my gut says: 'Uh oh, not safe.'*
>
> *"As far as we can tell, the information highway between the three brains is the vagus nerve. 70–80% of the nerve relays go up, not down. That's why, when your gut and your heart are already in reaction mode, it's hard to talk yourself out of it."[2]*

---

[1]Marvin is one of only five people in the world who have been accorded the rare title of Certified Master Behavioral Modeler. Additionally, Marvin was one of the first five people to achieve the accredited status of a Certified NLP Master Trainer in the field of neuro-linguistic programming (NLP).

[2]Oka, M. (2016). "The Three Brains: Why Your Head, Heart and Gut Sometimes Conflict." https://spinalresearch.com.au/three-brains-head-heart-gut-sometimes-conflict/ (Accessed 25 September 2021).

Bad decisions are only harmful if we don't heed the lesson. More accomplished investors, however, learn to tap into the internal feedback provided by the three decision-making faculties: the head, the heart-brain, and our enteric system (guts).

Who's in Charge?

The left brain may be the master of processes, but it is devoid of the ability to draw perspectives provided by the right brain, set principles (heart-brain), and ultimately pull the trigger (gut-brain). Decisions are rarely just cognitive; studies now prove that our emotions and intuition also play equally major roles.

The left brain is the equivalent to a computer. Data in, data out. Among the three brains, though, it is the most useful to build a structured investment model. Yet it is also the most limited in its ability to render decisions. It can be easily fooled by data, trends, and current events. It relies heavily on assumptions to eliminate inconvenient data. In the face of bad outcomes, a headstrong decision-maker, those who rely heavily upon rules, systems, and procedures will attempt to refine their model and implement new rules. While this purely logistical approach may sound reasonable, the use of modeling to predict the future relies entirely on hindsight. And the future is always very uncertain. To render better decisions, we need to engage more brain power.

North Star Compass

Beware the Assumption

The use of assumptions in framing an argument is a clear indication that an individual is relying more heavily on the logic and reasoning from their left brain rather than listening and engaging with their heart and guts. Assumptions allow incoherent and inconvenient data to be explained away. According to Kendra Cherry, MS,[3] the overuse of assumptions and heuristics (rules of thumb) is reflective of a poorly functioning decision-making complex.

Assumptions conveniently allow our thought process to dismiss the unknowns for the sake of expediency.

---

[3]Cherry, K. "What Are Heuristics?" https://www.verywellmind.com/what-is-a-heuristic-2795235 (Accessed 25 September 2021).

The Head: A Tale of Two Halves

In his book *Thinking, Fast and Slow*,[4] Daniel Kahneman, PhD, points out that about 2% of the time, the left brain methodically processes information. The other 98% of the time, our subconscious right brain fervently tries to make sense of the data (relevancy and perspectives). Alpha waves generated in the right hemisphere are responsible for innovations and creating those excess performance returns (alpha) that investors crave.

Where O Where Art Thou Alpha?

One of the strongest motivators behind the DIY explosion is due to the investment management industry's inability to generate consistent alpha returns. By its very nature, generating alpha is like chasing the wind. We know it exists, but it takes innovation to capture it. Due to the costs, time, and effort required to innovate, the investment industry favors instead charging high fees for beta (index) returns.

Alpha Requires Unique Thinking

To create alpha returns requires doing what no one else is doing. This is the domain of the right brain and takes inherent curiosity, wisdom, and confidence to trust the discovery process. Plus, it requires uninterrupted time to self-educate and process the ideas.

Tactical trading, as preferred by most retail investors to generate alpha, introduces several mismatches:

1. The assurance of long-term gains are replaced with short-term gambles.
2. Trading is dominated by highly refined algorithms. Teams of motivated analysts and PhDs put hours of mindful thought into programming their algorithms to perform thousands of precise transactions per second. Retail investors struggle to deploy, at most, one trade per minute.
3. Every trade for an algorithm is independent of past trades. For the average investor, trading can be physically, mentally, and emotionally exhausting, which increases the probability of costly errors. Worse, we are burdened with the hippocampus, which regurgitates painful memories of past events and can result in emotional linkage between trades.

---

[4]Kahneman, D. (2011). *Thinking, Fast and Slow*. New York: Farrar, Straus and Giroux.

Trading, by its very nature, is reactionary to a given situation and relies heavily on gut instincts. Decisions which bypass our rational thoughts and principles tend to be deployed spontaneously. This is where most of our investing mistakes are made. While there can be merit to periodically trading on instinct, it should not be the primary method by which to build wealth.

> *"None of my scientific discoveries came from rational thought."*
> —Albert Einstein (1879–1955)

The Heavy Lifting Is Already Done

The Investing Oasis already provides the foundational blueprint to build a core portfolio. Then, through a combination of logic and creativity, two tiers of incremental alpha-generating tactics are introduced: covered calls and cash-secured puts. Without having to reinvent the wheel, an investor can quickly get up to speed.

Heart Principles

Meanwhile, our heart grounds and calms the head and guts. A well-developed heart-brain helps us ponder the choices and whether a decision feels right, much in the same way a CEO steers a corporation with their vision but does not get involved with the actual day-to-day decisions. Investment decisions are essentially a process of deciding between multiple choices that require a sense of sacrifice that only the heart can perceive (the choices not taken). Experience helps.

Having principles and holding to them despite the noise will reward those with patience. Our worst decisions come when we ignore our principles and make decisions to fit the situation.

Learn It the First Time

Studies show that longer-term performance improves with lower trading activity (see "Fees and Accountability" at the companion site: www.theinvestingoasis.com). A reduction in trading activity requires stepping away from the markets and willfully neutralizing our emotions. Yet, no matter how disciplined we think we are, it's hard not be triggered by "Mr. Market." *The Investing Oasis* reinforces five processes to diminish spontaneous trading:

1. A well-diversified portfolio of quality stocks should already engender higher convictions to hold through periods of volatility.
2. Adopting more professional standards encourages only deploying trades to improve performance, better diversify a portfolio, or eliminate undue risks.
3. Setting defensive trades proactively (trailing and stop loss orders) means not having to make on-the-fly trading decisions during a sell-off.
4. Building a cash reserve offers an investor the opportunity to treat market pullbacks as opportunities to invest.
5. Equal sizing all stocks in the portfolio simplifies and promotes contrarian rebalancing.

While these processes are discretionary and require judgment, together they could be consequential to shift an investor's paradigm toward seizing the advantages of being a contrarian investor. Adopting any of these will already set an investor on a better alpha-generating path. And we've yet to explore the alpha generating ideas in Tiers 2 and 3.

> *"The first steps to happiness are understanding that negative emotions are harmful and that positive emotions underlie constructive behaviors."*
>
> —The Dalai Lama

Moral of the Story: It should only take one market correction to learn our lesson.

Guts: The Ultimate Decision-Maker

The gut-brain is the "triggerman." This is our core identity. That queasy feeling before, and after, a decision is your gut talking. It's also a source of courage. While absolute fear can paralyze us into doing nothing, our amygdala can overrule all rational thoughts and force us to instigate action.

It requires tremendous discipline to stand your ground to do nothing or, even better, to well up the courage to buy more shares during market tumult. This is when deep-seated intuition and wisdom are required to overcome our primal fears. The gut knows no logic, it only learns by trial and error. It takes wisdom (time + experience) to learn that our head, heart, and gut-brains may not always be on the same page.

> *"If you're relying on your guts rather than a rule-based approach to investing, it is almost certain that your feelings of risk or safety are exactly the opposite of what they ought to be."*
> —Daniel Crosby, PhD,
> *The Laws of Wealth: Psychology and the Secret to Investing Success*[5]

Our best decisions are when the three brains are in alignment. Only once an outcome is known will our head fully comprehend what our heart- and gut-brains had been communicating. Well-honed gut instincts are rarely wrong (except through outright fraud and deceit), but they usually learn very quickly from bad decisions.

> *"My best trades turned out to be the ones*
> *where my hand was shaking when I submitted the trade ticket . . ."*
> —Bob Hager, founder of Phillips,
> Hager & North Investment Management Inc.

Common Sense: Since "Mr. Market" will always be the wild card, the investor should deploy their tactics as consistently as possible.

Harnessing the "Three Brains"

If alpha were so easy to generate, everyone would achieve outperformance. Yet those who can harness the power of their "three brains" will have a probability edge over the rest.

The Investing Oasis is the fusion of intellectual insights and perspectives (head), personal principles (heart), and market experience (guts) to enact an investment plan. With *The Investing Oasis*, investors are given a running start. No need to rethink the model or the management style. Start by establishing a meaningful core portfolio and deploying purposeful trades. Once the foundation is built, if desired, the investor can then move forward to generate alpha returns in Tiers 2 and 3.

---

[5]Crosby, D. (2016). *The Laws of Wealth: Psychology and the Secret to Investing Success*. Petersfield, UK: Harriman House.

Building Backbone

Conquering the behavior gap requires having rock-solid convictions:

- **Belief in your plan.**
- **Confidence in your decisions.**
- **Holding faith in the markets.**

Of course, all convictions are subjective. But like a mother bear guarding her cubs, true convictions should be resolute; nothing should get between you and them.

So, when the market eventually descends into correction mode, your confidence should remain unwavering that a portfolio of quality investments bought at reasonable prices will not only survive, but these high-quality businesses will likely engage in opportunistic M&A. Your duty should be to lean into the sell-off with your cash reserve and add to existing positions. Ultimately, the market will return to its long-term growth trajectory.

"Conviction" means that it should take much more than day-to-day price fluctuations or a periodic market swoon to cause capitulation. Aside from finding a legitimately better candidate stock, or needing the cash for obligations, the only other truthful reason to sacrifice a stock should be when something corporately material transpires.[6]

> *"We think [. . .] that we're much more rational than we are. And we think that we make our decisions because we have good reasons to make them. [. . .]*
>
> *"We believe in the reasons, because we've already made the decision."*
> —Daniel Kahneman, PhD,
> 2002 Nobel Prize Laureate, Professor of Psychology
> and Public Affairs Emeritus at the Woodrow Wilson School,
> the Eugene Higgins Professor of Psychology Emeritus at
> Princeton University, and a fellow of the Center for
> Rationality at the Hebrew University in Jerusalem

---

[6]Material and non-material criteria are explained in Chapter 15.

Volatility, Our Teacher

If a stock did not tick enough of your conviction boxes to begin with, then it was always going to be a candidate for abandonment. Market downturns expose our weakest decisions. While volatility is unforgiving, it is also a moment of honesty. Each sell-off is an opportunity to learn about ourselves.

Ideally, don't compromise on your principles and put yourself into a position for potential failure. The winning edge requires making consistently good decisions (or non-decisions) and minimizing unnecessary mistakes. Stick with quality.

North Star Behavioral Compass

What Did You Do?

Investing is not real until you have skin in the game. So, how did you react when:

- The market collapsed 55% in the Great Financial Crisis of 2007–2009?
- The market fell 32% in one month (March 2020) in the COVID-19 bear market?
- The market peeled off 30% from January 2022 to June 2022?

These three events could tell you everything you need to know about your market manners and your risk tolerance limits. Everyone hates a bear market. But how it is handled precisely defines an investor's capital markets character.

Bad Behavior – sold into a downturn.
Good Behavior – held through the downturn.
Best Behavior – bought more during the panic.

How we handle ourselves during market mayhem (or any crisis) reveals our truest character. Each one is an opportunity for improvement. *The Investing Oasis* offers many ways to prepare yourself and your portfolio for the next downturn. So, the next time you are faced with a rampaging herd, step aside. In exchange for the safety of your cash, they will hand you their highest-quality assets . . . at a discount.

At the Oasis: Chapter 5

- Better trading decisions happen when all three brains are involved:
  - Head = logic and perspectives to see the opportunity.
  - Heart = principles and framing the choices.
  - Guts = taking action using experience and intuition.
- Common sense and simplicity tend to get better results than trying to outsmart "Mr. Market."
- Solid convictions are krypotnite to volatility.
- Winning consistently isn't complicated:
  - Have a plan.
  - Buy quality.
  - Stay on the path (avoiding temptations; minimizing mistakes).
  - Trade less.
  - Trust the capital markets.

"Investing is not about beating others at their game.
It's about controlling yourself at your own game."

—Benjamin Graham,
author of *The Intelligent Investor*

Chapter 6

The Case for a Planner/Advisor

Source: fineartamerica.com

Objective:

Building better relations with your Advisor.

A Professional Backstop

The benefits of hiring a professional to create, deliver, and implement a financial plan cannot be overstated. Having a trusted Advisor is much like having a private mentor in support of your life's journey. During better times, their merits may be underappreciated, yet during life's unexpected moments, their counsel and intervention could prove immeasurable.

This chapter will walk through how an investor may benefit from engaging a professional and how the investor has a role to play in ensuring that the relationship with their financial professional is mutually beneficial:

- Distinguishing the roles of Financial Planners and Financial Advisors.
- Traits of a good financial services professional.
- Measuring a financial professional's value proposition.
- What to do if a change is necessary.
- Pros and cons of DIY investing.

Critical Moments

Through our lives, we will all experience upheavals and transitions:

- Career changes (compensation/negotiations).
- Moving between jurisdictions (new tax laws/estate rules).
- Changing life partners (births, death, divorce, a new significant other, remarriage).
- Small business growing pains.
- Challenges with the tax authorities.
- Leaving the workforce (retirement/severance).
- Planning for higher education.
- Managing through market corrections.
- Handling a windfall (sale of property, an inheritance).
- Caregiving across generations.
- Deterioration of health.
- Estate and life succession planning.

And on it goes. Progress toward our lifetime goals is rarely in alignment with our intentions and best-laid plans. Periodically, we all could benefit from having access to an experienced professional to reassess our situation and outline the choices.

Planner vs. Advisor

The right financial professional can help to translate and project your current situation into a tangible future. Is it the one you envisioned? Perhaps, but more likely periodic adjustments are required to smooth the path forward. To ensure engagement with the most appropriate professional, it pays to know what different functions they serve. The following descriptions are intended to distinguish between these two roles.

Financial Planners (FPs) are hired for their expertise, independence, and objectivity. They are positioned best in the financial community to provide either a detailed financial plan, a generalist financial plan, or stand-alone modules to address more specific financial matters, including, for example:

- Cash flow/budgeting shortfalls.
- Debt consolidation and management solutions.
- Navigating government benefits programs.
- Projecting retirement possibilities.
- Budgeting for long-term health care needs.
- Designing family income tax effectiveness.
- Counseling through a tax audit.
- Reviewing insurance coverage and identifying risk gaps.
- Outlining equitable estate planning solutions.
- Crafting an investment policy document and asset mix.

According to the Certified Financial Planner Board of Standards, Inc. and the equivalent organization in Canada, titled FP Canada, a financial plan typically culminates in tailored investment recommendations based on information collected about the client's current situation, goals, needs, priorities, and risk exposures. A plan should use clear and concise language to convey the benefits, as well as the risks and costs of those recommendations.

When an investor is ready to move forward from the financial planning stage to implementation, they could then consider hiring a Financial Advisor to manage some or all their wealth.

Financial Advisors (FAs) are hired for their investment knowledge and expertise to implement a portfolio of investments on your behalf. Working titles will vary depending upon their individual licensing and the securities registration of their firm (i.e. portfolio managers, securities advisors, investment counsel, wealth advisors, or investment executives). However, all will be registered with either national or provincial authorities. Their investment recommendations should be outlined in a personalized investment policy document.

If you decide to hire an FA, inquire how much investment discretion they have. Depending upon the licensing and registration, there may be limitations:

1. A **non-discretionary manager** (restricted) can set up a portfolio of investment products; however, all portfolio adjustments would require your approval. Periodic meetings are the opportune time to review the progress and address making changes. Most FAs in the industry are registered to provide non-discretionary (restricted) services.

2. A **discretionary manager** is a fiduciary hired to manage a portfolio with day-to-day discretion according to an investment policy statement tailored to the individual client. Periodic meetings offer the opportunity to discuss what has transpired in the portfolio and how the manager intends to handle the portfolio going forward.

Before proceeding to do business with either a discretionary or non-discretionary manager, however, a professional should provide an "engagement letter" outlining their services, their compensation method, and a fee schedule.

Traits of a Quality Professional

Consider some of these following traits when interviewing a financial professional:

- **Listening and Interviewing Skills**. Are you being heard? Does the FA demonstrate an interest in understanding not just your situation but the circumstances and challenges that underlie your situation? Would you be willing to be vulnerable with them?
- **Leadership** is a cornerstone. To place your trust in the hands of another, you should want to know that they can lead you through critical challenges. Ask personal questions to learn of an FA's character and relevant experiences. They are being hired to act in your better interests during life's more difficult moments.
- **Competency** should be observable through a presentation of the FA's education, life experiences. and areas of expertise. A professional should also know when to defer to other professionals. Clear responses to your questions are as important as the content of those answers.
- **Objectivity.** Ideally, an FA will stand apart from the sales process and introduce thoughtful perspectives relative to your agenda. Ultimately, your gut instinct will decide whether an Advisor is being fair and impartial in their guidance.

Checklist for Hiring a Financial Professional

If you don't yet have a Planner or an Advisor, shop around. There are plenty of service models and personalities, each with strengths and weaknesses. Ultimately, this should be a long-term relationship, so trust and chemistry are intangibles. Here are 9 pragmatic aspects to consider in assessing their value proposition:

1. The firm's reputation
   - Google for news about the firm.
2. The professional's status
   - LinkedIn can provide insight on a professional's education and experience.
   - To verify a financial professional's registration status:
     - In the USA:
       - Securities and Exchange Commission (SEC)[1]
       - CERTIFIED FINANCIAL PLANNER™ Board of Standards[2]
     - In Canada:
       - National Registration Search, MFDA, IIROC or La Chambre de la sécurité financière[3]
       - FP Canada™ [4]
       - Check a CERTIFIED FINANCIAL PLANNER® professional for disciplinary actions.[5]
3. A Planner/Advisor's current client base
   - Ask for a profile of their average client and whether that matches well with yours (life stage, average wealth, level of sophistication).
   - Ask for client references.
4. Breadth and depth of expertise and financial planning services offered
   - Do they have the relevant experience for your needs?
   - Are more comprehensive wealth management services available in the firm?

---

[1] https://www.sec.gov/oiea/investor-alerts-bulletins/ia_checkfinpro.html (Accessed 26 September 2021).
[2] https://www.letsmakeaplan.org.
[3] https://investorcentre.ific.ca/ensuring-a-financial-advisor-is-registered-and-in-good-standing/ (Accessed 26 September 2021).
[4] https://www.fpcanada.ca/findaplanner.
[5] https://www.fpcanada.ca/canadian-public/disciplinary-actions.

5. What types of investment services and products are offered (if any)?
   - Are investment management services discretionary or non-discretionary?
   - House brand products or open market solutions?
6. Ask about the firm's conflict of interest policies and dispute resolution mechanisms.
7. What type, and frequency, of communications should be expected (webinars, newsletters, statements, email, telephone, social media, Zoom)?
8. Clarify fees and compensation structure. Ask for a sample engagement letter.
9. Do some research. To ensure your initial meeting goes well, use this list as a template along with the checklist available at the CFP Board Center for Financial Planning website.[6]

Some of the greatest value offered by a professional, however, could be the intangibles:

- Proactive outreach when rules and laws materially change.
- Acting as an emotional buffer when the markets are in turmoil.
- Being a trusted source of wisdom through intergenerational challenges.
- Ease of accessibility during business hours and beyond.
- Chemistry and fit.

Before choosing, talk to friends, family, and peers. Word of mouth is still the most common method of referral. Interview several professionals before making a final decision.

To provide effective advice, an FA should eventually need to know everything about you. It's only when an individual faces difficult personal circumstances (death, disability, moving, loss of job, difficult markets, etc.) might their worth be truly proven.

To locate a local CERTIFIED FINANCIAL PLANNER™ professional in the US,[7] use the accompanying URL in the footnote.

1 800-487-1497 (Toll-Free)
https://www.letsmakeaplan.org

---

[6]https://www.letsmakeaplan.org/getting-ready/checklist-for-your-first-visit-with-a-financial-planner (Accessed 26 September 2021).
[7]https://www.letsmakeaplan.org (Accessed 26 September 2021).

To locate a CERTIFIED FINANCIAL PLANNER® professional in Canada,[8] use the accompanying URL in the footnote.

1-800-305-9886 (Toll-Free)
https://www.fpcanada.ca/findaplanner

Performing an Annual Assessment

At least once per year, an investor should expect their FA to conduct a portfolio and service review. In this exercise, the client typically takes a more passive role while the Advisor presents relevant information and performs a KYC (Know Your Client) update (now an annual obligatory requirement). This is often a moment when investors feel nervous and vulnerable. Being better prepared can help develop a more productive interaction. Table 6.1

Table 6.1 CFA investor rights.

Investor Rights[1]
CFA® Institute Standards
Abbreviated Version

1. An investor's financial interests take precedence over those of the professional and the financial institution.
2. Honest, competent, and ethical professional conduct that complies with all applicable laws.
3. Independent and objective advice and assistance based on informed analysis, prudent judgment, and diligent efforts.
4. Fair treatment with respect to all clients.
5. Disclosure of existing or potential conflicts of interest in providing products or services to the investor.
6. Advice rendered is suitable relative to an investor's financial objectives, constraints, and circumstances.
7. Clear, accurate, complete, and timely communications using plain language and effectively presented.
8. Full disclosure of all fees and costs charged, and that these expenses are fair and reasonable.
9. Accurate and complete records are kept.
10. All information is to be kept confidential.

[1]https://www.cfainstitute.org/-/media/documents/support/future-finance/investor-rights/translations/statement-of-investor-rights-english.ashx (Accessed 27 September 2021).

---

[8]https://www.fpcanada.ca/findaplanner (Accessed 26 September 2021).

presents a summary of universal investor rights as outlined by the CFA® Institute.

Yet instead of remaining passive, why not conduct your own annual review with the FA to assess the value proposition delivered and whether any changes need to be made to the portfolio or to the services to better meet your interests. Here are four pragmatic ways to assess their value proposition:

1. Assessing Service Standards
2. Identifying Expertise
3. Measuring Portfolio Performance
4. Reviewing the Cost of Services Rendered (Fees)

1. Assess Service Standards

To help perform an annual review of your FA's service quality, Rob Carrick, a personal finance columnist with *The Globe and Mail* newspaper, has created a downloadable service checklist comprised of 18 questions.[9] Simply download the checklist and complete it in the privacy of your home. Upon doing the review, add up your "Yes" answers and compare the numbers with the Advisor Test Ranking Chart in Table 6.2.

Table 6.2   Advisor test ranking.

14+	Solid Value
11 to 13	Not Bad
8 to 10	Just OK
5 to 7	Weak
4 or less	Bye-bye

This report card is founded in common sense and should help to create a dialogue around any areas of concern. A good FA should want to know how they can improve their practice.

[9]Carrick, R. (2021). Are you getting value from your adviser? Try Rob Carrick's checklist. *The Globe and Mail* (February 25). https://www.theglobeandmail.com/globe-investor/investor-education/are-you-getting-value-from-your-adviser-try-rob-carricks-checklist/article33649964/ (Accessed 7 November 2021).

2. Identify Expertise

This is another qualitative measure. A competent FA should be able to handle most financial planning challenges. However, on occasion, matters may require outside counsel or expertise (i.e. deploying an estate freeze, corporate buy-sell insurance agreements, international property and trusts, generational tax and succession planning, separation/divorce agreements, etc.). Use this opportunity to inquire whether more complex financial matters can also be handled.

3. Measure Portfolio Performance

Measuring the performance of a portfolio is the third stage of an assessment. Your annual statements already include your annual performance information.

To better understand your portfolio's performance, it could be compared to:

- an objective benchmark.
- the original projected required rate of return.
- the performance from previous years.
- whether the degree of volatility incurred was problematic.

These four additional relative metrics could provide valuable insight to affirm whether your investment plan is on track.

Note: Since the degree of portfolio volatility is less tangible of a topic, it might not be addressed unless the year was unusually turbulent. However, if volatility is a cause for concern, this should be discussed. Sleep matters.

4. Review the Cost of Services Rendered

Being able to assess an FA's value proposition also requires knowing the costs/fees incurred. Each financial institution is required to provide an annual fee/cost statement. Fees can be assessed as follows:

- Have the total fees increased from prior years?
- When measured against the total services provided, do you feel you are getting value for your money?
- Can you negotiate better fees by consolidating more assets?

The Overall Value Proposition

Measured altogether, the services provided, the expertise displayed, the performance generated, the volatility experienced, and the fees charged comprise a relatively full assessment. As in any business for hire, an investor deserves to know not just how they are doing relative to their stated objectives but also whether their FA is delivering tangible value. The costs incurred should justify the value received.

Ultimately, what does your gut say? Your intuition may be the best assessment tool.

An annual review is an opportunity for transparent discussion, education, and reassurance. Like any healthy relationship, periodically, it should be assessed and discussed to affirm its value for both parties.

Changing a Planner or Advisor

What if a tipping point has been reached? According to an interview with Money Coaches Canada CEO and co-founder Karen Mizgala, client dissatisfaction with their current FA is not usually due to high fees, nor even portfolio performance.[10] The primary reasons were lack of transparency and poor communication, leading the client to believe their concerns were not being heard or listened to.

If you are unhappy for any reason and are thinking about making a change, don't be intimidated. It is not that uncommon. Sometimes changing "doctors" is the right medicine to address your needs. Yet, since your financial professional knows most everything about you, it may feel very personal. To expedite as smooth a transition as possible, here are several keys:

- Know why you are leaving. Like a change in any relationship, some self-reflection should be required in order not to repeat the same mistakes with the next FA.
- Make sure it is mutually agreed with your life partner. To change without gaining support could open an unexpected avenue of dissonance.
- Review the original "Letter of Engagement" to know the termination terms.
- Determine the costs of transferring assets to a new firm. There may be incentives offered by the new FA to entice this new business.
- Deliver the decision professionally. It should be respected as a business relationship.
- As a courtesy, provide the ex-FA with critical and fair feedback to help improve their business going forward. This decision can be delivered in person or by phone, email, or letter.
- Set a reasonable date by when to expect the existing services to be terminated. In most cases, the new FA can handle the transition details and would benefit from having the most recent investment statements.

---

[10]Carrick, R. (2021). The surprise factor that kills adviser-client relationships-no, it's not stock market plunges or high fees. *The Globe and Mail* (March 13). https://www.theglobeandmail.com/investing/markets/inside-the-market/article-the-surprise-factor-that-kills-adviser-client-relationships-no-its/ (13 March 2020) (Accessed 26 September 2021).

Going DIY

To go DIY, there are two big questions:

1. **How good is your personal value proposition?**
   In other words, do you feel competent enough, do you have the confidence, and do you have the temperament to manage investments? Opening a discount trading account and managing capital to save on management fees also comes with the responsibility for making all the investment decisions. Do you have the time? Do you want to do the research? Are you willing to make gut-wrenching decisions and be exposed to the emotions that come from second-guessing your decisions? Are you prepared for sleepless nights? And there will be mistakes. How much are you willing to pay for this education?

2. **How much money should you manage?**
   If you already have an FA, how much to invest DIY may be influenced by your:

   • Degree of motivation.
   • Level of self-confidence and ability to form decisions.
   • Prior investing experience.
   • Area of personal expertise to be exploited.
   • Time to spend on the investment process.
   • Willingness to embrace market hours (depending upon the time zone).

If you just want to dabble in the markets (e.g. a hot stock or an IPO), *The Investing Oasis* may offer only modest value. However, if you desire to learn and apply a more professional approach to investing, this guide could be greatly beneficial as an investment plan, as a source of education, and as a reference tool. The bonus is that an investor can choose their desired level of engagement.

Building a portfolio independent of the style offered by your Advisor would be most appropriate. After all, it's not meant to be a competition. There are many alternative routes by which to get to a desired destination.

DIY Pros

• **Save on professional fees** – Cutting professional costs is a very strong motivation. And by using a discount, or a commission-free trading platform, retail investors gain an enviable advantage over the costs of professional money management. But can you control your trading activity?

- **More investing choices** – Investors will have access to a world of investments. Advisors may be constrained to invest in a limited number of pre-approved investment vehicles, let alone not being able to invest in individual securities.
- **Simplicity** – Investing could simply be comprised of a portfolio of low-cost exchange-traded funds (ETFs) plus a few preferred stocks. Sleep well.
- **Education** – Everyone learns more by doing.
- **Personal challenge** – Perhaps you want to exploit a personal expertise or a strategic knowledge advantage.
- **Accountability** – Some investors just want to control their own destiny and don't require checks and balances.

DIY Cons

- **Behavior gap** – Despite that most professionally managed portfolios underperform the markets, retail investors underperform by an even greater margin. To do better requires a sincere commitment to control behavior and improve capital markets behavior and practices.
- **Professionalism** – A necessity to minimize the behavior gap. You may already have a full-time job or have retired from one. Do you want another?
- **Day-to-day vigilance** – It can be tedious watching a terminal for hours and dealing with the sundry administrative matters.
- **Need for discipline** – No plan, no limits, and poor discipline tend to equal mistakes and reduce performance.
- **Trading challenges** – Every trade will evoke an emotion. Second-guessing your decisions adds to the trauma. Investing requires confidence and conviction to stay the course.
- **Stress** – Market corrections can be enormously stressful. Having an FA can help buffer the worst moments of the market. Retail investors are most vulnerable to closing their investment accounts just after market corrections.

Best of Three Worlds: The Hybrid Model

(Advice, Management, and DIY)

Being a DIY investor and hiring a professional are not mutually exclusive concepts. A Financial Planner can be hired to design your financial plan and be available to handle your interim financial matters/crises.

A Financial Advisor can be hired to manage some, or most, of your investments. And you could tackle the remainder. A well-founded relationship with competent, trusted professionals could even buoy a decision to go DIY.

More education, building perspectives, and greater confidence in your investment decisions should also translate into a better working relationship with your financial professional(s).

At the Oasis: Chapter 6

- Engaging a professional money manager and DIY investing are not mutually exclusive.
- The experience of a professional should be invaluable during life's critical moments.
- Deploying a structured assessment of your financial services professional should be a mutually beneficial exercise.
- Fee savings alone may not justify taking on the risks and frustrations of DIY investing.
- How much to manage will depend upon confidence, competence, and your free time.
- To find a good Advisor, "word of mouth" is the strongest invitation. Bring a checklist and a friend. Like investing, better decisions happen by triangulating resources.
- A Financial Plan + Pro Management + DIY = Best of Three Worlds.

Foundation Comments

No matter the mission, investing should never be a series of high-stakes decisions that just happen to play out favorably. And building and maintaining wealth requires much more than tactical trading. In the foundation, the focus is first on the investor.

Preparation is critical for any adventure, let alone one as long and arduous as traversing the stark capital markets "desert." Success rests primarily on an investor's guile, mindfulness, and ability to navigate the unknown. Learning to read the market's subtle signs and avoid temptations are as critical as having chosen a good stock of "camels" for the journey ahead. This foundational stage has been purposefully designed to reinforce preparation of self to make better decisions. Visions of riches too often blind us to the risks. For the unprepared, the capital markets will exploit our weaknesses. And although mistakes are expected, taking unnecessary discretionary risks could subvert the whole expedition.

In the next step, Tier 1, the focus will be to design and manage a portfolio of exceptional growth stocks.

As in most adventures, staying close to the beaten path should be the more assured route. At the outset most decisions will have been derived through left-brain logic. But as temptations are introduced along the journey, the guide will explore how to better use one's intuition to explore safely "into the beyond."

"Know yourself and you will win all battles."
—Sun Tzu (544–496 BCE), *The Art of War*

THE INVESTING OASIS: Tier 1

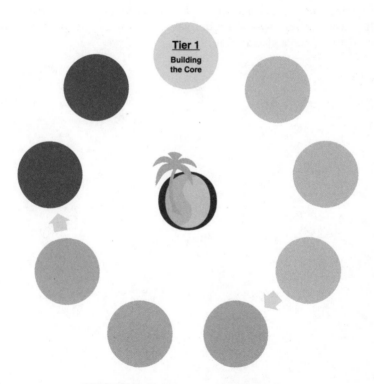

Tier 1
Building
the Core

MISSION #1: To Improve on the Status Quo

	Mission #1
	To Improve on the Status Quo
Tier 1 – Building a Core Growth Portfolio	✓

At this stage, the status quo should no longer be acceptable. To generate better results with diminished volatility and fewer mistakes requires applying portfolio management principles more diligently and adopting more mindful practices. Investing is a long-term endeavor. An investor should not have to rethink their stock positions and rehash decisions on a daily or even a weekly basis. The Tier 1 mission is to build a manageable, sustainable, and diversified portfolio to generate beta performance. Further ahead, there will be higher value–creating concepts that deserve more of your time and attention.

Chapter 7

The Oasis Growth Fund (OGF) Model

"To make money in stocks, you must have 'the vision to see them, the courage to buy them, and the patience to hold them.' Patience is the rarest of the three."
—Thomas William Phelps *(1923–1992),*
100 to 1 in the Stock Market

Objective:

Design overview of a comprehensive, holistic portfolio.

Choose Your "Camels" Well

Without a healthy stock of dromedaries, there would be no commerce in the desert. Camels are brilliantly adapted to the harshness of their environment. Every aspect of these "beasts of burden" provides their cameleer with a mode of business and life-critical support: transportation, shade, evening warmth, storm and predator protection, dung for fires, milk for consumption, and nutrition when they pass away. The average camel lives for 40 years and is minded protectively to generate a lifetime of service. After all, an owner's life depends on their well-being.

This analogy with a portfolio of stocks is fitting. Eventually, investors will depend on deriving as much revenue as possible over 30+ years of retirement from their assets. It may stretch the imagination that a portfolio of stocks could endure our lifetime but each is a thriving, dynamic business. Picked well, these "beasts of burden" will provide for you.

RMP #6: Filtering for Quality Stocks

Winning Should Never Be by Chance

Investing in a company is a vote for the world you want to see. As such, a portfolio should not be a random accumulation of opportunistic stocks.

As the chief decision-maker, it is essential to know why and how each business incrementally augments a portfolio. Only by understanding a current portfolio's composition can an investor know which next stock to introduce into the portfolio to augment performance or diversify away risk. A portfolio should reflect an investor's outlook toward the next decade of economic growth.

A well-designed portfolio should reflect your personal convictions. The importance of such a commitment will be necessary at the market's direst moments.

The steps ahead in Tier 1 will help identify approximately 50 of the highest-quality companies filtered from a universe of approximately 8,000 candidate stocks. From this select group, 20–35 stocks will eventually form the core portfolio. The remaining quality names could then prove valuable in Chapter 19.

Respectfully, most investors likely already hold favored stocks. These may act as a foundation from which to construct the rest of a portfolio. However, consider screening even preexisting stocks through the following 16 filters to confirm their merit.

At the Core

Here is what to expect from a well-designed core portfolio:

- Performance results exceeding that of an uncoordinated accumulation of stocks and directly competitive with the S&P 500 benchmark.
- Less surprises and volatility in line with the S&P 500.
- Modest ongoing maintenance.
- Lower costs than the average professionally managed equity fund.
- Stronger conviction to hold the selected securities in periods of high volatility.
- Opportunity to focus on the higher-gain value-creating tactics in Tiers 2 and 3.

At the Oasis

The Build

A fully diversified core portfolio of 20–35* premium growth stocks can be crafted in eight steps using "bottom-up" research and 16 selection filters. Stocks are then bought with discipline according to QARP (quality at a reasonable price) and periodically rebalanced using a built-in Relative Strength model.

As the journey progresses, three optional tiers of portfolio enhancement will be gradually introduced:

- Tier 2 – Supplementary income from covered calls
- Tier 3 – Additional returns from put contracts on discounted non-core, quality stocks
- Tier 4 – Portfolio protection techniques

*The ideal number of stocks in a portfolio is a debated topic. However, most experts agree that a portfolio comprised of 20–35 uncorrelated stocks (diversified between economic sectors and industries) will provide the most effective diminishment of volatility. Investing in a greater number of stocks renders little additional reduction in volatility.

The Investing Oasis *Investment Style*

The large circle in the equity style box (Figure 7.1) identifies the investment style: large cap/growth model. While "Market Capitalization" is easy to understand, the differences between "Value" and "Growth" deserve a few comments.

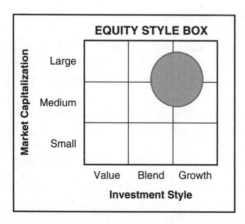

Figure 7.1   Equity style box.

Value vs. Growth

These terms reflect the opposite ends of the stock valuation continuum. A growth business is one that is healthy and competitive. This should be the normal aspiration for all companies. The term "value" is applied to stocks whose share price has been deeply reduced relative to their earnings. This could be due to seasonal or longer-term cyclical trends that affect an industry (e.g. commodities) or due to a material matter specific to a company rendering it less competitive.

For value stocks, the key is assessing whether the situation is a temporary imposition or worse, that it has become a value trap. In the professional world, there is a perennial debate about which style, value vs. growth, is currently in favor. This is a false argument.

Growth is the aspiration for all stocks. Value is the "penalty box" for individual stocks incurring challenges, whether due to seasonal industry trends or corporate material issues. They tend to remain value stocks until appropriate measures are taken to restore their corporate competitiveness or that seasonal/secular cyclicality has returned their industry back to favor. In other words, value is a state of devaluation enforced by the market and remains as such until a corporation can overcome their challenges. From an investing standpoint, value investors tend to be contrarians, believing that superior rewards can be earned once these price-challenged businesses eventually recover. This requires longer-term patience. Cycles and turnaround stories take time. *The Investing Oasis* model, however, prefers to own healthy, growing businesses yet deploys six contrarian tactics to manage the portfolio. Overall, it's valuable to understand how and why corporations fall into the value abyss and then what is necessary for them to regain their growth trend.

Filtering Toward Quality

Through eight steps, *The Investing Oasis* will introduce 16 filters to help investors select high-quality, mid- to large-cap growth stocks and then form the candidates into a well-diversified, equal-weighted portfolio.

> *"If you own a collection of quality companies then making, money is just a matter of time."*
> —Peter Lynch,
> manager of the Magellan Fund at Fidelity Investments
> (1977–1990)

While there are many investment styles and techniques that can be deployed, the following study strongly influenced the methodology as deployed by the author in the Oasis Growth Fund (OGF).

The Influence

Figure 7.2 depicts the graph of a 24-year study[1] (January 1, 1983, to December 31, 2006) comparing the performance of nearly 8,000 individual stocks of all market capitalization sizes and differing degrees of corporate success to the Russell 3000 Index (a good proxy for the best US corporations by market capitalization).

One might have expected the graph to have been split almost evenly between winning securities and losing securities. However, only 36% (the dark bars on the right side of the graph) of 8,000 stocks generated total returns greater than the Russell 3000 Index over those 24 years.

This demonstrates that quality, growing businesses not only generated greater returns and endured longer but that the very best business models (6.1%) dominated the competition. In other words, winning companies know how to keep winning.

This research directly influenced how to build a portfolio with the highest-quality mid- to large cap North American–based growth stocks with dominant, and often industry-critical, business models.

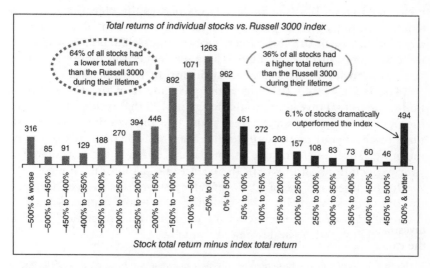

Figure 7.2   Total returns of individual stocks vs. Russell 3000 Index.
Source: Reproduced with permission of Cole Wilcox, CIO of Longboard Asset Management, LP, and Eric Crittenden, CIO of Standpoint Asset Management, LLC.

---

[1]Conducted by Cole Wilcox, CIO of Longboard Asset Management, LP, and Eric Crittenden, CIO of Standpoint Asset Management, LLC, was published by Meb Faber in his book The Capitalism Distribution: Fat Tails in Action,". December 2, 2008, https://mebfaber.com/2008/12/02/the-capitalism-distribution-fat-tails-in-action/.

Eight Steps to Designing a Core Growth Portfolio

Here are the eight steps toward building a core growth portfolio:

Step 1. Setting the Investment Policy
Step 2. Six Quantitative Filters
Step 3. Choosing a Stock Screening Platform
Step 4. Profiling a Stock's Performance and Volatility Character
Step 5. Choosing a Stock Research Platform
Step 6. Four Qualitative Screens
Step 7. Diversification Techniques
Step 8. Equal Allocations

Step 1. Designing a Purposeful Portfolio: Setting the Investment Policy

The very first step in charting a course is to craft an investment policy statement[2] (IPS). The IPS (see Table 7.1) establishes the objectives and constraints around which a portfolio manager's investment decisions must align. In the case of DIY, this is a contract with yourself to honor plans made when you were of rational mind. These guidelines will define the target securities and degree of acceptable risks in pursuit of the financial objectives.

The IPS in Table 7.1 reflects the parameters of the Oasis Growth Fund. Individual investors should design an IPS that reflects their genuine personal objectives and constraints. Use this sample IPS as a template to chart your course but don't leave it so wide open that it has no meaning. High performance at low risk is unlikely. Be reasonable in your expectations and be realistic in setting risk tolerance limits.

In the absence of regulatory oversight, a supervisor, or peer feedback, the IPS essentially sets investing boundaries. It is also a promise to your future self. No one else needs to see it but, for it to have relevance, it should be crafted thoughtfully and reviewed annually.

> **Note:** Some of the IPS terminology and their purpose will become more relevant upon review of Chapters 8–11.

---

[2]CFA Institute (May 2010). "Elements of an Investment Policy Statement for Individual Investors." https://www.cfainstitute.org/-/media/documents/article/position-paper/investment-policy-statement-individual-investors.ashx (Accessed 26 September 2021).

Table 7.1 The Oasis Growth Fund investment policy.

INVESTMENT OBJECTIVES	• Long-term growth and capital preservation
EXPECTED RETURNS:	
• **Average annual return required**	• 6%.
• **Average annual return desired**	• 8+%[1] (Historical average annual return of the S&P 500).
• **Income required**	• None. (Dividends to be reinvested.)
RISK PROFILE:	
• **Risk Capacity**	• High.
• **Risk Tolerance**	• Moderate to High.
PORTFOLIO CONSTRAINTS:	
• **Target Asset Mix**	• 80–100% equities / 0–20% cash reserve.
• **Time Horizon**	• 10+ years.

• **Stock Selection**	• Mid- to large-cap growth stocks listed on North American exchanges.
	• Non-duplication of industries.
	• Metrics:
	  • ROE >20%.
	  • Betas (~1).
	  • Sharpe ratios >1.
	  • 4-year track record of growing revenues and profitability.
	  • Healthy balance sheets.

• **Portfolio Management Metrics**	• Equal-weight positions. • Economic exposure across all 11 sectors. • Rebalance according to thresholds (−15% / + 20%). • No high-frequency trading. • No speculative use of options. • (Discretionary) Use of leverage limited to compelling situations. • (Optional) Passive income from writing covered calls – Tier 2. • (Optional) Passive income from writing puts – Tier 3.
• **Short-Term Liquidity Needs**	• None. Quality stocks offer daily liquidity.
RISK MANAGEMENT MEASURES	• Avoidance of all asset categories above and below large- and mid-cap stocks and REITs (see Chapter 13). • Deploy multiple degrees of diversification (see Chapter 11). • (Optional) Portfolio protection – Tier 4.
LEGAL and REGULATORY FACTORS (e.g. trust or pension regulations)	• Portfolio subject to jurisdictional security laws (likely unnecessary for DIY portfolios).
TAXATION CONSIDERATIONS	• Plan favors generating tax-preferred dividends and capital gains.
UNIQUE CIRCUMSTANCES (e.g. FX management, ESG preferences, SRI limitations, foreign market inclusions/exclusions, etc.)	• FX positions will be unhedged. • ESG overlay (trading platform compares corporate ESG principles with personal principles and flags differences for action).

[1] If an investor desires to generate returns greater than the long-term historical average of 8%, it requires taking on either more risk, leverage, or inclusion of the alpha-generating activities of Tiers 2, 3, or 4.

Like a country's founding constitution, an investment policy statement (IPS) is foundational and provides the framework for investment decisions. While the individual investor and their situation will evolve over time, the IPS should remain relatively steadfast. However, an IPS may be adjusted to allow for operational flexibility as life's circumstances evolve.

The following schematic diagrams in Figures 7.3, 7.4, and 7.5 provide a visual overview of the security selection process. Each filter will be explained in more detail in subsequent chapters.

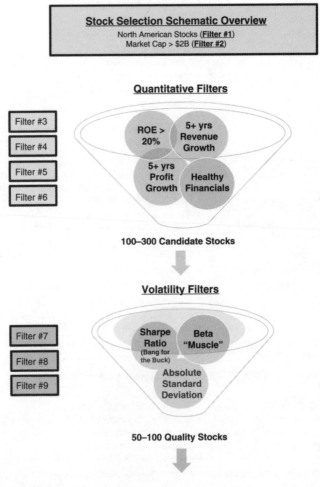

Figure 7.3   Stock selection filters (1–9).

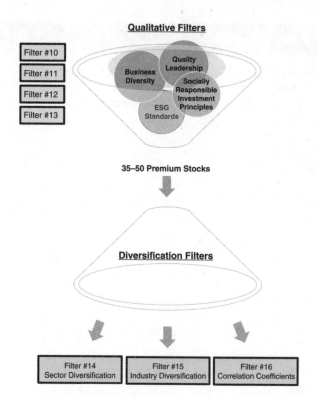

Figure 7.4   Stock selection filters (10–16).

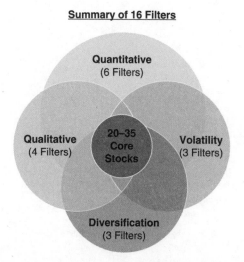

Figure 7.5   Venn diagram summary of 16 stock selection filters.

At the Oasis: Chapter 7

- An investment policy statement will set the course. Like a promissory note, it is a commitment to onself to stay on the path.
- Before buying that next stock, reconsider the overall design of your portfolio. A more conscious design should lead to:
  - Improved returns.
  - Reduced volatility.
  - Elimination of undue risks.
  - Better cost controls.
  - Time efficiencies (i.e. less monitoring required).

Chapter 8

Stock Selection

Quantitative Filters

"For all its hazards,
picking individual stocks is a fascinating game."
—Burton Malkiel,
A Random Walk Down Wall Street

Objective:

Introducing six quantitative filters to identify
high-quality businesses.

From a universe of ~8,000+ publicly traded stocks, 16 filters will be deployed over the next four chapters to cull the universe down to approximately 50 high-quality stock candidates. Some stocks may be agreeable with you, some less so. But by using filters, all should be proven, financially sound, and sustainable businesses. Each filter offers an investor the opportunity to tailor their portfolio toward businesses they can believe in.

Note: ESG- (environmental, social, and governance) conscious investors may prefer to build in ESG parameters at an earlier stage rather than applying them later. Our thesis is that, for investing purposes, it is better to first determine the economic viability of a business before introducing other qualitative measures. ESG filters can be applied at any stage, but for the purpose of this model, they are applied at the later stages of this selection process (see Chapter 10).

These filters are provided as a guideline. We respect that investing requires investigation and mental dexterity. Be mindful to understand why a filter makes sense or not. Why is a preferred company not appearing on your short list? How might the filters be adjusted without compromising the end results? Of course, an investor can still invoke exceptions but with a clear understanding as to what vulnerabilities are being introduced.

Before investing in that next company, though, an investor also needs to be mindful that all may not be what it seems. Tom Fisher's work *Common Stocks and Uncommon Profits*[1] is so well presented that Warren Buffett has often cited his work. Warren is a big believer in asking why a stock should warrant his capital. In essence, the goal of using filters is to gradually cull the less worthy stocks. Eventually, the gems will stand out.

Keeping Track

As you whittle down the list of candidate stocks to a more reasonable number (<100), consider setting up a spreadsheet based upon the specific filters used. These will help track and compare data between the final pool of candidate stocks. Both Google Sheets and Excel allow the importation of stock ticker and sundry stock-specific data.

Step 2. Designing a Purposeful Portfolio: Six Quantitative Filters

"Moats are lame – nice and quaint in a vestigial way. But if your only defense against invading armies is a moat, you won't last long. What matters is the pace of innovation – that is the fundamental determinant of competitiveness for any given company."
—Elon Musk, CEO, Tesla

Above is a Twitter comment from Elon Musk levied at Warren Buffett. Warren sees "moats" as integral to defend existing businesses against their competition. Elon's perspective is that only constant innovation will defend a company against the competition. Realistically, it's just semantics. Technological innovation is another word for "moat."

An exceptional company should always sum greater than its parts. In other words, to defend against marauding armies, a corporation's moat needs to be staunch, multilayered, and constantly reassessed.

---

[1]Fisher, T. *Common Stocks and Uncommon Profits*. New York: Harper & Brothers, Revised edition, 1960.

Note: Although it would be easy to build an entire portfolio around technology stocks, instead relax the parameters and follow where the filters take you. In the early phases of filtering, be industry agnostic.

Q: What is a quality growth stock?

A business generating sustainable surplus cash flows greater than required to maintain, update, innovate, and grow their ongoing operations.

Ideal Traits of a Growing Business

- Has a motivated leadership team and a healthy corporate culture.
- Offers a clear value proposition and an easy-to-understand business model.
- Retains high profit margins by exploiting competitive advantages.
- Has a significantly addressable market and scalability to grow.
- Is dominant in its industry with a well-established brand.
- Is integrated and expanding internationally.
- Deploys debt responsibly.
- Consistently generates surplus revenues and profits.
- Deploys R&D to generate new revenue streams.
- Deploys stakeholder-friendly practices:
  - Mindful of ESG obligations
  - Holds respectful relationships with employees, community, and suppliers
  - Treats capital providers with respect:
    - Grows dividends
    - Buys back shares
    - Pays down debts
    - Accretive M&A activity
    - Spawns spin-off businesses.

Note: Many of the traits listed above require qualitative research that cannot be easily determined from traditional financial statements. Picking good stocks also requires good detective skills. Several more subjective qualitative filters will be introduced in Chapter 10.

Note: Several stock screener platforms and alternative filters are presented at the end of this chapter.

Begin the hunt by seeking businesses in a more favorable jurisdiction.

FILTER #1

North American Stocks: A preference for North American (NA) companies with global business models is based on the following rationales:

- **Sets a trustworthy foundation** – North American corporations are subjected to high degrees of regulatory, accounting, and legal standards. Gaining exposure to international business opportunities is better left to competent NA business teams to handle foreign issues and risks.
- **Primary consumption markets** – On a per capita basis, the NA consumer has a higher amount of discretionary income and can be segregated for marketing more easily than the peculiarities found in foreign cultures. NA companies have the homefield advantage.
- **Enhanced trading** – North American stock and options markets are more liquid and efficient than most other global jurisdictions.
- **Many quality foreign stocks are also listed on NA exchanges** – If investing in foreign firms is still desired, numerous worthy foreign stocks are also dually listed on North American exchanges as American Depository Receipts (ADRs).

At the Oasis

Tracking Global Revenues (Figure 8.1)
   To confirm that North American–based businesses are a good proxy for global investing, we review corporate quarterly/annual reports for geographic dispersion of their revenues. The domicile listing of a stock does not reveal its true geographic exposure. Review revenue sources at least once a year to properly track the geographic reach of your core stocks.

- USA
- Canada
- Europe
- Rest of the World

FILTER #2

Market Cap: Figure 8.2 identifies that a business's growth rate is highly correlated to its market capitalization. Once a business gets past the critical

Figure 8.1   Oasis Growth Fund geographic revenue as of March 31, 2021.

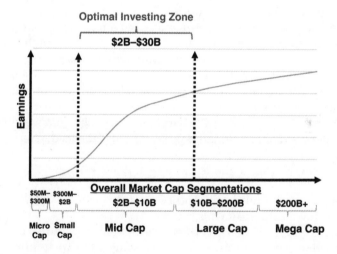

Figure 8.2   Optimal investing zone.

start-up phase (micro- and small-cap zones), corporations gain easier access to capital, economies of scale begin to work in their favor, profitability leads to surplus cash flows, allowing the business to grow organically and through mergers and acquisitions (M&A). A growing market cap also invites more analyst coverage, which tends to help expand a company's price/earnings multiples (P/Es). Equally, a growing business in the range of $2B to $30B remains an attractive size to be opportunistically bought or merged with a larger business.

FILTER #3

High ROE Ratios: ROE (return on equity) is a reliable measurement of management's ability to generate revenues from the capital invested into a business. Companies that can sustainably develop and exploit a market niche will typically have a higher ROE. We set the annual ROE filter at 20%. These are the growth engines of the global economy. There are three elements that influence ROE generation:

a. High margins on product/services (also known as a "wide moat").
b. High turnover of inventory
c. The use of leverage.

We favor businesses with multiple products, technological advantages, high margins, and loyal clients (a).

Low-cost products with low margins but high turnover (b) are not attractive because of a heavy reliance on the supply chain, high fixed costs, and an inability to control the product and delivery costs.

Beware businesses that embrace M&A through excessive leverage (c). If deployed poorly, higher revenues and profitability may eventually implode (e.g. Valeant Pharmaceutical, Laidlaw, RJR Nabisco, Nortel, Concordia International, Loewen Group). Hearing of a management's commitment to repay debt is vital and should only be trusted if the leadership has previously proven credible.

Examples of business models with high ROEs (a) are:

- High-end manufacturing processes (aeronautics, defense contractors, medical instruments, autos).
- Service to niche markets (biomedical, human resources).
- Providing core infrastructure (5G, semiconductor testing, fintech, cloud services, energy storage).
- Subscription-based revenues and lease agreements, Software-as-a-Service [SaaS] firms, utilities, real estate investment trusts [REITs].

ROE data is readily available from most discount trading stock platforms or stock analytic sites. Compare current and historical ratios to see the trend. When a high-ROE company is discovered, drill down to ensure that the high growth is due to high margins and not due to high turnover or excessive leverage (check the balance sheet).

FILTER #4

Top-Line Revenue Growth: Align Technologies in Figure 8.3 is a good example of a healthy business generating consistently growing revenues, whether through the introduction of new products, services, M&A, or a growing client base. Even though revenues may fluctuate seasonally, annualized profitability should still show a consistently growing trend over 5+ years.

FILTER #5

Bottom-Line Profitability: Also notable in Figure 8.3, Align Technologies' net profits have been improving year/year. This reflects management's ability to translate sales revenues into shareholder value. A lean company with a relatively flat management hierarchy and minimal need to carry inventory underscore a more effective business model. Measure profitability across 4+ years to ensure a favorable trend.

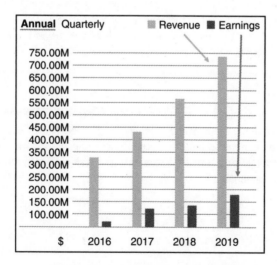

Figure 8.3   Align Technologies Inc. revenue & earnings (2016–2019).

Shareholder-Friendly Practices

When revenues are generated sustainably beyond all necessary corporate capital expenditure requirements (to maintain operations), the following practices reflect a shareholder-friendly business:

- Paying down debts.
- Steadily raising dividends.[2]
- Declaring special dividends.
- Deploying share buy-backs.
- Spinning out separate business divisions to shareholders or as IPOs.
- Pursuing accretive corporate mergers and acquisitions (M&A).

Note: To confirm a corporation's shareholder-friendly practices, periodically check news releases on their website. Corporations are motivated to share good news.

Investment Tip

Temptation of the "Sirens"

Don't be deceived by high dividend–paying companies. High payout ratios are rarely sustainable, and likely reflect that current management is in denial of a need for change in the company's practices. When management disagrees with the market, trust the market. Leadership unwilling to make tough decisions should be questioned.

Note: Quarterly earnings reports are a reality check. Four times a year, a stock's valuation is confirmed or adjusted according to all publicly available information. Better companies tend to meet or exceed prior projections. To keep an eye on upcoming earnings expectations, Zacks.com is a well-respected stock screening tool (subscription required).

---

[2]When it comes to building a portfolio, capital growth is the focus. Dividends are valued but are not critical in the selection process. However, even pure growth stocks periodically issue special dividends and/or buy back shares.

Investment Tip

Beware "Icarus"

Commodity stocks (precious metals, oil, gas, mining, agricultural, and forestry firms) are not considered as long-term growth stocks because they are "price-taking" business models. Quality commodity business models can be distinguished by their cost disciplines, quality assets, and astute acquisitions. Otherwise, their revenues fluctuate with the underlying commodity prices during very long economic cycles. The greatest gains come from buying them out of favor. If considered, place a high emphasis on their leadership (running efficient operations and M&A discipline). Be most wary once the returns approach the "sun."

Special "Rule of 40" for Software-as-a-Service Companies

At 27% of the S&P 500 Index, Info Tech has now come to dominate all other economic sectors and continues to grow. Yet traditional accounting practices makes it difficult to measure the true profitability for digital companies, particularly for SaaS firms. These are B2B companies that make their software available by subscription. Due to the labor intensiveness of software, these costs tend to overwhelm an income statement. This creates the impression of non-profitability, possibly for many years. As such, using traditional tax accounting methods, the profitability and growth of SaaS firms is often underrepresented. Instead, professional analysts prefer to use a multiple-step process called "The Rule of 40"[3]:

1. SaaS businesses are perceived to be more attractive investments if their combined revenue growth rate (%) and their EBITDA[4] margin rate (%) (also known as "current margin ratio") add up to 40% or better (simple addition of the two ratios). Fast-growing software firms invest as much as any other industry, yet traditional accounting methods result in immediate write-offs for sales and marketing expenses, thereby rendering the perception that SaaS firms are unprofitable. Meanwhile, other industries that invest in depreciable assets and amortize their capital expenditures over multiple years

---

[3]Erdem, S. (2017). "What Is the Rule of 40 and How to Calculate It and Use It for SaaS?," https://userguiding.com/blog/rule-of-40/.

[4]Earnings before interest, taxes, depreciation, and amortization. Analyzing a corporation's EBITDA essentially means that the earnings reported before these deductions are more meaningful to explain a business's operations than the earnings being reported after these deductions.

(e.g. trucking firms and airlines) would appear more profitable. As such, SaaS firms remain well under the radar far longer than more traditional companies, due to the tax system. The Rule of 40 helps to reveal worthy SaaS businesses sooner. The following two sets of data points can be found on most stock research platforms:

   i. **Revenue Growth Rate** = [Total Net Sales from the current period – Total Net Sales from the previous period] / Total Net Sales from the previous period. This reveals year/year growth in sales.
   ii. **EBITDA Margin Rate (Current Margin Ratio)**[5] = [Total Year's Sales – Total Year's Selling Expenses] / Total Year's Sales. This ratio reflects how effective management is in generating sales.

  2. Add (i) and (ii). If they are greater than 40, there would appear to be value for the growth being generated. The higher the number, the more attractive the current share price.

FILTER #6

Healthy Financial Statements: Review corporate quarterly or annual statements:

  1. **The Balance Sheet** reports a firm's assets, liabilities, and owner's equity at one moment in time. It's better to compare a firm's year-to-year balance sheets to identify progress in a company's financial fortunes (hopefully increasing assets, decreasing liabilities, and increasing shareholder equity). An increase in the firm's book value should also reveal successful M&A activities. A growing reserve of retained earnings confirms long-term profitability.
  2. **The Income Statement** reports the operating income and expenses over quarter-to-quarter and year-to-year periods. Hallmarks of an effectively run business are increasing revenues from diverse geographic regions while containing operational costs, therefore improving profitability over time.
  3. **The Cash Flow Statement** reveals how a corporation's cash is being generated and deployed since the last report. Like blood in our body, the cash flow statement discloses a company's true state of health.
     Unhealthy budgeting practices require borrowing more, issuing more shares, or selling assets to cover the bills. Excessive leverage

---

[5]Investopedia. "What Is the Formula for Calculating Profit Margins?" https://www.investopedia.com/ask/answers/031815/what-formula-calculating-profit-margins.asp (Accessed 26 September 2021).

ratios and declining debt service ratios are signs of poor business practices. To quickly assess a business's soundness, look at the following three critical vital signs. The information is drawn from both the balance sheet and the income statement, but these ratios are now readily available on most analytics sites:

i. **Liquidity** – The current ratio[6] is a straightforward calculation revealing how well a corporation can cover its short-term liabilities in the ordinary course of operations. Divide the company's current assets by its current liabilities. Current assets are those that can be converted into cash within one year, while current liabilities are obligations expected to be paid within one year. A ratio >1 is preferred.

ii. **Solvency** – The ideal debt-to-equity ratio[7] (D/E) would be less than 1. A ratio of 1 means that 50% of the business is being funded by debt. Occasionally, investing in M&A activity may result in temporary D/E >1. However, well-managed companies usually focus surplus cash flows toward debt servicing to bring this under control. A trustworthy corporation will announce its debt repayment plan.

iii. **Operating Efficiency** (Operating Income/Sales Revenues[8]) – A ratio greater than 10% is a well-managed business. Net revenues generated are being assessed whether they would be adequate to cover non-operating outflows, like servicing debts and dividend payments. Lenders and investors pay close attention to the operating efficiency (OE). Operating margins that vary significantly from period to period are another indicator of business risk.

Note: OE ratios are commonly used to assess businesses with large asset bases, such as airlines and railroads. Yet, since OE ratios can vary significantly between industries, only use this ratio for comparing companies within the same industry.

Finding great companies is no mystery. Setting high filter standards, then using discerning judgment will ultimately reveal the gems.

> *"An investor should act like he had a lifetime decision card with just 20 punches on it."*
> —Warren Buffett

---

[6]Fernando, J. (2021). "Current Ratio." https://www.investopedia.com/terms/c/currentratio.asp (Accessed 26 September 2021).
[7]Fernando, J. "Debt-to-Equity (D/E) Ratio." https://www.investopedia.com/terms/d/debtequityratio.asp (Accessed 26 September 2021).
[8]Hayes, A. "Operating Margin." https://www.investopedia.com/terms/o/operatingmargin.asp (Accessed 26 September 2021).

Step 3. Designing a Purposeful Portfolio: Deploying a Stock Screening Platform

Screening Checklist for Quality Growth Businesses

- North American–listed firms with global scalability
- Market cap from $2B to $30B
- ROE consistently greater than 20%
- 5+ years of positive revenue growth
- 5+ years of increasing profitability
- Healthy financials = low to moderate debt
- Commitment to research and development
- Satisfied stakeholders (employees, customers, suppliers, creditors, shareholders, and community)
- Positive ESG ranking (see Chapter 10)

Investopedia offers a list of stock screening websites.[9]

Shhh . . . Shortcuts

If building a portfolio from scratch is not overly appealing, consider cherry-picking securities from other notable sources:

The Top Hedge Fund Managers[10]
The Gurus[11]
Past Pro Picks[12]
Fortune Survey: 100 Best Corporations to Work For[13]
(Note: This list has annually outperformed the S&P 500 Index.)

---

[9]Best, R. "Best Stock Screeners." https://www.investopedia.com/best-stock-screeners-5120586 (Accessed 26 September 2021).
[10]https://www.tipranks.com/hedge-funds/top (Accessed 26 September 2021).
[11]https://www.gurufocus.com/guru/list (Accessed 26 September 2021).
[12]https://stockchase.com.
[13]https://docs.google.com/spreadsheets/d/1NF48A0p6L4V_79XkJVdOCT_jAdP1vKlC3ix5e44xXXM/edit#gid=0.

Insider Reports – US[14]
Insider Reports – Canada[15]
These sites, and more, are also presented in Chapter 27.

Next: Chapter 9 will filter stocks according to crucial reward/risk parameters.

Investment Tip

The temptation of shortcuts also introduces risks. All stocks deserve due diligence, even if recommended by the pros or bought by insiders, and those already held in your portfolio. A portfolio constructed from the selections of others will likely lack the valuable diversification techniques as outlined in Chapter 11. Do your own research to confirm that each stock is merited and fits well within your portfolio with the other stocks.

At the Oasis: Chapter 8

- The screening process is a chance to build a portfolio that reflects your worldview.
- Experiment with different stock screener apps and filters. The process can lead to new discoveries.
- Set the search criteria high, then gradually lower them to develop a list of worthy names.
- Overall, great growth stocks should require very little introduction.

---

[14]https://www.insidertracking.com (Accessed 26 September 2021).
[15]https://undervaluedequity.com/insider-trading-canada-3-free-resources-for-tracking-the-change-in-canadian-insider-ownership/#:~:text=Step%20 1%3A%20Go%20to%20www,click%20on%20the%20Next%20button (Accessed 26 September 2021).

Chapter 9

Stock Selection

Brains and the Brawn

"When it comes to investments, there's no such thing as a perfect 10.
You have to choose where to compromise."
—Seth Klarman,
billionaire hedge fund manager
and founder of Boston-based Baupost Group

Objective:

Learning to influence the performance character
of a portfolio.

RMP #7: Profiling for Stock Performance and Volatility Traits

This chapter will outline how to profile candidate stocks using four quantitative methods. Even if the top investment stocks are a forgone conclusion, use these tests to confirm your decisions. This is an opportunity to shape the performance character of your portfolio.

So far, the selection process has focused on simply identifying quality growth businesses. The other side of the coin is that growth stocks are also volatile assets: reward vs. volatility. Filling a portfolio with performance stocks without considering their historical ranges of volatility could render a portfolio unnecessarily susceptible at critical market moments.

Step 4. Designing a Purposeful Portfolio: Profiling a Stock's Character

Depending on an investor's stock choices, the overall performance character of the core portfolio can be influenced. Consider the following example.

In Figure 9.1, five years of performance data (for the period ending March 31, 2021) for 11 securities (10 stocks and the SPDR Gold Shares ETF) are compared to the S&P 500 Index on a platform called the "Portfolio Visualizer."[1] The performance profile of up to 50 stocks can be compared side by side across 4 categories (A, B, C, and D).

1. Annualized Performance (A)
2. Annualized Standard Deviation (B)
3. Sharpe Ratio[2] (C) – A calculation to reveal which stocks offer the most performance per unit of volatility.

	A	B	C	D
	Annualized Return	Annualized Standard Deviation	Sharpe Ratio = [(A-Rf)/B]	Beta (Relative to Market = 1)
Apple Inc.	40%	30%	1.34	1.2
Microsoft Corporation	34%	18%	1.88	0.79
Amazon.com, Inc.	37%	29%	1.29	1.15
MercadoLibre, Inc.	71%	44%	1.63	1.47
Paycom Software, Inc.	64%	42%	1.53	1.38
ServiceNow, Inc.	45%	32%	1.41	0.93
Danaher Corporation	27%	18%	1.44	0.64
IDEXX Laboratories, Inc.	47%	26%	1.81	0.89
Mastercard Incorporated	31%	23%	1.34	1.18
Visa Inc.	24%	19%	1.27	0.99
SPDR Gold Shares	12%	14%	0.85	0.11
> Portfolio Averages	39%	27%	1.44	0.98
SPDR S&P 500 ETF Trust (SPY)	15%	15%	1.00	1.00

Figure 9.1   Sample portfolio performance profile data.

---

[1]https://www.portfoliovisualizer.com/asset-correlations
[2]The Sharpe ratio is used to help investors understand the return of an investment compared to its degree of volatility. The ratio is the average annual return earned in excess of the prevailing risk-free rate per unit of volatility or the standard deviation. Fernando, J. (2022). "Sharpe Ratio." https://www.investopedia.com/terms/s/sharperatio.asp (Accessed 26 September 2021).

4. Beta[2] (D) – The degree to which share prices are expected to vary with movements in the market.

Each reveals a different aspect of a stock's performance profile and each will be explained in more detail.

Suppose an investor desires to add only 3 of the 11 securities to their portfolio. For each of the four categories, the three most likely choices are circled. Depending upon which performance trait(s) are preferred, the choices will vary. This allows an investor to actively tailor the expected future performance character of their portfolio over the medium to long-term.

Note: Figure 9.1 is a condensed version of a larger comparison chart presented in Chapter 11.

Column A – Performance Caveat: Stock decisions are often made according to recent performance. However, simply choosing the highest-performing stocks from Column A could render a portfolio overly vulnerable to a market pullback. Column A in Figure 9.1 highlights the three stocks with the highest annualized performance over the 5-year period.

FILTER #7

Column B – Review the Absolute Volatility of Candidate Stocks: Imagine a sports team where the team's leading scorer was a high-strung athlete who could win games but was either hot or not. Everyone wants to win, but championship teams favor consistency. The same can be said for stocks.

It should be worth knowing whether the outstanding performance from some stocks is worth the pain of their overall volatility. Great days can be followed by nail-biting, sleepless nights. Review column B to compare the absolute volatility for all stocks. Consider setting a maximum cut-off point where the heightened range of volatility is not worth holding a stock. One with a more moderate volatility profile might be preferred. Column B in Figure 9.1 highlights the three stocks with the lowest annualized volatility (standard deviation).

Ideally, the average standard deviation (SD) for the overall portfolio would be equal to or less than the long-term average volatility of the

---

[2]Kenton, W. (2021). "Beta." https://www.investopedia.com/terms/b/beta.asp (Accessed 26 September 2021).

S&P 500 (15%). A portfolio's average volatility could be adjusted by populating the portfolio with lower-SD stocks to offset the more volatile high-performance stocks. However, if a stock's SD is above 15%, it still might be worthy to hold as a core position if its Sharpe ratio is above 1 (see Filter #8).

FILTER #8

Column C – Manually Calculate Each Stock's Sharpe Ratio: Subtract the 1-year Treasury yield (~3%) from a stock's annualized performance (Column A), then divide the result by the annualized SD (Column B). The Sharpe ratio helps to identify the stocks offering the better reward per unit of volatility. With volatility being kept constant in the denominator, the higher the ratio, the better the performance character of a stock. A reasonably performing stock with low volatility could be a portfolio's real superstar. Stocks with ratios >1 should be preferred. This means that the rewards exceed the range of volatility.

Q: Is there a way to predict how much a stock might move with the markets?

FILTER #9

Column D – Filter According to a Stock's "Beta Muscle": The beta of a stock reflects the degree of the stock's movement relative to the markets. Some move more. Some move less. For example, if a stock has a beta of 1.2, in a rising market, the stock would be expected to rise by 20% more than the market. Equally, when the markets are in decline, that stock would be expected to fall by 20% greater than the returns of the market. Although a stock's beta may evolve with time, it should be relatively stable from year to year for high-quality stocks.

An investor can control the amount of growth or defensive bias in the portfolio simply by adjusting the weights of different stocks with different betas in the portfolio, like a thermostat. In a weakening economy, the portfolio can be rendered more defensive by lowering exposure to cyclical growth stocks (financials, industrials, materials, energy, technology, consumer discretionary) and increasing the exposure to more defensive stocks (utilities, consumer staples, telecom, health care, REITs [real estate investment trusts], etc.). And vice versa if the economy appears to be moving back into growth mode.

Note: Unfortunately, managing beta is not foolproof. During market corrections or worse, most stocks react in absolute unison. For example, during the great COVID Bear Market of 2020, there were no safe havens. Even traditionally defensive REITs were sold off along with the cyclical stocks and the ensuing recovery was particularly muted for defensive stocks. Unfortunately, in that case, a rising tide did not lift all boats.

Individual stock beta data are available on most trading platforms, as should be the weighted beta for the entire portfolio. An investor would benefit to track their portfolio's overall beta and to know which stocks have outlier betas (high and low).

Note: A portfolio with a weighted-average beta of 1 should mimic the performance and volatility of the broad market (S&P 500 Index). Inherent to growth portfolios, the weighted-average beta is usually >1.

In Figure 9.1, we highlighted stocks with the highest betas. However, we equally could have identified the stocks with the lowest betas. Depending upon an investor's preference for growth or defensiveness, the portfolio beta could be increased or decreased, respectively.

Managing a Portfolio's Performance Character

As outlined above, an investor can control the performance profile of their portfolio by purposefully choosing between stocks according to four select reward/risk characteristics:

- Moderate to high average annual returns.
- Moderate annual volatility (standard deviation).
- Sharpe ratios >1.
- Weighted-average beta ranging between 0.8 and 1.2.

So, in the example, depending on which characteristics are to be emphasized, an investor could pick completely different stock choices.

Before making that next trade, learn to use the "Portfolio Visualizer" program. Although it is a subscription model, the basic version is complimentary and the data can be copied, pasted, and managed in Excel. Data from an Excel spreadsheet can even be copied and pasted directly back into the app. However, before launching this application, review the segment outlining correlation coefficients in Chapter 11. This same platform can also help select stocks to improve portfolio diversification.

By embracing performance profiling, an investor can periodically adjust their portfolio depending upon the economic and market outlook: sometimes sacrificing on performance to gain a reduction in volatility, or vice versa when anticipating a period of economic expansion.

Step 5. Designing a Purposeful Portfolio: Choosing a Stock Research Platform

Ideally, your candidate list is now becoming more manageable. Consider using a subscription-based professional-grade stock analytics site to allow more in-depth analysis of each candidate stock. Here are three platforms. More choices are presented in Chapter 15.

1. **StockCalc Reports**[3] – Quickly evaluates companies and ETFs. This screener helps to find fundamentally undervalued securities. StockCalc is complimentary for clients of Interactive Brokers, Amazon.com (Alexa), and GlobeandMail.com.
2. **StockReports+**[4] – Analyzes each stock across six widely used quantitative data sources and then conveniently averages them into a single score. Each firm is ranked on a scale from 1 to 10 and updated weekly. Rankings are also directly compared to all competitors within their respective industries. StockReports+ is complimentary for clients of Interactive Brokers or the GlobeandMail.com.
3. **Top US Stock Research Sites**[5] – The website Youngandinvested.com is well presented. It highlights 18 highly respected sites, their track records, and their respective costs.

Next: Chapter 10 introduces qualitative measures to ensure that the remaining candidate stocks also operate according to principles closely aligned with yours.

---

[3]https://www.stockcalc.com/Welcome.aspx (Accessed 26 September 2021).
[4]https://www.stockreportsplus.com/ (Accessed 26 September 2021).
[5]https://youngandtheinvested.com/best-stock-investment-research-websites-software/ (Accessed 26 September 2021).

At the Oasis: Chapter 9

- More beta = more "muscle." Depending upon your market outlook, consider tailoring your portfolio's overall beta between .8 and 1.2.
- Stocks with Sharpe ratios >1 are desirable at most any time.
- Set limits on stocks with high variances. Be wary of stocks with SDs > 15% unless the Sharpe ratio > 1. Star stocks may offer average performance but low volatility.
- Reject stocks with lower long-term returns than the S&P 500.

"Son, if you really want something in this life, you have to work for it.
Now quiet! They're about to announce the lottery numbers."
—Homer Simpson (*The Simpsons*)

Chapter 10

Stock Selection

Qualitative Filters

*"He who knows, does not speak.
He who speaks, does not know."*
—Lao Tzu, *Chinese philosopher*

Objective:

Refining stock selection with qualitative filters.

Step 6. Designing a Purposeful Portfolio: Four Qualitative Screens

When building a portfolio, start with quantitative analysis to ensure that a company is a financially viable operating business. Then introduce filters to select qualitative traits according to your preferences and principles.

This could mean selecting companies with visionary leadership, diverse business models, or clear environmental, social, and governance (ESG) protocols and/or admirable socially responsible investing (SRI) standards. Belief in the corporate philosophy or mission should serve to buttress an investor's convictions, particularly valuable during periods of market stress.

Here are four categories to review in weighing the qualitative merits of a business:

- Quality Leadership Traits (Filter #10).
- Business Model Diversity (Filter #11).
- Environmental, Social, and Governance (ESG) Standards (Filter #12).
- Socially Responsible Investment (SRI) Principles (Filter #13).

FILTER #10

Quality Leadership Traits

Great businesses usually have visionary leaders who surround themselves with a competent team of professionals.

- Leaders who can articulate their vision and inspire others to follow.
- A corporation's consistency in generating positive earnings surprises (see Chapter 15).
- Ability to raise capital for business growth (review cash flow statements).
- A corporation's willingness to invest in R&D (supports innovations).
- M&A successes (growing the company through accretive acquisitions).
- Enforces stakeholder-friendly practices – including suppliers, distribution channels, customers, lenders, community employees, and shareholders (see Chapter 8).
- Minimal turnover in the C-suite.
- Holding significant ownership in the firm:
  - US corporations, check either EDGAR or Investopedia, which offers a list of free sites.[1]
  - Canadian corporations, a list of three insider ownership sites.[2]

---

[1]Tun, Z. T. (2021). "Buy Stock with Insiders: How to Track Insider Buying." https://www.investopedia.com/articles/investing/040915/buy-stock-insiders-how-track-insider-buying.asp (Accessed 26 September 2021).
[2]https://undervaluedequity.com/insider-trading-canada-3-free-resources-for-tracking-the-change-in-canadian-insider-ownership/#:~:text=Step%201%3A%20Go%20to%20www, click%20on%20the%20Next%20button. (Accessed 26 September 2021).

"I try to buy businesses that are so wonderful that even an idiot can run them. Because, sooner or later, one will."
—Warren Buffett

Finding businesses with quality leaders and management teams is a learning experience. Since all businesses undergo periods of challenge, an investor must determine just how much challenge they are willing to accept before making a change.

- C-suite turnover and public discord in the boardroom.
- Companies compensate by borrowing excessively or by diluting shareholders to raise new capital.
- Beware legacy-building management types or those who undertake excessive M&A activity to transform the company. This rarely ends well.
- Be cautious of leadership whose personalities garner news headlines. Good leaders should let the results do the talking.

Investment Tip

The Merit of Short Sellers

When leadership is suspected of making poor business decisions, short sellers will notice. While most stocks have some outstanding shares sold short, rising short positions deserve investigation. A short interest ratio[3] exceeding 10 "days to cover"[4] suggests trouble is brewing. Even though corporations like to keep their decisions "close to their chest," short sellers tend to be very good detectives.

Conversely, already heavily shorted shares are also known to be a contrarian sign. Positive news could send a heavily shorted stock skyrocketing as short sellers scramble to exit their position by buying back shares.

Periodically check how much short sales have changed. Professionals are required to share this data monthly. Links to both US and Canadian short seller positions can be found in Chapter 27.

---

[3]Chen, J. (2021). "Short Interest Ratio." https://www.investopedia.com/terms/s/shortinterestratio.asp (Accessed 26 September 2021).
[4]Ganti, A. (2021). "Days to Cover." https://www.investopedia.com/terms/d/daystocover.asp#:~:text=Days%20to%20cover%20is%20a,signal%20a%20potential%20short%20squeeze (Accessed 26 September 2021).

Business Model Diversity

FILTER #11

Business Model Diversity: Businesses typically start with a value proposition comprised of a single product or service. With time, the business model broadens and deepens through organic growth, R&D, and M&A. Companies that generate revenues from a more diverse and integrated business model, and whose client base extends globally, tend to weather recessions better. In addition to measuring a business's success quantitatively, review your candidate stocks with fresh eyes. What are some of the intangibles that make a company stand out? When debating between stock choices, peruse their respective corporate websites, news sources, and analyst reviews. Some of the unique intangible elements of a business may sway your decision:

- **Brand loyalty.** This allows a business to endure economic hardships or corporate miscues better than most. Meta has made many miscues in advancing its corporate policies, yet consumers remain loyal and so have the corporate advertisers.
- **Core relevance to other highly valued companies.** The smartphone industry would not exist without semiconductor chips. Chipmakers will be integral in the future of smartphones, the evolving EV car industry, and the entire IoT industry for the foreseeable future.
- **A competitive cost advantage over rivals.** Innovations at Amazon .com and Tesla continue to create further cost advantages over their competition. For Amazon.com, AI-driven robots have replaced higher-cost labor and will eventually extend these cost savings through overnight/same-day, drone-to-home deliveries.
- **Breadth of geographic dispersion.** A company that resonates broadly with their constituents is likely to withstand regional economic disparities better than niche businesses. Starbucks now operates more than 5,000 cafes in China. Starbucks went forward to win hearts and minds with consumers, employees, and local governments. They pay higher wages than their competition, gave ownership benefits to employees, offered critical illness insurance for the parents of employees, and now requires that employees regularly engage in local community charity work.
- **Level of employee satisfaction.** Happy employees do translate into corporate outperformance. According to research submitted to Seeking Alpha, over the past 10 years, the publicly listed companies identified as "Best Places to Work" on the employee feedback site Glassdoor.com have significantly and consistently outperformed the

S&P 500.[5] This study has been repeated and confirmed by different authors. Companies that rank highly in terms of employee satisfaction consistently generate stock returns exceeding the S&P 500 Index in subsequent years.

All great companies will have unique factors that give them an edge, whether obvious or intangible. Since you plan to own a stock for the next decade, it should be worth knowing what makes a stock so special to be in your portfolio.

Investing with Purpose

For years, consumer spending was the only way to sway the corporate world. Today, investors are becoming more activist in the capital markets. The following offers a brief introduction into the ever-progressing realm of investing with purpose:

- **ESG** filters assess and rank corporate environmental, social, and governance practices, revealing to what degree businesses are being good corporate citizens.
- **Socially responsible investing** (SRI) imposes personal ethical guidelines whether to include/exclude a particular stock/industry in a portfolio.
- **Impact investing** is deployed by targeting capital into a project with an expected beneficial outcome to society. However, since corporate bonds are the primary tool of impact investing, this topic will not be addressed further.

FILTER #12

ESG standards[6] can be used by investors as a filter to discern whether a corporation is deserving of their capital. ESG is often termed "green" investing. **Environmental** criteria consider how a company's practices impact the environment. **Social** criteria examine how

---

[5]App Economy Insights (2019). "The Best Places to Work: Delivering Strong Results Compared to the S&P 500 Over 10 Years." https://seekingalpha. com/article/4270853-best-places-to-work-delivering-strong-results-compared-to-s-and-p-500-over-10-years (Accessed 13 December 2021).
[6]Investopedia (2022). "Environmental, Social, and Governance (ESG) Criteria." https://www.investopedia.com/terms/e/environmental-social-and-governance-esg-criteria.asp (Accessed 20 November 2021).

it manages relationships with employees, suppliers, customers, and the communities in which it operates. **Governance** addresses a company's leadership, executive pay, audits, internal controls, shareholder rights, and generally how well a company is managed.

Historically, corporations considered ESG matters secondary to their shareholder-driven interests. The exceedingly obvious impacts of climate change and the COVID-19 pandemic of 2020–2021 have accelerated the public demand for corporations to pursue higher standards of ESG responsibility. The good news is that this heightened awareness has spawned more than 114 agencies to track corporate data and summarily present their ESG rankings. The bad news is that at least 114 agencies are now presenting their own proprietary versions of ESG rankings.

ESG parameters are now being incorporated into professionally managed portfolios in more sophisticated ways than simply binary decisions of avoidance or engagement. These include thematic investing, impact investing, and multiple degrees of shareholder engagement and activism. Further, with rising ESG sensitivity, corporate best practices are being challenged and even new industries are being formed, such as carbon capture, energy storage, electric vehicles, and bio-friendly manufacturing, to name but a few. Corporations are no longer getting a free pass.

For educational purposes, MSCI has produced an informational video[7] (3½ minutes) offering insights on the investment merits of ESG.

Environmental, Social, and Governance (ESG) Standards

As an introduction, Figure 10.1 is a general overview of the ESG landscape.

Imperfect but Improving Standards

Integration of ESG standards into the portfolio selection process is regularly used to reveal risks and growth opportunities not captured by conventional analysis techniques. With improved data analytics, ESG rating agencies allow investors to be more discerning in their investment choices on issues such as human rights, gender inequities, race relations, and adherence to eco-friendly climate policies, etc.

Respectfully, though, ESG standards are a moving target. It is an industry built on relativity. How data is derived, to what it is compared, and by whom, could lead to far different investment decisions. Further confusion stems from differing terms, definitions, and standards between these agencies. Even the definitions of core ESG terms, such as "responsible investing"

---

[7]"ESG Rating Explained: What Are MSCI ESG Ratings?" Youtube, uploaded by MSCI, 27 January 2020. https://www.youtube.com/watch?v=79rZm7F CkOU (Accessed 26 September 2021).

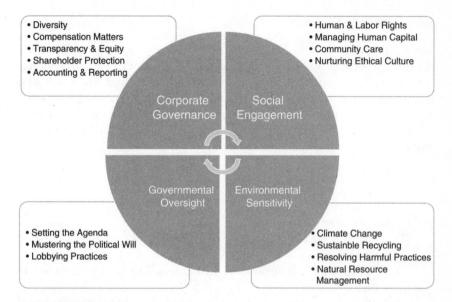

• Diversity
• Compensation Matters
• Transparency & Equity
• Shareholder Protection
• Accounting & Reporting

• Human & Labor Rights
• Managing Human Capital
• Community Care
• Nurturing Ethical Culture

Corporate Governance

Social Engagement

Governmental Oversight

Environmental Sensitivity

• Setting the Agenda
• Mustering the Political Will
• Lobbying Practices

• Climate Change
• Sustainble Recycling
• Resolving Harmful Practices
• Natural Resource Management

Figure 10.1 ESG categories of assessment.

and "sustainable investments," are still being debated. Nonetheless, substantial progress has been made globally.

Realistically, ESG violations can be found in every business across every industry, even amongst the very highest ranked ESG firms. And a high ESG ranking does not necessarily translate into a good investment. ESG rankings are important, but they are just one more tool in a lengthy assessment process. If corporations were required to follow absolute standards, businesses would be shuttered.

Investors should remain flexible. Start by becoming familiar with the ESG issues that hold the highest degree of personal importance and then seek a rating agency that better reflects those values (more on this below). This will require investigation and self-reflection. While each ratings agency will provide their methodology, whether their methods resonate will be up to the individual investor. Yet, without universal ESG standards, the biggest challenge for investors will be to know where to draw the line.

For a well-presented introduction to ESG education, the RIA (Responsible Investing Association) offers introductory education.[8] Equally, the Interactive Brokers site offers an excellent educational overview of their ESG assessment process.[9]

---

[8]https://www.riacanada.ca/responsible-investment/ (Accessed 14 July 2022).
[9]https://www.interactivebrokers.com/en/index.php?f=45158.

ESG Research Platforms

To help construct an ESG-focused portfolio, there are specialized ESG stock research platforms. Since there are more than 150 platforms, the challenge is to determine which firm's methodology matches best with your ESG standards. Below are just four of the many respected reporting platforms. To understand their differences, review their methodologies and then input several similar stock candidates into each method and compare the assessment results.

- MSCI[10]
- Morningstar[11]
- Sustainalytics[12]
- Interactive Brokers[13]
    i.   Provides analytic graphics that outline a portfolio's current ESG status.
    ii. Calculates a "Controversies Score" revealing which stocks are in violation.
    iii. Affirms the potential impact on a portfolio's ESG status for pending trades.
    iv. Proactively offers alternative investment choices where a stock choice fails an investor's identified values.

ESG Investing Choices

For the retail investor, implementing a personalized ESG model is not difficult but can be daunting. Before launching into an ESG mandate, learn which social causes are likely to trigger you into action. Then decide on an investing method:

- **Passive Overlay** – Build a core diversified portfolio according to *The Investing Oasis* then compare the ESG attributes for each company using an external ESG rating assessment platform. While this ESG methodology is passive and deployed in hindsight, it would still reveal those companies in a portfolio that are not up to your ESG standards. It won't, however, reveal new ESG industries and companies.

---

[10]https://www.msci.com/esg-ratings/issuer/ (Accessed 26 September 2021).
[11]https://www.morningstar.com/company/esg-investing (Accessed 26 September 2021).
[12]https://www.sustainalytics.com/esg-ratings (Accessed 26 September 2021).
[13]https://download2.interactivebrokers.com/mtws/assets/esg/IBKR_ESG_Scores.pdf (Accessed 26 September 2021).

- **Integrated** – Consider deploying an ESG filter early in the fundamental analysis stage. This would potentially allow an investor to incorporate a more ESG-themed approach. However, to build a well-rounded portfolio, this proactive approach requires more intensive research and may result in the inclusion of foreign-listed stocks if best practices are sought.
- **Impact Investing** – Investing according to personal principles often means prioritizing a desired ESG initiative over financial performance. To find a worthy project, contact a trusted Financial Advisor/Broker that specializes in impact investments.
- **Simplest** – Alternatively, investors can choose to passively invest in broad market or themed ETFs dedicated to ESG standards, such as the S&P 500 ESG Index.[14]

ESG Performance

Table 10.1 is a comparison of annualized performance between the S&P 500 ESG Index and the S&P 500 Index. While the impact on long-term performance of incorporating ESG standards is still not statistically relevant, the greatest rewards can be found at the grassroots level. Investing and caring for our planet are no longer mutually exclusive concepts. By embracing ESG protocols, it should further improve an investor's level of conviction toward their investment decisions. Pragmatically, integrating ESG standards into a portfolio is an opportunity to vote for your worldview.

Table 10.1 Annualized Performance S&P 500 vs. S&P 500 ESG.

	Annualized Returns (as at Sept 23, 2021)			
	1 Year	3 years	5 Years	10 Years
S&P 500 Index	**32.58%**	14.48%	15.09%	14.55%
S&P 500 ESG Index (Tracker)	32.54%	**15.82%**	**15.76%**	**14.68%**

---

[14]https://www.spglobal.com/spdji/en/indices/esg/sp-500-esg-index/#overviewl (Accessed 26 September 2021).

Caution

Marketing over Substance

"Greenwashing" is the superficial act of a corporation appearing to be progressive on ESG matters but instead incorporating the bare minimum of change due to the inherent costs or concerns of disruption to their business model. Investigation may be required to ensure that corporations are truly "walking the talk."

FILTER #13

Socially Responsible Investment Principles (optional): While ESG standards are used to objectively rank corporations according to socially beneficial metrics, the application of an SRI filter is more specific to the individual. SRI places a higher priority on personal moral and ethical parameters as determined by an investor (e.g. no gambling, military, or tobacco products) and a lower priority, if any, on a corporation's profitability. Security selections tend to be binary: that screening will either be inclusionary or exclusionary. Since SRI standards are based on an investor's convictions, they become an extra filter over and above the ESG standards being applied by an investor and the other quantitative filters being deployed up to this point in the stock selection process.

Example: ESG vs. SRI

An example highlighting differences between ESG and SRI standards – An energy company might be considered a responsible ESG investment if it embraces carbon capture technology, has a solid safety record, and is charitable to the local communities, yet according to a person's SRI standards it may not be a responsible investment due to a negative filter that dismisses all extraction corporations from investing consideration.

> *"We need to talk about money in ways that subject it to*
> *human ethics and standards of love and decency."*
> —Joel Solomon, *The Clean Money Revolution:*
> *Reinventing Power, Purpose, and Capitalism*

Next: Chapter 11 will demonstrate how diversification can be prioritized into portfolio design.

At the Oasis: Chapter 10

- Qualitative filters prioritize principles and ethical standards over financial metrics.
- Deploying ESG and SRI filters are ways that an investor can actively support their worldview.
- To confirm specific qualitative traits, stocks can be manually filtered by:
  - Quality Leadership Teams (invest in whom you trust).
  - Business Model Diversity (seek the intangibles).
  - ESG Standards (according to qualitative rankings).
  - Socially Responsible Metrics (according to personal principles).

Source: Cartoonstock.

Chapter 11

Stock Selection

3+ Degrees of Diversification

*"Diversification is a protection against ignorance.
It makes little sense if you know what you are doing."*
—Warren Buffett

Objective:

Enhancing portfolio performance through
diversification.

---

arren Buffett openly holds disdain for diversification, as well as for the concepts of portfolio management. His perspective is that managing a portfolio of 3–5 small businesses should already be enough for a prudent investor. To him, a portfolio constructed of 30–40 stocks is near madness.

But Warren is talking out of both sides of his mouth.

According to the website GuruFocus.com, as of August 2021, the publicly listed stocks held in the Berkshire Hathaway (BRK) portfolio[1] totaled $324B. The top five (Table 11.1) represent approximately 75% of the portfolio. BRK also holds positions in over 100 more publicly traded stocks

---

[1]https://www.gurufocus.com/guru/warren+buffett/current-portfolio/ portfolio?gclid=CjwKCAjwkJj6BRA-EiwA0ZVPVh6WzsyXD2hC2zaGh3VT ueVig_5Deas6Hi0MyBvO9iE_FkjHfaxGtxoC7ckQAvD_BwE (Accessed 26 September 2021).

Table 11.1   Berkshire Hathaway top five holdings (as at March 31, 2022).

Stock	Value (as at March 31, 2022)	Sector	Portfolio
Apple	$135B	Info Tech	42%
Bank of America	$31B	Financials	10%
Coca-Cola Co	$25B	Consumer Staples	8%
Chevron Corporation	$21B	Energy & Gas	7%
American Express Company	$21B	Financials	7%

but these positions are so relatively small they don't move the diversification needle.

With regard to practicing minimal diversification and zero allegiance to portfolio management principles, Warren seems to be true to his word.

However, BRK also wholly owns a broadly diversified portfolio of 65 high-quality private businesses worth another approximately $600B (not included in the publicly disseminated numbers).

So, despite his deference to diversification and portfolio management theory, with the accumulation of so many companies over the years, Warren wholeheartedly embraces portfolio management principles. It's just that he got there through the back door.

Warren's mission has always been to find a well-managed, quality growth businesses irrespective of their sector or industry and buy them at reasonable prices. To him, the opportunity cost of diminishing portfolio volatility through diversification is not worth sacrificing the opportunity to generate higher returns through a concentrated portfolio of great companies.

Since most of us will never hold the number and diversity of businesses that populate BRK, the benefits of following portfolio management principles and deploying diversification should still be considered. *The Investing Oasis* is founded on the tenets that a well-diversified array of 20–35 great companies will not only enhance performance and reduce volatility but can also be easily managed.

RMP #8: 3+ Degrees of Diversification

Benefits of a Well-Diversified Portfolio

- Captures innovations and growth emanating from all economic sectors.
- Moderates portfolio volatility through balanced economic exposure.

- Reinforces purposeful trading and reduces spontaneous trading.
- Reinforces conviction in the investment plan, particularly beneficial during vulnerable markets.

Although there are many opportunities to deploy diversification in a portfolio, the three active diversification methods deployed are:

- Economic Sector Diversification (Filter #14).
- Industry Diversification (Filter #15).
- By Correlation Coefficients (CC) (Filter #16).

Step 7. Designing a Purposeful Portfolio: Diversification Techniques

> **FILTER #14**

Sector Diversification: It used to be that investing across the 11 different economic sectors introduced distinctly different stock profiles into a portfolio. Utilities and Health Care for their defensive characteristics. Financial Institutions and Non-discretionary Consumer stocks for the cyclicality. Industrial and Technology stocks as engines of growth. However, in an ever-converging world, with innovation and technology spanning all sectors, value creation is happening everywhere. While the diversification merits between sectors may be questioned, they should still be embraced.

Expect to build a portfolio in relative proportion to the global economic sectors (Table 11.2). Chapter 12 will demonstrate the allocation of stocks per sector according to an equal-weighted portfolio.

Note: More than 63,000 publicly listed global businesses are categorized according to the Global Industry Classification Standard (GICS).[2] This structure consists of 11 economic sectors, 24 industry groups, 69 industries, and 158 sub-industries.

---

[2]MSCI (2020). "Global Industry Classification Standard (GICS®) Methodology: Guiding Principles and Methodology for GICS." https://www.msci.com/documents/1296102/11185224/GICS+Methodology+2020.pdf (Accessed 20 November 2021)

Table 11.2   Sector allocation of the S&P 500 Index as at July 30, 2020.

	Sector	Percent of the S&P 500 Index
1	Information Technology	27.48%
2	Health Care	14.58%
3	Consumer Discretionary	11.18%
4	Communications Services	10.50%
5	Financials	9.89%
6	Industrials	7.90%
7	Consumer Staples	7.05%
8	Utilities	3.13%
9	Real Estate	2.80%
10	Materials	2.56%
11	Energy	2.53%
		100%

Source: Berkshire Hathaway Inc. https://berkshirehathaway.com/qtrly/2ndqtr21.pdf.

Investment Tip

Sector Predictability

Cyclical sectors, like mining, forestry, energy, and agriculture, may periodically be exceptional investments but require a contrarian mindset. Such stocks should rarely be bought and held. Once they've rebounded from the depths of despair to match their previous long-term highs, pat yourself on the back and consider taking profits. Commodity stocks should hold a zero long-term weighting in a portfolio comprised of value-creating businesses.

FILTER #15

Industry Diversification: On your candidate spreadsheet, segregate the candidate stocks according to their respective sector and industry categories. With the world's businesses divided into 69 industry categories according to the MSCI Global Industry Classification Standard Methodology,[3] it

---

[3]MSCI (2020). "Global Industry Classification Standard (GICS®) Methodology: Guiding Principles and Methodology for GICS." https://www.msci.com/documents/1296102/11185224/GICS+Methodology+2020.pdf (Accessed 20 November 2021).

should not be difficult to build a portfolio of 20 to 35 stocks without duplication of an industry. Compare your candidate list to the S&P 500 Index Industry Classification Overview[4] to identify opportunity gaps in your industry categories. This comprehensive graphic uniquely outlines each sector and a breakdown of the affiliated industries in proportion to their respective capitalization sizes. Industry selection allows an investor to consciously design a portfolio across industries that reflect your worldview.

Best diversification practices would be that all 11 sectors would be proportionately covered by your candidate stocks and that no two stocks would represent the same industry. At 27.5% of the S&P 500, Info Tech is the largest sector. A portfolio should benefit by choosing individual candidate stocks from the sector's 13 different industries.

Investment Tip

Doubling up could mean doubling down.

The danger of industry duplication, however, is not when markets are performing well but when they aren't. If tempted to hold more than a single stock from the same industry (i.e. Meta, Twitter, Snap, etc.), verify their diversification merit using the stock correlation coefficient matrix (outlined below).

Risk Mitigation Benefits of Diversification

Studies have repeatedly demonstrated that the full benefits of diversification begin with a minimum of 8 uncorrelated stocks and diminish around 25, beyond which the benefit of more diversification is negligible. Filter #16 demonstrates how to efficiently deploy diversification across a portfolio.

FILTER #16

Correlation Coefficients[5]: Diversification works best when stocks react independently to outside variables. Stocks that move in close tandem are

---

[4]https://advisor.visualcapitalist.com/wp-content/uploads/2020/08/s-p-500-sectors-sectors-industries.html (Accessed 20 November 2021).

[5]Fernando, J. (2021). "Correlation Coefficient." https://www.investopedia.com/terms/c/correlationcoefficient.asp (Accessed 26 September 26, 2021).

considered highly correlated. A "correlation coefficient" is the degree of variance between two stocks. Running your prospect stocks through the "Portfolio Visualizer" program[6] succinctly reveals whether there are any unnecessary duplications within your group of prospect stocks. The following scale will help to compare the range of diversification benefits.

Correlation Coefficients Scale

Figure 11.1 is a correlation coefficient scale. A perfect correlation between two stocks would be +1. This would mean that two stock prices move identical to one another. Such a relationship implies that these stocks come from the same industry, like Mastercard and Visa. This would offer very little diversification value to a portfolio. On the other hand, two stocks with a perfectly negative correlation (−1) would reflect a perfect hedge, like airlines and energy refining stocks. As the price of jet fuel rises, airlines are typically negatively impacted. However, a perfectly negative hedge would not likely benefit a portfolio in the long term with the constant seesaw of share prices. Instead, best-fit diversification is found at "0," where two stocks react entirely independently from one another. Realistically, the best range of correlations is anywhere from −.50 to +.50 and even up to +.80, beyond which the price correlation between two stocks is too similar to offer any reasonable diversification value.

- Stocks with correlations from −1 to −.50 are best used for hedging against another stock holding. This will be revisited in Chapter 23.
- Stocks with correlations between −.49 and +.50 offer the **greatest** diversification benefits.

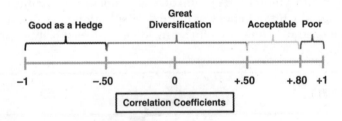

Figure 11.1 Correlation coefficient scale.

[6]https://www.portfoliovisualizer.com/asset-correlations (Accessed 13 February, 2022).

- Stocks with correlations between +.51 to +.80 still offer **acceptable** diversification benefits.
- Stocks with correlations > +.80 imply **poor** diversification benefits. With a high degree of correlation between two securities, a portfolio should benefit by eliminating one of them. Likely, the two stocks come from the same industry.

Correlation Coefficient Example

Figure 11.2 is the Correlation Coefficient matrix for the 5-year period ending March 31, 2021, for the same sample of 10 stocks and a gold ETF as was presented in Chapter 9 (Figure 9.1). This also includes the performance profile statistics (RHS) previously provided. Pairs of securities were purposefully chosen and listed side by side under five industry categories to highlight several potential dilemmas when choosing between two related securities.

> **Note:** Correlations are not proof of causation between two securities (that they impact each other). The correlation coefficients in the matrix only show the strength of movement between two securities over time in response to external stimuli.

Stock Comparison Analysis

The following examples demonstrate an assessment of the relative fit for individual securities into a portfolio comprised of 11 securities according to Figure 11.2.

	Tech Infrastructure		Online Retail		Tech Services		Healthcare		Fin Services			A	B	C	D
												Annualized Return	Annualized Standard Deviation	Sharpe Ratio = [(A-Rf)/B]	Beta (Relative to Market = 1)
	AAPL	MSFT	AMZN	MELI	PAYC	NOW	DHR	IDXX	MA	V	GLD				
Apple Inc.		0.67	0.51	0.27	0.37	0.39	0.29	0.31	0.60	0.59	0.07	40%	30%	1.34	1.2
Microsoft Corporation	0.67		0.65	0.34	0.42	0.49	0.48	0.28	0.66	0.71	(0.10)	34%	18%	1.88	0.79
Amazon.com, Inc.	0.51	0.65		0.40	0.45	0.65	0.57	0.54	0.60	0.57	0.11	37%	29%	1.29	1.15
MercadoLibre, Inc.	0.27	0.34	0.40		0.53	0.61	0.47	0.50	0.50	0.58	0.13	71%	44%	1.63	1.47
Paycom Software, Inc.	0.37	0.42	0.45	0.53		0.62	0.49	0.58	0.61	0.61	0.01	64%	42%	1.53	1.38
ServiceNow, Inc.	0.39	0.49	0.65	0.51	0.62		0.52	0.77	0.68	0.56	0.03	45%	37%	1.41	0.93
Danaher Corporation	0.29	0.48	0.57	0.47	0.49	0.52		0.42	0.39	0.40	0.24	27%	18%	1.44	0.64
IDEXX Laboratories, Inc.	0.31	0.28	0.54	0.50	0.33	0.27	0.42		0.36	0.36	0.21	47%	26%	1.81	0.89
Mastercard Incorporated	0.60	0.66	0.60	0.50	0.58	0.68	0.59	0.36		0.90	0.00	31%	23%	1.34	1.18
Visa Inc.	0.59	0.71	0.57	0.58	0.61	0.56	0.40	0.36	0.90		0.00	24%	19%	1.27	0.99
SPDR Gold Shares	0.07	(0.10)	0.11	0.13	0.01	0.03	0.24	0.21	0.00	0.00		12%	14%	0.85	0.11
> Average Correlation per Security	0.41	0.46	0.51	0.42	0.44	0.47	0.43	0.36	0.53	0.53	0.07				
> Total # Correlation Coefficients > .79	0	0	0	0	0	0	0	0	1	1	0				
> Portfolio Averages												39%	27%	1.44	0.98
SPDR S&P 500 ETF Trust (SPY)												15%	15%	1.00	1.00

Figure 11.2   Five-year correlation coefficient matrix.

Let's now review these pairings and assess their relative merits for diversification.

- **Amazon.com** (AMZN) and **Mercado Libre** (MELI) are both from the Internet Commerce industry.
  - Relative CC of .40 is attractively low. Despite being from the same industry, share prices are not highly correlated.
  - MELI had a better fit with the rest of the portfolio (.42 vs. .51).
  - MELI offered superior annualized performance (71% vs. 37%).
  - AMZN had better annualized volatility (29% vs. 44%).
  - MELI had a superior Sharpe ratio (1.63 vs. 1.29).
  - MELI also had a higher beta (1.47 vs. 1.15).
  - **Verdict:** Depending upon the economic/market outlook, an investor could choose Meli when growth is expected (superior Sharpe ratio and higher beta) or Amazon.com for less volatility if the outlook is less promising.
- **Paycom** (PAYC) and **ServiceNow** (NOW) are both from the same industry of Tech Services, Human Resources, and workflow analytics firms.
  - Relative CC (.62) is third highest but is acceptable (less than .80).
  - Either fit well with the rest of the portfolio (.47 vs. .44).
  - PAYC generated the stronger annual performance (64% vs. 45%).
  - NOW incurred lower volatility (32% vs. 42%).
  - The Sharpe ratio slightly favors NOW (1.53 vs. 1.41).
  - NOW had a much higher beta (1.38 vs. .92).
  - **Verdict:** For absolute performance, PAYC is the better choice. But if an investor is sensitive about volatility, similar solid Sharpe ratios would suggest choosing NOW, particularly if the economic/market outlook is weakening.
- **Danaher** (DHR) and **IDEXX Labs** (IDXX) are both Health Care companies from the same industry (Diagnostics and Research) but their business models don't overlap. DHR serves human health care needs. IDXX focuses on veterinary needs. So, they are not really competitors.
  - The relative correlation coefficient (.42) is low.
  - They both fit well with the rest of the portfolio (.43 vs. .36).
  - IDXX generates a significantly higher annualized return (47% vs. 27%).
  - DHR incurs lower annualized volatility (18% vs. 26%).
  - IDXX offers better performance per unit of volatility (1.81 vs. 1.44).
  - Both betas are <1, so both should act defensively when the economy slows.
  - **Verdict:** IDXX has generated significant outperformance, even on a volatility-measured basis (Sharpe ratio). But with such low

average CCs, they could both be held and could contribute differently to the portfolio.

- **Apple** (AAPL) and **Microsoft** (MSFT) are both Info Tech giants and, although considered as foundational holdings, are categorized in different industries (Consumer Electronics vs. Software).
  - Their relative CC of .67 is second highest pairing in the portfolio but is still lower than .80.
  - AAPL and MSFT have almost the same average individual correlation coefficients (CC) (.41 vs. .46), representing excellent fit with the rest of the portfolio.
  - APPL had higher annualized returns (40% vs. 34%).
  - MSFT had lower annualized volatility (18% vs. 30%).
  - MSFT generated a better Sharpe ratio (1.88 vs. 1.34).
  - MSFT had a much lower beta (.79 vs. 1.2) over 5 years.
  - <u>Verdict:</u> APPL holds the edge in performance, but MSFT has generated better results per unit of volatility and has exceptional defensive characteristics. Both fit well with the rest of the portfolio. A portfolio could benefit from owning both.
- Since **Mastercard** (MC) and **Visa** (V) are from the same industry, a high correlation (.90) could have been predictable. Which one should be removed?
  - MC has had higher annualized performance (31% vs. 24%).
  - MC has a higher Sharpe ratio (1.34 vs. 1.27).
  - The annualized standard deviations are similar (19% vs. 23%).
  - V is more defensive exhibiting a lower beta (.99 vs. 1.18).
  - <u>Verdict:</u> With minimal difference in volatility characteristics, MC should be the better choice to retain based upon better annualized performance and a better Sharpe ratio.
- **Gold** is presented to highlight its exceptionally low correlations with all listed stocks.
- If an investor desires to hold two or more highly correlated stocks, consider instead owning an industry-specific ETF to gain the benefits of broader industry exposure.

Creating a Correlation Matrix

To construct a coefficient matrix similar to Figure 11.2, launch the Portfolio Visualizer Asset Correlation platform.[7] Input up to 50 stocks. Leave the rest of the details blank. These other parameters will populate automatically.

---

[7]https://www.portfoliovisualizer.com/asset-correlations (Accessed 26 September 2021).

Copy and paste the resulting spreadsheet data into a blank Excel chart. This will allow you to perform manual calculations (see Chapter 9) similar to Figure 11.2.

> **Note:** When the correlation results are first presented, the platform will highlight any limitations during the process. Read their notes to understand what might be deficient. Some stocks may have no data and must be removed. As well, if a stock with a short corporate history is included (i.e. recent IPO), the entire data set will be curtailed to this shorter time frame for all stocks. Consider removing any stocks that have less than 5 years of public data.

Stock Comparison Metrics

Peruse the chart to first seek out high correlation coefficients > +.80. By removing one, a portfolio's diversification merits could be immediately improved. To decide between two highly correlated stocks, consider which other performance characteristics are preferable: growth, defensive, or a relative combination. The following five parameters might help to better frame investment decisions:

    i. Average Annual Performance – Which has generated the best annual returns?

    ii. Absolute Variance – Which stock is the more volatile?

    iii. Sharpe Ratio – Which has the best returns relative to the amount of volatility?

    iv. Beta (degree of volatility relative to the market) – Which responds more to market movements?

    v. Correlation Coefficients – Which are better for portfolio diversification (i.e. lower correlation coefficients)?

If still undecided, compare other qualitative traits such as quality of leadership, ESG standards, and business model diversity (see Chapter 10).

Investment Tip

Stop what you are doing!

Before buying or selling that very next stock, assess its diversification value against the rest of your current portfolio using the "Portfolio Visualizer" program. This process could significantly reshape how to construct a winning portfolio.

Summary of Diversification Techniques

Diversification is the proverbial "free lunch." While it won't counter overt corrections or bear markets, diversification can improve a portfolio's overall volatility and performance characteristics during ordinary markets. Here is a recap of the techniques.

> **Note:** The asset mix decision introduced in Chapter 4 (stocks, bonds, cash) offers the single best opportunity to diminish volatility. However, in this guide, the asset mix is not counted as a diversification technique because bonds are ignored due to their relative underperformance over the long term and cash is intended for investing opportunities (see Chapter 18).

i. **Filter #14 – Stock Selections across All Economic Sectors** (Active Filter): Incorporating stocks from all 11 economic sectors in similar proportion to their global weights reduces the impact of any one sector during times of economic stress.

ii. **Filter #15 – Non-duplication of the 69 Industries** (Active Filter): Avoidance of industry duplication reduces portfolio vulnerability during periods of high market volatility.

iii. **Filter #16 – Minimization of Correlation Coefficients** (Active Filter): A portfolio comprised of lower-correlated stocks should exhibit lower overall volatility.

Here are three additional non-active diversification filters to consider when choosing between stocks.

i. **Mid- and Large-Cap Stocks** (Manual Screen): Large-cap businesses offer revenue stability, while mid-caps introduce more dynamic, faster-growing business models and introduce potential for accretive mergers or becoming acquired.

ii. **Corporations with Globally Dispersed Revenues** (Manual Screen): Verifying the geographic source of a corporation's revenues (Figure 11.3) is not an active filter. Yet by perusing quarterly reports, an investor can quickly discern the breadth and depth of a corporation's revenues per region. A portfolio comprised of stocks with global reach should weather better during periods of regional economic stresses.

iii. **Corporate Revenue Models** (Manual Screen): While this is not an active filter in the stock selection process, performance and stability can be further enhanced by consciously introducing a variety of different corporate revenue models: bricks and mortar, online retail, advertising, leasing, licensing, SaaS, freemium/premium, auctions, franchising, fractionalization, disintermediation, or roll-up (M&A), etc.

Prioritization of Diversification

Without considering each stock's diversification potential, a portfolio could be unnecessarily vulnerable the next time the market roils. Instead of treating diversification as a cumulative afterthought, reverse the process and make it a priority. Every stock trade (buy or sell) is a chance to add incremental value to the portfolio, contributing either to improved performance or to the moderation of volatility. Understanding the different types of diversification and how stocks interact with one another could improve the performance characteristics of a portfolio.

Investor Tip

Periodically review your portfolio's correlation matrix to confirm that the portfolio is not being exposed to bad diversification.

Caution: No matter how well you pick your stocks and build a balanced, diversified portfolio, during market corrections, stocks tend to act in unison. In other words, in a crisis, most stocks will suffer together. Diversification may help to soften the blow, but there will still be pain.

The good news is that quality businesses usually rebound faster and often take advantage of a crises with M&A activity. They are usually the ones with cash reserves.

Wisdom: Aside from introducing fixed income assets (i.e. bonds) into your portfolio, the next best security to help reduce volatility is gold (see "The Yin of Gold" at the companion site: www.the investingoasis.com).

At the Oasis: Chapter 11

- Prioritize diversification. Each trade is an opportunity to purposefully enhance performance, reduce volatility, or eliminate specific risks from the portfolio.
- Learn the limits to diversification. Over-diversification (i.e. too many stocks) will introduce redundancies and potentially increase volatility if industries are duplicated.
- A well-diversified portfolio should bolster an investor's confidence and calm behavior.

"In my 45-year career as an investment counselor, humility did show me the need for worldwide diversification to reduce risk. Over time, I became even more humble because statistics showed that about one-third of the time, my stock selections should have been ignored."

—Sir John Templeton (1912–2008),
founder of the Templeton Funds

Chapter 12

Portfolio Construction

Equal-Weighting a Portfolio

*Simplify investing by
deploying portfolio democracy.*

Objective:

**Applying the final steps to allocate capital equally
between stocks.**

Step 8. Designing a Purposeful Portfolio: Equal Allocation

Through the 16 filters deployed in Figure 12.1, the stock prospect list should now reflect most of an investor's very best investment ideas. In this chapter, capital will be allocated equally between stocks.

Advantages of an Equal-Weighted Portfolio

Since growth can happen within any industry at any time, investing the same amount into all stocks places corporate leaders and their respective businesses on equal footing, irrespective of the size of a business or its sector or industry. An equal-weighted portfolio offers the following advantages:

1. **Easier portfolio building.** Building and adding new positions is simplified. Investing equal amounts into each stock reduces the time spent on over-weighting or under-weighting sectors, industries, and indvidual stocks.

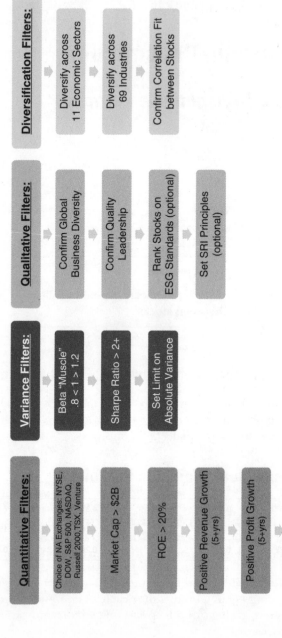

Figure 12.1   Summary of stock selection filters.

2. **Allows corporate leaders to manage.** Let market democracy prevail. A portfolio's long-term growth comes from the intelligent decisions undertaken by corporate management teams. With growth happening in all sectors and most industries, equal-weighting the securities in a portfolio allows the performance of these leaders to be objectively measured.

3. **Potential for enhanced performance.** Figure 12.2 demonstrates that the equal-weighted S&P 500 Index significantly out-performed the market cap weighted S&P 500 Index over a 16-year period ending in 2016. This was likely due to the increased exposure to smaller, faster-growing companies, lower exposure to the slower-growing mega-cap stocks, and greater exposure to potential value stocks,

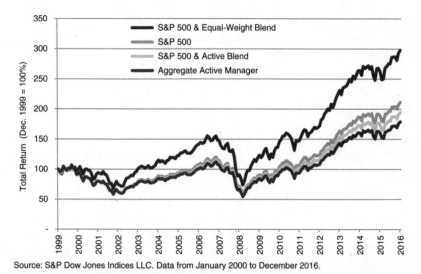

Source: S&P Dow Jones Indices LLC. Data from January 2000 to December 2016.

Risk/Return Comparison

METRIC	S&P 500	ACTIVE MANAGERS	S&P 500 EQUAL WEIGHT	S&P 500/ ACTIVE BLEND	S&P 500/ S&P 500 EQUAL WEIGHT BLEND
Annual Return (%)	4.8%	3.7%	9.3%	4.3%	7.1%
Annualized Volatility (%)	14.8	14.7	17.1	14.8	15.8
Return / Volatility	0.32	0.25	0.54	0.29	0.45

Source: S&P Dow Jones Indices LLC. Data from January 2000 to December 2016.

Figure 12.2 Outperformance of an equal-weight index.

which periodically outperform their growth counterparts.[1] Note, however, that annualized volatility is higher for the equal-weighted portfolio relative to the S&P 500 Index (17.1% vs.14.8%). The good news is that the Sharpe ratio for the equal-weighted index is higher (.54 vs.32). This suggests that the higher potential returns are justified for the minimal added volatility.

4. **Easier rebalancing decisions.** Periodic rebalancing (see Chapter 15) is simplified. By having predetermined thresholds, the process becomes an objective and visual exercise rather than relying upon economic forecasting and using human judgment for periodic reallocation. Time and energy can be quickly focused on the outliers (leaders and laggards).

5. **Redirect energy toward more valuable decisions.** Instead of wrestling with an economic forecasting model and constantly rethinking the relative weighting of each stock position, once an investor buys quality and allocates their capital equally between core positions, their time can be focused on implementing more value-added decisions in Tiers 2 and 3.

Final Steps

Equal-weighting a portfolio is recommended but is discretionary. Use the next four steps to create a sector-diversified, equal-weight core portfolio:

1. Decide on the number of stocks to be held in your core portfolio. Table 12.1 provides six different equal-weighted portfolio combinations. Pick one column with the closest approximate number of stocks expected to be held in the core portfolio (i.e. 10, 15, 20, 25, 30, or 35). Each column shows the target number of stocks to be allocated per sector, according to the S&P 500 sector breakdown (Table 12.2). For example, to maintain a sector-diversified portfolio of 20 stocks with 5% allocated per stock, an investor would buy four Info Tech stocks, three Health Care stocks, two Consumer Discretionary stocks, and so on, down the column.

---

[1]Edwards, Tim, Lazzara, Craig J., Preston, Hamish, and Pestalozzi, Oliver. January 2018. "Outperformance in Equal Weight Indices." Index Investment Strategy. https://www.spglobal.com/spdji/en/documents/research/research-outperformance-in-equal-weight-indices.pdf (Accessed 19 December 2021).

Table 12.1 Equal-weighted portfolio allocations.

Economic Sectors	S&P 500 Sectors **	Total Number of Stocks in the Portfolio*					
		10 10%/stock	15 6.7%/stock	20 5%/stock	25 4%/stock	30 3.3%/stock	35 2.9%/stock
Info Tech	27.48%	3	4	4	6	9	10
Health Care	14.58%	2	2	3	3	4	5
Consumer Discretionary	11.18%	1	2	2	3	3	4
Communication Services	10.90%	1	2	2	3	3	4
Financials	9.89%	1	1	2	2	3	3
Industrials	7.90%	1	1	2	2	2	3
Consumer Staples	7.05%	1	1	1	2	2	2
Utilities	3.13%	0	1	1	1	1	1
Real Estate	2.80%	0	1	1	1	1	1
Materials	2.56%	0	0	1	1	1	1
Energy	2.53%	0	0	1	1	1	1
Total	**100%**	**10**	**15**	**20**	**25**	**30**	**35**

*To calculate the total number of stocks per sector, divide 100% by the total number of positions in the full portfolio. Then divide the S&P 500 Sector Weightings by that percentage to determine the number of stocks per sector.
**S&P 500 Weightings as of July 2020 (Figure 12.2).

2. Separate the list of candidate stocks into their respective economic sector. Ideally, there will be representation across all 11 economic sectors. If any sector lacks at least two candidate stocks, either adjust your search filters or use some other means of research to introduce additional prospective stocks (without duplicating industry exposure).

3. Now re-rank your candidate stocks by one of the following four priorities, depending upon the desired performance characteristics:

   i. Pure growth stocks – highest ROE (return on equity) (see Chapter 8).

   ii. Growth relative to the market – beta between 0.8 and 1.2 depending upon desired relative movement with the market (see Chapter 9).

   iii. Lower standard deviations (defensive stocks with some growth) (see Chapter 9).

   iv. Highest Sharpe ratio (best growth stocks relative to equal degrees of volatility) (see Chapter 9).

   No matter the ranking, these stocks should all hold your highest conviction. Yet all may not be included in the final portfolio. Depending upon how many stocks are to be held, each sector should be limited as per the columns identified in Table 12.1.

4. On your spreadsheet, highlight the top stocks per sector ranked according to the desired performance profile traits (#3). These stocks will become your core portfolio.

Note: An equal-weighted portfolio does not mean creating equal-weighted exposure to the 11 economic sectors. Through the grid process in Table 12.1, sector exposures are purposefully kept approximately in proportion to the S&P 500 Index (Table 12.2).

Note: To invest an equal amount in all stocks, remember to adjust the amount invested in Canadian stocks by the prevailing FX rate. Since the $CAD continues to be weak relative to the $USD, to maintain relatively equal amounts in both Canadian and US stocks, allocate proportionately more into each Canadian stock (i.e. 20–30% more according to the prevailing FX).

Note: For the candidate stocks not chosen to invest in the core portfolio, continue tracking them on your spreadsheet. They could yet again be prospects in Tier 3 (see Chapter 18).

The Starting Line

This chapter was the final step in building a purposeful portfolio, each chapter having built upon the previous ones.

However, if you do not yet have a viable list of candidate stocks from across all 11 economic sectors, please review and refine the filtering process outlined in Chapters 8–10 or defer to a preferred research method.

Investing Process Review

Easy as A–B–C–D

A. 16 Quantitative and Qualitative Filters enable ~8,000 North American stocks to be narrowed into a core portfolio of 20–50 of the highest-quality, globally diverse, growth businesses.

B. Purposeful Diversification across all 11 economic sectors and among diverse, innovative industries create a well-rounded team of stocks, aligned with the global economy, while also moderating portfolio volatility.

C. Equal Allocation into each stock divides the business burdens democratically between world-class leadership teams, while also greatly simplifying ongoing portfolio management.

D. Focus on Alpha. Investors can then focus their attention on creating valuable incremental returns in Tiers 2 and 3.

At the Oasis: Chapter 12

- Investing equal amounts per stock offers more effective portfolio management:
  - Performance is expected to generate higher absolute results per unit of volatility than a portfolio designed around market weights.
- Simplifies target amounts to invest per stock.
- Rebalancing is visual and objective.
- Performance profiles (returns and volatility) can be compared more easily between stocks.
- With stocks allocated proportionately to the 11 economic sectors, performance can still be compared to the S&P 500 Index.
- An investor's time can be better focused on Tiers 2 and 3.

"You're not rich until you have something money can't buy."
—Garth Brooks, singer,
songwriter

On either hand the hazards of believing temptations and taking short cuts can be crippling. As in travelling abroad it risks all, misunderstood or just starved, then stepping off the beaten path will be at one's peril.

Chapter 13

Beware Those Temptations

"Speculation is most dangerous when it looks easiest."
—Warren Buffett

Objective:

Differentiating between the good, the bad, and the ugly risks.

Wandering Spirits Beware

The desert is filled with thorny plants, pesky insects, venomous creatures, contaminated water, and a host of unsavory characters. If the harsh sun and barren landscape did not already pose enough threat, such other dangers could be lethal, especially in combination. This analogy embodies the capital markets journey.

Along the route, wily vendors will persistently tempt an investor to stray from their mission, where the dangers are more clearly defined. The greatest risk of investing in quality assets is periodic volatility. Easily survivable. On the other hand, the hazards of following temptations and taking shortcuts could be crippling. As in traveling abroad, if risks are misunderstood or just ignored, then stepping off the beaten path will be at one's peril.

RMP #9: Speculation and Leverage

If the intention is to build a consistently winning long-term portfolio, why introduce investments of questionable uncertainty? This is rhetorical.

Most investors know why they stray off the beaten path. Yet the topic still deserves a reminder.

Circled in Figure 13.1 are four ranges of asset categories: the "Good," the "Bad," the "Ugly," and the "Discretionary." In the zones above the "Good," investments are either lacking acceptable performance or creating exposure to undue risks.[1] As mentioned in Chapter 4, the return/risk line suggests a linear relationship between ever-increasing risky investments and the returns they could be expected to generate, if any at all. Again, this is far from realistic. As the spectrum advances, the returns become more sporadic (less predictable), and the degree of risks are multiplied. This chapter reveals in escalating order many (but not all) of the temptations lying off the beaten path.

> **Note:** If an investor already perceives volatility in their core stock portfolio to be uncomfortable, likely they should avoid exposure to the riskier categories. Unfortunately, the true riskiness of an investment choice is usually only realized in hindsight.

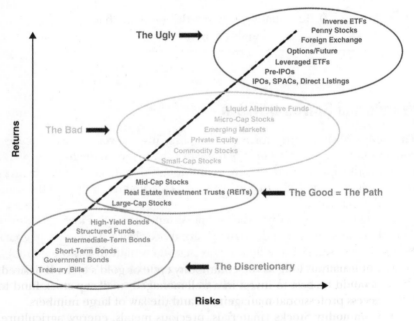

Figure 13.1   The asset zones of the reward/risk spectrum.

---

[1]Investments that introduce greater risk than the expected rewards. In other words, investments with risks that an ordinary investor would consider to be excessive (poor Sharpe ratios).

The Discretionary

Fixed income assets (i.e. guaranteed certificates, term deposits, government bonds, corporate bonds, etc.) are best valued for their lower degree of volatility and consistency of generating income. Their merit is greatest when aligned with repaying outstanding fixed obligations. However, holding fixed income assets for long investing periods has historically realized performance inferior to investing in a portfolio of quality blue-chip stocks. Review Figures 4.3 and 4.5 of the rewards and risks to see the relative difference between a portfolio comprised of bonds and a portfolio comprised of quality stocks. Despite the lower range of volatility, the rewards pale relative to the long-term growth of a portfolio of quality stocks.

The Good

Chapters 7–10 should have established the reasoning underlying the beneficial nature of building a portfolio comprised of high-quality mid- to large-cap stocks and REITs as identified in Figure 13.1. Relative to all the other investing zones, the "Path" more consistently offers the best rewards relative to the degree of volatility. History has shown that the higher-quality investments have a Sharpe ratio > 1. This means they generate greater annual performance than the degree of volatility.

The Bad

Investments with bad risks can generate decent returns, yet the additional risks (unprofitable businesses, illiquidity, cyclicality, and products with high management fees) warrant greater scrutiny before investing and greater vigilance post-investment. Your time could be better spent in Tiers 2 and 3.

- **Small-Cap Stocks** (market cap $500M–$2B) – Big upside when well chosen. Small-cap companies are subject to multiyear cycles, though not usually as long as the commodity cycle or gold's cycle. If desired, it would be best to invest in a well-managed small-cap stock fund to access professional management and the law of large numbers.
- **Commodity Stocks** (materials, precious metals, energy, agriculture, and forestry, etc.) – Resource extraction businesses depend on prices determined by external supply and demand factors. Creating value is primarily achieved by operational cost-effectiveness and M&A activities. Cyclicality of commodities favors contrarian investing. Buy during a recession. Sell in euphoria.

- **Private Equity Investments** – Where a corporate insider desires to sell their shares in a privately held corporation to an outside investor, often at a premium. Although the eventual returns can be exciting, they come with a high degree of illiquidity and a lack of transparency for the outsider to see the underlying business. Consider this money unavailable and at risk until the company goes public.

Educational Note: Private Placements – Alternatively, a private placement is an investment into a publicly listed company by invitation only and usually at a discount to a company's current public share valuation. Such opportunities are reserved by brokerages for high-net-worth clients.

- **Emerging Markets Exposure** – Investing offshore involves unique risks not present when investing in the domestic capital markets: transparency of earnings, ESG violations, political interference, foreign exchange devaluations, liquidity concerns. Even if a foreign stock is listed as an ADR (American Depository Receipts) on a North American exchange, it could still be forcibly delisted by political persuasion (either by country of domicile or by country of listing). If considered, invest through a reputable EM investment fund or ETF.
- **Micro-Cap Stocks** (stocks less than $500M in market cap) – As new and growing businesses, micro-cap stocks engender unpredictability. Visionary founders may be different than the leaders needed to take a business forward. The transition may not be fluid. Best to invest through a reputable investment professional that does their homework. A micro-cap is more highly influenced by their business opportunity, quality of leadership, and access to funding capital.
- **Liquid Alternative Funds**[2] – Alternative assets could enhance a portfolio with performance or defensively by the addition of unique assets that were, historically, only available to wealthy investors, for example:
  - Venture capital funding
  - Private equity
  - Pre-IPO stocks
  - Distressed debt
  - Crowdsourced real estate
  - Managed futures
  - Collectibles (i.e. reserve wines, rare wines, fine arts)
  - Timberlands
  - Cryptocurrencies

---

[2]Chen, J. (2020). "Liquid Alternatives." https://www.investopedia.com/terms/l/liquid-alternatives.asp (Accessed 26 September 2021).

Although each liquid alternative fund will be managed professionally, accessibility through publicly traded ETFs masks the inherently high risk of the underlying assets. In a tight market, prices of such specific assets could be subject to illiquidity and steep corrections due to an inability of the underlying fund managers to find buyers. Equally, the more exotic the nature of the assets, the higher the fees. Read the fine print. Alternative investments are better suited for long-dated institutional investment mandates, like pension plans, or investors with deep pockets.

Note: Before venturing into an alternative investment, read an insightful commentary from Bain Capital at this URL: https://www.bain.com/insights/adjacency-strategy-global-private-equity-report-2019/.

The Ugly

"Ugly" assets carry the highest potential for permanent losses. Surrounded by gross uncertainty and multiple degrees of ill-defined risk (i.e. speculation, leverage, lack of fundamentals, heightened volatility, and time constraints), the return/risk ratio is immeasurable. Tread with deep caution, if ever.

- **IPOs, SPACs, and Direct Listings** – Be aware that when a business finally gets floated on the capital markets, the retail client is the last after a long line of insiders have already received their rewards. No matter the method of entry, usually the fundamentals rarely justify the valuations. Without clear fundamentals, it could be many quarters before their worthiness can be confirmed.
- **Pre-IPOs** – In the early stages of a start-up, without defined business models or confirmed revenues, dreams and volatility reign supreme. It's less about the concept and more about the leadership's track record. Be knowledgeable about the capital-raising stage of the start-up:
  1. Seed Capital
  2. Angel Investor Funding
  3. Venture Capital Financing
  4. Mezzanine Financing and Bridge Loans
  5. IPO (Initial Public Offering)
- **Leveraged ETFs** – While there may be fundamentals underpinning a broad-market leveraged ETF, the downside is that they introduce extreme volatility relative to the market (2×, 3×, 5×). In rising markets, the returns can be exhilarating, yet during a sell-off, the losses will be staggeringly quick. If you're willing to use leveraged ETFs, make sure

the opportunity is compelling (i.e. buy during an absolute market sell-off), then use a stop-loss trade to prevent any runaway grief.

Caveat: An ETF of 3× means an investor only needs to invest one third of the size of a usual investment to mimic the regular markets.

- **Buying Options/Futures Contracts** – Options are leveraging tools with a limited life. They require strong market experience. Buying puts (for protection) or calls (for increased offense) introduces time limits on getting results at the risk of losing the premiums paid. Chapters 16 and 19 outline how to build in advantages to generate supplementary, reduced-risk income by selling options to speculators.
- **Foreign Exchange (FX) Trading and/or Cryptocurrencies** – No matter whether a currency is fiat or crypto, allocating capital into currencies is a speculative venture left for specialists. Until crypto-currencies are accepted openly by corporations as legal tender, non-fiat currencies will remain speculative. Development of the metaverse, though, could be the tipping point to legitimize cryptocurrencies.
- **Penny Stocks** – Despite the high risk of fraud and bankruptcy, overly promoted penny stocks continue to find willing speculators. The old-fashioned "boiler room" is now replaced by a never-ending barrage of clickbait emails from seedy offshore locations. Don't click.
- **Inverse ETFs** – Used as protection when markets appear overbought but guaranteed to lose your capital if held beyond several trading sessions. As evidenced in Figure 13.2, the long-term negative trend tells the story. These ETFs are "ugly" risks because:
  i. The long-term trend will always be negative. Such ETFs are made up of near-term futures contracts, which are in a state of constant decay as they mature and are replaced with next-month contracts. Inverse ETFs require high time-wasting vigilance.
  ii. The sporadic positive upticks are too far in between. Making money using an inverse ETF hinges entirely on timing. Good luck.

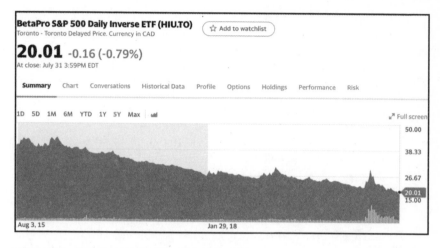

BetaPro S&P 500 Daily Inverse ETF (HIU.TO)
Toronto - Toronto Delayed Price. Currency in CAD

☆ Add to watchlist

20.01 -0.16 (-0.79%)
At close: July 31 3:59PM EDT

Summary   Chart   Conversations   Historical Data   Profile   Options   Holdings   Performance   Risk

1D 5D 1M 6M YTD 1Y 5Y Max

⤢ Full screen

50.00

38.33

26.67

20.01
15.00

Aug 3, 15   Jan 29, 18

Figure 13.2 BetaPro S&P 500 Daily Inverse ETF.

Summary

The further an investor ventures away from the "Path," the greater the scrutiny required before and after investing. Equally, the allocation of capital should be progressively smaller. Caveat emptor applies to any investment off the Path.

At the Oasis: Chapter 13

If planning to invest in off-the-path investments, first consider a reputable investment fund where the risks are already being vetted by professional management teams and the benefits of diversification can counter some of the risks. Otherwise, for the true adventurer:

- Draw a line in the sand. Limit extraneous, non-core investments to < 10% of the portfolio.
- Allay the risks by investing small amounts across multiple risk categories.
- Be opportunistic. Look at historical trends. Be patient for maximum pessimism.
- Use stop-loss orders to limit your losses.
- Once profitable, change your protection to trailing stop-loss orders to protect your capital.
- Periodically trim for profits. Most won't survive the long term.
- When the market sinks, if cash is needed, sacrifice these riskier assets first.
- Leverage is a strategic weapon. Never speculate off-the-path with debt (see Chapter 18).

"I can resist everything but temptation."

—Oscar Wilde

Tier 1 Summary

To improve on the status quo and generate better beta results, Tier 1 encourages introducing an investment plan with methodical construction and adopting more professional standards. Building an equal-weighted, diversified portfolio comprised of quality NA stocks relies on using our head and our heart-brains. Each investor must do their own research, but *The Investing Oasis* already provides the road map.

Tier 1 principles and methodology are timeless, which is appropriate, since investing is a lifelong undertaking. In this lightning-fast digital world, slow and steady methods can still win the day.

When you feel ready, Tier 2's rewards will require more time and effort but will also bring greater low-risk rewards.

THE INVESTING OASIS: Tier 2

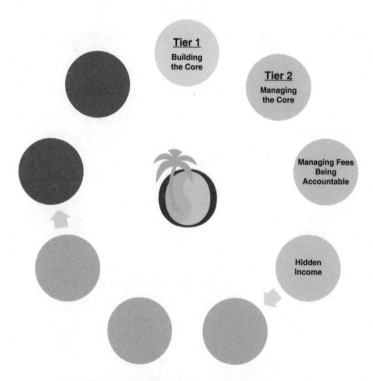

Tier 1
Building
the Core

Tier 2
Managing
the Core

Managing Fees
Being
Accountable

Hidden
Income

MISSION #2: To Outperform the Average Investor

	Mission #2
	To Outperform Average Retail Investors
Tier 1 – Building a Core Growth Portfolio	✓
Tier 2 – Core Management and Income from Covered Calls	✓

Tier 2 introduces three processes to launch and then enhance portfolio performance:

1. Buying stocks.
2. Contrarian rebalancing.
3. Income and protection from covered calls (CCs).

Chapter 1 encouraged building competency before tackling each successive tier.

Chapter 14

The Buy-in

"Your one chance to create value is when you buy.
The rest is up to the market."
—Warren Buffett

Objective:

Buying stocks on your terms.

Who doesn't want to buy quality stocks at a discount? But don't confuse being a good stock picker with being a good negotiator. According to Warren Buffett, investing involves four value-creating skills:

1. Finding quality stocks (see Chapters 8–10).
2. Waiting for a discount.
3. Negotiating to get your best price (this chapter).
4. Patience to let the market do the heavy lifting.

This chapter focuses on a fifth value-creation skill: proactive, contrarian trading tactics.

Trading Challenges

Since trading is a binary game, being a good negotiator is key to getting a better deal. Retail investors have just as much chance of getting it right as any professional. They even hold several key advantages over the professionals:

- No formal protocols or plan to be followed.
- No supervision.
- Unrestricted investment choices.
- Agility to trade on instinct.

Yet, without discipline, these freedoms can also become disadvantages.

Professionals set target prices, deploy protection strategies, and are held accountable for every trading decision. At any given moment, professionals have multiple trade orders outstanding, each with a specific purpose (i.e. adding to a position, stop-loss orders for defense, selling covered calls, etc.). Familiarity with the markets allows them to see and feel the trends but not get attached to any single trade. Trades are set proactively and adjusted incrementally until completed. Since the need for execution is usually secondary, trades may sit for extended periods.

Conversely, retail investors are more vulnerable. The focus tends to be on deploying singular trades to get in on the action. The money is personal, which intensifies the decisions and may breed impatience. Further, an investor may have other distractions, particularly if multitasking on a mobile phone. Without constraints or accountability, frequent trading serves more to feed hungry algorithms, brokerage platforms, and the market makers.

A market maker is an intermediary between buyers and sellers to ensure that trades are deployed efficiently. In the industry, this is viewed as being helpful to keep markets orderly. However, during the manipulated rise in GameStop shares by followers of the Reddit forum *WallStreetBets* in the Spring of 2021, it was revealed that Robinhood Markets Inc. had a "payment-for-order-flow" (PFOF) contractual relationship with several market makers. Trades on the Robinhood platform were being steered through outside brokers. While this assured revenues for Robinhood, it also ensured that most retail trades would be delivered at less than market prices. A few pennies shaved on a trade would not be noticeable to the average investor; however, when deployed over millions of trades, this practice is clearly not friendly to the retail investor community, writ large. Investors should know whether their broker deploys a PFOF system.

Note: Brokerage firms that have previously engaged in PFOF services are Robinhood, E-Trade, Ally Financial, Webull, Tradestation, The Vanguard Group, Charles Schwab Corporation, and TD Ameritrade. Brokerage firms that have not used PFOF services are Interactive Brokers, Merrill Edge, and Fidelity Investments.

Since there could be hundreds, or even thousands, of transactions over an investor's lifetime, there should be high motivation to improve one's trading practices.

> **Note:** Throughout *The Investing Oasis*, where trade orders are mentioned (e.g. buy, sell, stop-loss, trailing stop-loss, etc.), the recommended order parameters are "GTC" (good 'til canceled) and "FORTH" (fill outside of regular trading hours). GTC ensures that the trade will remain open until settled and FORTH allows the trade to be filled after the markets close.
>
> Further, all orders should be set as limit orders, to buy or sell a stock at a specific price or better. A buy limit order can only be executed at the limit price or lower, and a sell limit order can only be executed at the limit price or higher.

Importance of the ACB

A stock's adjusted cost base (ACB) may only be relevant to the individual investor but, as the combined average of all transactions for a stock, it offers two behavioral insights:

1. If positive, the investor is sitting on unrealized gains. This is proof that patient investing is creating value. Keep it up.
2. If negative, a position is not yet profitable. This possibly implies impatient buying. Sitting on any number of unrealized losses for extended periods should prompt reflection about buying practices.

Since buying a quality stock is the first chance to create value in your portfolio, when you buy and how you buy can also affect how much value creation is achieved during the buy-in process. Let's review three buy-in methods:

1. Lump Sum
2. Dollar-Cost Averaging (DCA)
3. Selling Put Contracts

Lump Sum

According to *TIME* magazine journalist Dan Kadlec, buying stocks in one lump sum has historically been a better way to invest than accumulating shares gradually through DCA because the market holds a perpetual positive bias over the long term.[1] On the other hand, buying stocks gradually with DCA often feels more comfortable but carries the potential opportunity cost of sitting on cash while the market marches higher. Choosing to invest by lump sum or by DCA depends primarily upon three factors:

1. The stage of the market cycle (nadir, uptrend, zenith, or pullback).
2. A stock's current price compared to its 52-week price history.
3. An investor's risk tolerance.

In a perfect world, investing a lump sum of capital would be deployed opportunistically when a share price is near its 52-week low while the markets are also plumbing new lows.

Equally, an investor should resist buying when a stock and the markets are at 52-week highs. Realistically, though, most trades will occur somewhere in mid-market and will rarely be perfect. It may take days, weeks, or months for a lump-sum investment to prove wise. But this evokes one of the greatest unstated lessons of the markets: The price paid for shares in a quality investment will eventually advance to overcome a poorly timed buying decision.

> *"The stock market is a 'no-called-strike' game. You don't have to swing at everything, you can wait for your pitch."*
> —Warren Buffett

Yet, when a targeted stock and/or the markets are well off their lows and moving toward 52-week highs, a better allocation tool may be dollar-cost averaging.

Dollar-Cost Averaging (DCA)

DCA refers to the discipline of periodically buying either an incremental number of shares or a set dollar amount of a targeted stock no matter the market trend. It places faith equally in owning quality stocks and that the market will eventually return to its long-term positive growth trend. This approach should appeal particularly to risk-sensitive or investors harboring doubts because DCA:

- Eliminates having to guess the market's short-term direction.
- Reduces buyer's remorse by empowering the investor to control the buy-in process (when, how much, and at what price?).

---

[1]Kadlec, D. (2012) "Is Dollar-Cost Averaging Dumb?" http://business.time.com/2012/11/15/is-dollar-cost-averaging-dumb/ (Accessed 26 September 2021).

- Buys more shares even at declining prices which lowers the break-even price (ACB) and ultimately helps to accelerate a rebound to profitability when the market recovers.
- Using DCA doesn't mean that an investor doubts their convictions about a particular stock. Instead, it demonstrates respect that markets are entirely random in the short run.

Note: The success of DCA requires conviction in the stock choice, faith in the markets, and a blindfold to keep buying more shares despite a sagging share price.

DCA Protocols

1. **Determine the average allocation per stock.** Divide the total portfolio value by the number of stocks to be held in the portfolio. This becomes the target allocation per stock.
2. **Calculate the average DCA tranche per trade.** Divide the average stock allocation (Step 1) by the number of DCA tranches desired. For smaller accounts, commission costs may be cost-prohibitive. The total number of tranches to deploy and over what time frame are both personal decisions.
3. **For the first tranche, set a limit order** at, or just slightly below, the current mid-market price. Once filled, don't worry about the valuation falling. This just gets you started.
4. **Set the second tranche** at 2–5% below the current market price (investor's choice). This will be the first attempt at lowering the ACB. This trade order will endure until it settles or is canceled.
5. **Set a series of GTC limit trade orders** at successively lower bids by increments of 2–5% (investor's choice). This invites the market to come to you until the orders are triggered or canceled.
6. **Consider accelerating the DCA process** with a partial or full lump sum if a share price falls significantly. Make sure the reason is non-material.
7. **Don't use DCAs on commodity stocks** (base minerals, precious metals, agriculture, energy, etc.). Averaging down on a stock is most beneficial when a corporation's fortunes are controlled by management's value-creating strategies (price-maker). Commodity stocks are price-takers and trends can last years, which would frustrate the DCA process.
8. **To prevent runaway failures,** set a trailing stop-loss order (TSL) at 10–15% below each stock's ACB because the average annual price fluctuation for a growth stock is about 15–20%. This order will either be triggered or will follow the share price into profitability.

DCA EXAMPLE

When investing $200,000 equally into 20 stocks (scale this example to your own situation), each stock allocation would be $10,000. The first purchase could be $2,000 (= 20% of the allotment). In subsequent sessions, gradually invest the remaining $8,000 (4 × $2,000, or 8 × $1,000, etc.).

The pace of the process could be influenced by an investor's degree of risk sensitivity and willingness to pay trading commissions (particularly if the account is small). The time between deployments could be days, weeks, or months. Growth share prices often gyrate by 15–20%. Don't be shy to set lowball limit orders at prices 5, 10, and 15% below a stock's ACB. Market openings can be quite erratic.

Important: If still sitting on cash and unable to deploy the remaining DCA tranches because the underlying share price continues to advance, consider waiting for a general market pullback (when all stocks are discounted) or sell short-term "cash-secured" out-of-the-money put contracts (see below).

Selling Put Contracts – A Wiser Buy-in (for More Advanced Investors)

An even smarter buy-in technique is to sell short-term put contracts on a targeted stock. Similar to deploying DCA, periodically selling put contracts allows the investor to pick a preferred buy-in price (strike price) and get paid while waiting for a contract to be exercised. The put seller (you) would receive a premium for taking on this potential obligation to own the shares. When a contract is finally exercised, the share's ACB would be reduced further than if those shares were bought at current market prices with DCA.

Note: Although selling put contracts is intended for more sophisticated investors, risk tolerance is not relevant since this method is an alternative to the deployment of cash through DCA. Risk tolerance would be more relevant in discerning which stocks to target.

Selling contracts to buy shares may be counterintuitive; however, this definition should help:

> A put option *is a financial contract which facilitates the transfer of shares at a stated price (called the "strike price") from the buyer of the put contract to the seller of the put contract (you) by a specified date.*

The contract is fulfilled only if the targeted share price is below the specified strike price at the maturity date. In exchange for this right to sell their shares at the strike price, the buyer of the put contract pays the seller (you) a premium. Put contract buyers usually own the underlying shares and desire to lock in a price, believing the price trend will decline. Sellers of the put contract, meanwhile, are more optimistic, believing that the price trend of the underlying stock will rise.

With put contracts, depending upon an investor's outlook for the underlying stock, there are three categories of strike prices:

1. OTM (out-of-the-money) – bearish. Low probability of being exercised. Low premiums.
2. ATM (at-the-money) – neutral. Medium probability of being exercised. Medium premiums.
3. ITM (in-the-money) – bullish. Higher probability of being exercised. Higher premiums. Consider selling an ITM put contract when a share price is expected to continue to rise during the limited time of the contract. However, the deeper the strike price, the more likely the contract may be exercised, which is desired if the intention was to buy the shares.

In all cases, at maturity, if the targeted stock's share price rises above the contracted strike price, the contract is terminated. The seller (you) keeps the premium and is not obligated to receive the shares.

However, if, at maturity, the targeted stock price is at, or lower, than the chosen strike price, the contract will be valid. You keep the premium but will now be obligated to purchase the contracted number of shares with cash at the contracted strike price.

Pros of Selling Puts:
• Flexibility of contract terms can be structured to fit a wide range of time horizons and risk scenarios (OTM/ATM/ITM).
• Premiums received are essentially interest paid on your idle cash.
• The premiums lower a stock's ACB when contracts are exercised.
• Provides leverage of ownership without interest costs.
• ITM puts will partially mimic market exposure to the underlying shares up to the chosen strike price.

Cons of Selling Puts:
• Not all stocks offer options streams.
• The share value of some stocks can be too large to accommodate selling even a single contract (i.e. Booking Holdings, Google, Tesla).

- Single contracts (representing 100 shares) may be too large for small accounts.
- Selling a contract does not guarantee the purchase of the targeted shares.
- American-style put contracts can be exercised prior to maturity (most NA stocks).

Example: The Trade Desk (TTD)

Setup

Your portfolio is $500,000 USD. You plan to own 20 stocks with the average value = $25,000. A targeted core stock is TTD, a self-service cloud-based business that allows buyers worldwide to create, manage, and optimize data-driven digital advertising campaigns. It otherwise meets all your selection criteria (see Chapters 8–10).

With TTD shares currently valued at $79 (August 2021), each contract would be valued at $7,900 (= $79 × 100). This equals approximately three contracts (= 3 × 100 × $79 = $23,700).

Base Position

To initiate a base position, you can either buy 100 ATD shares with cash at the current FMV, or you can sell one, 1-week ATM put contract at a strike price of $79 (ATM). At maturity, if the TTD share price is at, or below, the strike price ($79), the contract will be exercised. You will have bought 100 shares of TTD. Due to the premium received, however, the stock's ACB would be lower than if the shares were to have been bought with cash.

At maturity, if the TTD share price is above the strike price, the contract will fail, and you keep the premium. You can then sell another 1-week ATM put contract. Continue this process until a contract is exercised and the TTD shares are "put" into your account.

You would still have two contract tranches remaining (2 × 100 × $79 = $14,800).

Periodic Investing with Put Contracts

With successful implementation of a first put contract, consider selling the next contract. Consider the three options in Table 14.1, each with a different strike price and maturity date.

Table 14.1   TTD sample put-selling comparison.

	OTM	ATM	ITM
Investor Outlook	Bearish	Neutral	Bullish
Duration	5 Days	12 Days	19 Days
Strike Price	$77	$79	$82
Premium to Be Received	$1.00	$2.80	$5.25

	OTM	ATM	ITM
ACB of Shares (if exercised)	$76 (= $77 – $1)	$76.20 (= $79 – $2.80)	$76.75 (= $82–$5.25)
Discount Relative to Buying Shares at FMV ($79) (if exercised)	3.8% = ($79 – $76)/$79	3.5% = ($79 – $76.2)/$79	2.8% = ($79 – $76.75)/$79
Pros	• Strike price ($77) is below current FMV ($79). • Low probability of being exercised. • High probability of keeping the premium.	• Earns a good premium if shares remain at or above current price ($79).	• Earns a higher premium. • Remains unexercised if the share price rises above the strike price ($82). • Slightly longer time period to give underlying shares a chance to rise above the strike price.
Cons	• Smallest premium. • Likelihood of repetitive contracts if shares continue to rise.	• With such a short time horizon, 50/50 chance of being exercised.	• Short time horizon. • Aggressive strike price. • High probability of being exercised and shares received.

TTD Outcome

Whether the put contracts are exercised, in all scenarios the seller keeps the premiums. This generates an attractive revenue stream while waiting for the targeted share price to fall below the contracted strike price. In all scenarios, when a contract is finally exercised, the ACB for the TTD shares will be improved relative to having bought shares via a cash DCA.

Contract premiums increase:

• The longer the time to maturity of the contract (your choice).
• The deeper ITM strike price (your choice).
• The higher the volatility of the underlying stock – e.g. technology stocks offer higher premiums than bank stocks – (again, your choice).

Whether buying shares lump sum, DCA, or selling near-term put contracts, the essential plan is to get the core portfolio established. Time in the markets is the key. At least by selling put contracts, revenues are being generated while waiting.

Caution

Selling put contracts is leverage but without the interest costs.

Investment Tip

Turning Back the Hands of Time

Who wouldn't want to buy a stock back when it was cheaper? Yet it's never too late.

Don't let fear of missing out (FOMO) trigger you into chasing a share price higher. If you think you've missed your chance, consider selling OTM put contracts at a preferred lower strike price. Only if that stock's share price falls back below the lower strike price by the maturity date will those shares be exercised into your portfolio. This allows an investor with a specific bargain price point to stick to their guns and earn income on the options while they wait. By selling successive OTM put contracts on a targeted stock at price points below the current FMV, they could perpetually earn premiums while waiting to have those shares exercised into their portfolio.

Before making that next significant investment whether by DCA, lump sum, or selling put contracts, also consult the following reliable indicators to reinforce when to deploy your decision.

Sentiment Indicators

Below are sentiment indicators: two for the general markets and three more specifically for stocks. The first two capture sophisticated concepts and translates them into easy-to-grasp visuals. Their purpose is to sensitize investors to how economic and/or financial risks are trending. The other three reveal valuation sentiments more specific to individual stocks. Triangulating your research will improve the accuracy of a trend assessment.

1. CNN Fear & Greed Index – Market Sentiment
2. The Warren Buffett Rule – Market Sentiment
3. P/E Ratio Comparisons – Stock Sentiment
4. Short Seller Reports – Stock Sentiment
5. Insider Trading Reports – Stock Sentiment

1. **CNN Fear & Greed Index**[2] – As an alternative to the VIX index, CNN has created a proprietary contrarian Fear & Greed Index. It uses a weighted average of seven sentiment indicators to measure investor sentiments. A trend line above 70 is a "greedy" sign and should prompt consideration to apply portfolio protection and

---

[2]https://www.cnn.com/markets/fear-and-greed.

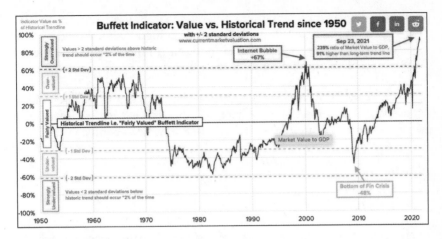

Figure 14.1   Buffett indicator.
Source: https://www.currentmarketvaluation.com/models/buffett-indicator.php.

portfolio trimming. When the index falls below 30, the sentiment is
"fearful" and likely a time to consider adding to positions.

2. **The Warren Buffett Rule** (Figure 14.1) – Widely followed, Warren
   presents a slightly different version of the P/E ratio. He measures
   the US stock market capitalization relative to the US GDP. In other
   words, he compares the present value of all future economic earnings generated by publicly listed stocks (sum value of all stocks listed
   on the S&P 500) divided by the country's current GDP (sum value
   of the current year's goods and services produced). This graph
   reveals when the willingness to pay for assets is distorted from historical norms. A ratio between –30 and +30 suggests fair valuation
   and reasonable returns. A graph line approaching a relative valuation of +80 implies lower returns over the next decade (if not an
   imminent correction).

3. **P/E Ratio Comparisons** – A stock's current price is meant to reflect
   the present value of all future net cash flows. The P/E ratio is a sentiment indicator reflecting the price investors are willing to pay for
   each $1 of net earnings generated by a company. There are three
   ways that the P/E ratio can help reveal the reasonableness of a
   stock's current price:
   i. Check that the market is not overpriced relative to historical aver-
      ages. The market's long-term average is 15–17×. Be more cau-
      tious when the market P/E trends above 22×.
   ii. Compare a stock's P/E ratio to its industry average. Significant
       deviations should be investigated.

iii. Compare a stock's current P/E ratio to its history.[3] Since stock P/Es should be relatively stable over time, a higher ratio should prompt investigation. Has market enthusiasm (P) increased or was there a problem with the earnings (E)?

So, comparing P/E ratios across three variables can quickly reveal the relative merit of a stock's current price. Alternatively, instead of relative measures, Warren Buffett uses an absolute P/E scale to confirm value:

- **P/E under 10 = Bargain**
- **11–19 = Fair**
- **20–25 = Overvalued**
- **Over 30+ = Bubble**

By following absolute P/E ratio thresholds, Warren keeps himself out of trouble. However, it can also park his cash on the sidelines for very long periods, which has been the case since the 2020 Bear Market. Warren was hesitant to commit capital, given the difficulty of confirming the market's P/E. This was a period when corporate earnings disappeared, yet the market soared.

In the long term, the rate of growth of a share should equal the growth rate of that share's earnings. Despite such common sense, P/E ratios can be pushed to extremes and can remain divorced from reality for very long periods of time.

4. **Short Seller Reports[4]** – These reports reveal the active efforts of short sellers to profit from a targeted company's demise. Avoid a stock if the short position is greater than 10% of the outstanding share float. Short position changes can reveal worsening or improving situations.

5. **Insider Trading Reports[5]** – Figure 14.3 is proof that insiders know best when to buy into their own company. When a number of insiders are selling, it also deserves scrutiny.

"Insiders might sell their shares for any number of reasons, but they only buy them for one reason."

—Peter Lynch,
legendary manager of the Fidelity Funds

---

[3]https://www.macrotrends.net.
[4]https://www.marketwatch.com/tools/screener/short-interest (Accessed 16 February 2021).
[5]https://www.marketbeat.com/ (Accessed 26 September 26, 2021).

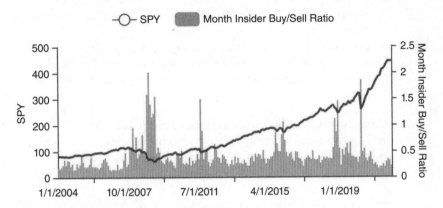

Figure 14.3   Monthly Insider Buy/Sell Ratio vs. SPY as at Oct 2021.
Source: Reproduced with permission of GuruFocus.com.

Trimming at market tops or buying near 52-week lows is usually the easier investing decision. It's the rest of the time in between that keep us on edge. Becoming better acquainted with the above-noted sentiment indicators can help build valued perspectives. Make a habit of checking the pulse of the markets. Yet, before deploying that next trade, use the following checklist to confirm its appropriateness. Stock trading creates value when performed with purpose.

Buy-in Checklist

1. **Confirm the quality of your stock pick:**

     Six Quantitative Measures (see Chapter 8):
     • Based in North America.
     • Market cap greater than $2B.
     • ROE consistently greater than 20%.
     • 5 years of positive revenue growth.
     • 5 years of increasing profitability.
     • Healthy financial statements (low to moderate debt).

     Three Variance Measures (see Chapter 9):
     • Moderate beta (1).
     • High Sharpe ratio (> +1).
     • Moderate range of variance (+/–15).

     Four Qualitative Measures (see Chapter 10):
     • Quality leadership.
     • Ranks well on ESG and SRI standards (optional).

- Meets acceptable socially responsible investing metrics (if desired).
- Diversity of business divisions and revenue models (bricks and mortar, online retail, advertising, leasing, licensing, SaaS, freemium/premium, auctions, franchising, fractionalization, or disintermediation).

Three Diversification Measures (see Chapter 11):
- Not overweighting any single economic sector.
- Not duplicating any of the 69 unique industry categories.
- Confirm low correlations relative to the rest of the portfolio.

"Buy a stock because you want to own the company.
Not because you want the stock to go up."
—Warren Buffett

2. **Estimate the Stage of the Market Cycle through Sentiment Indicators**
   Periods of relative market pessimism can be revealed through sentiment indicators signaling an opportunity to deploy cash. Smart money is patient and discerning. Look for contrarian signals:
   - CNN Fear & Greed Index <30.
   - The Warren Buffett Rule –30.
   - S&P 500 P/E ratio <16 and falling.
   - Target stock's P/E ratio is below the industry average and its own average.
   - Reduced short interest on a stock likely reflects an improving trend.
   - Increased insider buying.

3. **Choose a Buy-in Method (Lump Sum, DCA, or Selling Puts)** (see Figure 14.4)
   Before buying that next stock or adding to an existing position, be conscious of the stage of the market cycle (2) and the state of taxability of the targeted shares. Either, or both, of these factors can influence the creation of value when buying.
   - **At 52-Week Lows** – Irrespective of a stock's tax situation, be bravest when mass fear and doubt are greatest. Investing by lump sum should be favored.
   - **During Ordinary Markets** (the time in between 52-week highs and lows):
     - Favor DCAs when:
       - i. Investing into an existing stock holding that has unrealized losses.

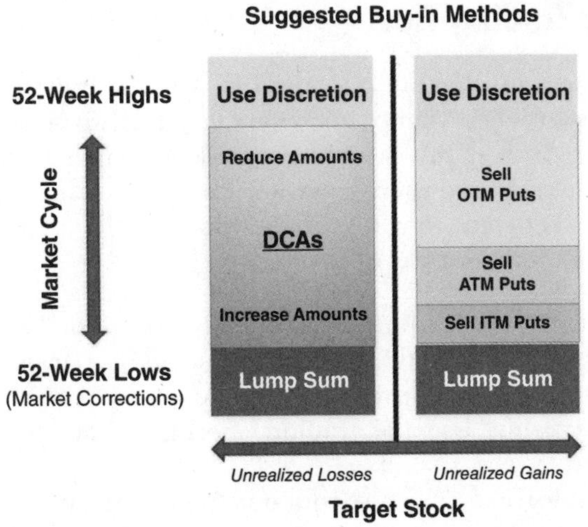
Suggested Buy-in Methods
52-Week Highs
Market Cycle
52-Week Lows
(Market Corrections)
Use Discretion
Reduce Amounts
DCAs
Increase Amounts
Lump Sum
Use Discretion
Sell
OTM Puts
Sell
ATM Puts
Sell ITM Puts
Lump Sum
Unrealized Losses
Unrealized Gains
Target Stock

Figure 14.4 Suggested stock purchase methods.

- This lowers a stock's breakeven price point (ACB).
- Increase the DCA when the market cycle is ebbing.
- Decrease the DCA when the market cycle is peaking.

ii. A stock has no options string.
iii. Buying for smaller-sized accounts where put contracts would be excessive.
iv. Buying highly volatile securities.

- Favor selling put contracts when:
  i. Initiating into a new core stock holding.
  ii. Investing into an existing stock holding with unrealized profits.
  - Consider selling short-term OTM put contracts to generate premiums while waiting for a share price pullback.

- **At 52-Week Highs** – Investing is not recommended. Await a sell-off either in a targeted stock or the markets. If selling put contracts, deploy deeper OTM contracts.

Early on, a checklist may challenge an investor to double-think their next trade. Eventually, the process should become second nature. If a trade does not tick all the required boxes, it doesn't mean that it won't be a good investment. But you should now know where potential vulnerabilities in your stock selections lie. Having a checklist is intended to confirm your conviction for each security held. Eventually the market will test you.

10 Smarter Trading Tips

As noted in the introductory quotation by Warren Buffett, the purchase price is an investor's best chance to create value. Instead of having to change an investor's behavior, these trading protocols can help build a buffer between the investor and their behavior. Preset the trade, then walk away and let the market come to you. A trade won't always get filled but when it does, your ACBs will improve.

1. Trade consistently from a calm, familiar location. Fewer distractions invite less mistakes and increase focus and objectivity.
2. Trust that you are buying a great company. Sixteen filters should assure quality. Use the trading checklist above to confirm your decision.
3. Only trade if it will improve your portfolio (better offense or defense).
4. Determine an acceptable price target for the transaction.
    • Recognize the stage of the market cycle. Heed the sentiment indicators.
    • Compare a stock's current P/E relative to the market, the industry, and itself.
5. With cash, be contrarian. Wait for declines in both the market and the targeted stock.
6. Be courageous to invest lump sums when markets ebb.
7. Depending on the ACB, either deploy DCA or sell put contracts.
8. Be proactive, not spontaneous. Invite the market to come to you.
    • Set low GTC RTH limit trade orders, or
    • Sell short-term OTM put contracts and earn interest on idle cash.
9. Be vigilant for stock disappointments during earnings season.
10. With rising stocks, it's never too late. Sell deeper and longer OTM put contracts.

The ad hoc decisions that get investors into trouble can be reduced by confirming the purposefulness of a trade, then preset the order and make gradual adjustments until triggered. Being proactive and thinking contrarian will decrease the management time and reduce the stresses induced through too much market vigilance. Set it and forget it . . . almost.

While poor trades will still happen, at least by sticking to quality and being patient, you won't fall victim to an algorithm. Time in the market is the key.

Your efforts can be better spent on creating real value in Tiers 2 and 3.

> *"Know yourself, and your enemy equally. Don't fight when it is in strength. Respect its strengths. But know when it is weak. That is the time to go for the kill."*
>
> —Sun Tzu, *The Art of War*

TRADING REMINDER

Before deploying any trade (buy or sell), do a cursory review of your portfolio. There may be outstanding open trade orders to consider (stop-loss, trailing stop-loss, covered call contracts, or put contracts). To check for current positions and open trade orders, rearrange your portfolio according to "Group by Underlying Securities." This allows an investor to pair up all outstanding holdings and trades grouped by each individual security.

At the Oasis: Chapter 14

- Learn when to use each buy-in method (lump sum, DCA, or selling puts).
- Each trade should have purpose – improving performance or reducing volatility.
- Buy on the three reds:
  - Negative-trending stocks.
  - Market pullbacks.
  - Setting lowball bid orders.
- Be even smarter: Wait until the insiders are buying.

"There are three winning investment strategies:

- *Be smarter than others.*
- *Be luckier than others.*
- *Be more patient than others."*

—Tweeted on October 2, 2019,
by Morgan Housel, partner at Collaborative Fund,
ex-columnist at the Motley Fool,
and author of *When Things Get Wild*

Chapter 15

Contrarian Rebalancing

Objective:

Learning the art of buying low and selling high.

RMP #10: Rebalancing

Comment: In the context of portfolio risk management, rebalancing is traditionally the periodic realignment of an asset mix between stocks, bonds, and cash. In *The Investing Oasis*, rebalancing is only deployed tactically between stocks and cash.

Less Is More

Although a buy-and-hold strategy should be simple to manage, it can be challenging to achieve. Stare at a trading screen long enough, and the "fidgety finger" syndrome becomes hard to quell. Daily market vigilance tends to seduce investors into more frequent and unnecessary trades, increasing the potential for mistakes and higher transaction costs (unless working from a commission-free platform).

Instead, by following a plan, every trade should result in purposeful improvement to the portfolio. In portfolio management, after buying quality at a reasonable price (see Chapter 14), the second chance at creating value is the art of rebalancing (buy low/sell high).

Buy Low / Sell High

Rebalancing is based on the concept of "reversion to the mean." In other words, "what goes up eventually comes down" (but not necessarily back to square one). Over time share prices ebb and flow around an intrinsic valuation that progressively increases as corporations deploy value-creating activities.

Rebalancing offers the opportunity to seize the advantage of this market "dance." It is most effective if performed proactively and with discipline. As stock prices rise, trim the leaders, and as individual stocks lag, buy more shares. Rebalancing assumes that the shares of all quality growth stocks will eventually contribute to a portfolio's performance.

Acting Contrarian

Which Stocks to Trim or Buy?

Rather than relying upon an external Relative Strength Index (RSI) to know when to buy or sell a stock, with an equal-weighted portfolio, the leaders and laggards will be visually apparent on the trading screen. In other words, the portfolio itself is an internal RSI.

Start by double-clicking on the "Market Value" column header to rearrange the stocks in order of overweight to underweight stocks (relative to the portfolio average[1]). In an equal-weight portfolio, this helps to quickly identify which stocks may require rebalancing.

At What Threshold?

Picking a rebalancing threshold is a function of your risk tolerance. Growth stocks typically vary up to 15–20% over a year. Lower risk-tolerant investors might be uncomfortable watching growth stocks gyrate too widely (e.g. +/– 20%). However, setting lower threshold limits (e.g. @ +/– 5%) would result in rebalancing too frequently and, therefore, more trading commissions.

With experience, an investor's risk tolerance should evolve to allow for greater stock price undulation before triggering a rebalance. Since markets have an inherent long-term growth bias, consider setting higher trim (i.e. +20%) and lower buy trigger points (i.e. –15%).

---

[1]The portfolio average is simply the total portfolio value divided by the total number of stocks expected to be held.

Rebalancing decisions should be framed against the prevailing market conditions:

1. **During Ordinary Markets** – As individual share prices drift above the target threshold percentage, trim them back to the core portfolio average. Consider proactively setting a limit sell order at a percentage (e.g. 20%) over the calculated portfolio average core stock holding. Calculate the share price and the number of shares to bring the stock back to the core average in one lump-sum trade. This will lock in a capital gain (selling high).

   Alternatively, once a stock reaches the upper threshold target, instead of immediately trimming the position, an investor can set a trailing stop-loss order to follow a rising share price higher. This would allow winning stocks to continue advancing with the fail-safe that once the shares began to pull back, a sell order would be triggered, yet likely at a higher share price than the original threshold target price.

   Eventually, the performance of all growth stocks will suffer. By deploying a set rebalancing threshhold, it makes it easier to deploy new capital (via DCA). Yet, if a share price continues to deteriorate, it deserves greater scrutiny. Either this position has become an even better bargain or it may be sinking into a value trap. Due diligence may be required to discern whether this discount is transient or material (Table 15.1).

   Rebalancing should follow the contrarian philosophy of implementing trades against the market trend: trim on green days, DCA on red days.

2. **During a Market Correction** – Most stocks will suffer during a market correction, irrespective of their individual promising fundamentals.

   "You can have clarity, or you can have undervaluation. You cannot have both."
   —Vitaliy Katsenelson,
   CFA, CEO at the IMA wealth management firm

   Since the best buying decisions require chaos to gain an advantage, once the market surpasses a 20% correction, it's time to consider averaging down across the portfolio. Resist any temptation to liquidate.

   Instead, acknowledge those queasy bodily sensations as signs of opportunity. Begin nibbling. Don't worry about whether you are getting the best prices. Set a series of incrementally lower limit buy orders. No trade will be perfect, but buying on either side of a market bottom should prove more valuable than not doing anything at all. Your future self will thank you. Being a contrarian involves taking action despite your fears.

Investment Tips

If you are an avid saver or anticipate receiving cash from other sources, trimming overweight stocks may not always be necessary. By regularly infusing new capital into the portfolio and investing into laggard positions, the overall portfolio average would be continually raised. With a higher portfolio average, previously overweight stocks may no longer require trimming.

As a portfolio value grows, the average stock value will also rise. Equally, some medium-growth/medium-volatility stocks may never require rebalancing if they grow at a similar rate as the overall portfolio.

"Such a policy will pay off ultimately . . . provided it is adhered to conscientiously and courageously under all intervening conditions."

—Benjamin Graham,
author of *The Intelligent Investor*

Relative Strength Indicators (RSIs)

To help determine when to make trades, professionals often use an RSI combined with other technical analytical tools (MACD or Bollinger Bands[2,3]).

RSI and technical analysis tools, however, require education and experience to be deployed effectively. They focus entirely on the trading patterns of individual stocks in isolation from the rest of a portfolio and introduce market timing "trigger points" when to trade stocks. They require vigilance to monitor price movements. Further, the signals are not always consistent.

---

[2]https://www.investopedia.com/terms/m/macd.asp (Accessed 26 September 2021).

[3]https://www.investopedia.com/articles/active-trading/100115/why-macd-divergence-unreliable-signal.asp (Accessed 26 September 2021).

A Built-in Relative Strength Indicator (RSI)

Instead, in a portfolio with equal-weighted stock positions, rebalancing is simplified because outperformers and underperformers stand out visually on the trading screen.

Leaders   Trimming should be straightforward. Once a stock achieves a pre-determined threshold, a quick trim back to the portfolio average infuses cash into the portfolio, to be reallocated opportunistically into a lagging stock at a later point.

Laggards   In a caravan of camels, all have a role to play. Yet, to help advance the entourage (portfolio), the cameleer should spend more time research-ing the trailing "camels." Progress of the whole will be held back by the lag-gards. Most growth stocks will eventually experience this challenge. Having a buy threshold allows objectivity when to begin infusing new cash (DCA). Yet, if a share price continues to deteriorate, it deserves greater scrutiny. Either this position has become an even better bargain or it may be sinking into a value trap. Due diligence may be required to discern whether this discount is transient or material (Table 15.1).

Table 15.1   Material vs. non-material matters.

MATERIAL RISKS (Requiring Significant Adjustments)	NON-MATERIAL RISKS (Transient)
• Questionable/bad business practices	• Missed quarterly revenues/poor earnings
• Pending lawsuits	• Weak earnings forecast
• Accounting discrepancies	• Supply and production problems
• Fraud or deception portrayed by management	• Distribution challenges
• Regulatory changes affecting an industry	• Speculative media comments
• Poor deployment of M&A activity	• Union strikes/lockdowns
• ESG violations (environmental, social, and governance)	• Loss of a significant client
• Unexpected changes of C-suite or management	• Limited lawsuit
• Bankruptcy threats	• Limited natural disaster

Material Risks   Material reasons should be a deal-breaker. In some way, the company will need to be transformed, likely requiring outside influences and resources (legal aid, capital, etc.). Material matters managed poorly result in value traps.[4] Corporate announcements outside of the regular quarterly reporting season often signal a material event. Triangulate with several sources to research your concerns. Before averaging down, wait for the corporation to publicly announce its plan of action to address the deficiencies. If doubts linger, sell and move on.

Non-material Risks   Non-material issues are typically more transient and more often associated with operational issues due to the traditional business cycle. While material and non-material matters may equally garner headlines, the latter usually can be resolved in a reasonable time and with only minor corporate adjustments. With confidence in the fundamentals and the management team, only the pace of rebalancing might be in question. Discounted, but otherwise unblemished, companies could be candidates for lump-sum rebalancing.

Secrets at the Oasis

Averaging Down

If a core stock has discounted by 10–15% and stabilizes, we deploy DCA to gradually bring the stock's value back in line with the portfolio average. Occasionally, though, if a stock continues to discount, further DCA may be suspended.

If we still remain hopeful, as an alternative, longer-term OTM (out-of-the-money) put contracts can be sold (see Chapters 14 and 19). This immediately increases exposure to the underlying stock but at a discount to the current stock price (depending upon how deep OTM). No cash is required, yet instead, selling put contracts will generate a cash premium.

To minimize the probability of a contract being exercised:

- Only consider selling contracts on core stocks devalued by +15%.
- Choose a strike price OTM. This allows for further share price weakness and only forces a purchase if the underlying share price falls below the strike price at maturity.
- Choose contracts of 3–6 months to allow the underlying share price to regain a positive growth trend.

---

[4]Chen, J. (2021). "Value Trap." https://www.investopedia.com/terms/v/valuetrap.asp (Accessed 26 September 2021).

Success

At maturity, if the underlying share price is below the strike price, the contract will be exercised, and new shares would be bought into the core portfolio at the strike price in exchange for the equivalent in cash. The ACB (adjusted cost base) of the existing shares would be averaged down due to these new shares being allocated into the portfolio.

By selling OTM put contracts in exchange for a premium, this method could result in adding new shares into the portfolio at a strike price lower than if they were bought with cash at current prices, plus a cash premium was earned on the transaction.

Successful Non-success

However, when the underlying share price rallies above the strike price, it annuls the contract. The premiums are kept but the shares are not received. At maturity, the process can be repeated by selling another OTM or ATM put contract. If the underlying share price keeps advancing, the investor wins in two ways:

1. Cash premiums are earned on the unexercised contracts.
2. The value of the shares already owned will be rising.

Note: Since each put contract equals 100 shares, the minimum number of shares enacted by selling even just one put contract may be too large for smaller accounts.

Benefits of Rebalancing

Once a portfolio has been set up, maintenance should be relatively modest. Here are five tangible benefits from periodic rebalancing with an equal weight portfolio:

1. **Simplicity.** Outlier stocks can be easily identified and the degree of rebalancing required can be measured quickly.
2. **Low maintenance saves time.** Proactively setting targeted threshold trades reduces the need for daily market vigilance.
3. **Trimming positions** regularly adds to the cash reserve for eventual DCA deployment on laggard stocks.
4. **Contrarian activity dampens volatility.** Trimming overweight stocks by lump sums and then redeploying the cash gradually via DCA with underweight stocks helps offset the ordinary market trends of rapid market corrections followed by slow-trending recoveries.
5. **Improves capital markets behavior.** DCA methodology is an easier process to follow and diminishes reactionary decisions.

Alternatively:

A Birthday Rebalance?

Instead of waiting for individual stocks to cross a rebalancing threshold, an alternative method would be to recalibrate all stocks back to the portfolio average on a select date (i.e. quarterly, annually, or on a specific annual date).

This concept is simple and objective. No discretion is required. Since both methods, the managed method described above and this alternative, would realize embedded capital gains and incur trading commissions, investors have a choice. Just remember to diarize the date. ☺

Investment Tip

Tax-Loss Selling

Near year-end, it is common practice to sell stocks with unrealized capital losses to offset taxable capital gains realized during the calendar year. This is a discretionary activity personal to each investor. In doing so, though, an investor needs to be mindful of the superficial loss rules that disallow capital losses if that same stock position is bought either 30 calendar days before or 30 calendar days after realizing a capital loss.

To keep a portfolio fully invested and appropriately diversified when selling to realize tax losses, consider investing the realized cash temporarily into appropriate sector ETFs until the 30-day grace period has ended (e.g. selling SVB Financial Group and buying the iShares IAT Regional Banking ETF). This would allow an investor to to realize tax losses yet to remain fully invested.

<u>Important:</u> Before tax-loss harvesting, consult with a trusted tax accountant.

North Star Compass

Rebalancing's Calming Effect

Establishing an equal-weighted portfolio of quality stocks and practicing disciplined rebalancing will help to overcome subjective, spontaneous decision-making, such as:

- All-or-none trading decisions.
- Selling winning positions too soon (note: "trimming" is acceptable).
- Hesitancy to average down on discounted stocks.

> A rebalancing plan effectively dismantles the emotional feedback loop that can override our rational thoughts. By methodically trimming advancing stocks, holding cash, then eventually redeploying the proceeds into lagging stocks, a rebalancing plan reinforces better capital markets behavior and helps to achieve better outcomes more consistently.
>
> More importantly, as a core activity in a long-term investing plan, the value of periodic rebalancing is most beneficial when the trades can be deployed contrary to the market trend: Sell high. Buy low.

Mindful Portfolio Design Equals Time Management

Management of the core portfolio can be as simple as presented. Once the primary growth stocks are chosen and the capital allocated, in an equal-weight portfolio, oversight becomes visual and simplified. The focus can then be steered toward the outliers (up and down). Overall, managing the core stocks should only require about 20% of your portfolio time.

If an investor desires to spend their time more constructively, consider selling covered calls (see Chapter 16).

At the Oasis: Chapter 15

- Rebalancing according to thresholds reinforces the adage "Buy low, sell high."
- Triggering taxable capital gains is an affirmation of investing success.
- Build your cash reserve. Trim the leaders on green days.
- Triangulate your research to understand the laggard stocks. Only buy on red days.
- Consider selling OTM puts to gain the premiums and even lower ACBs, if exercised.
- Since the market is progressive, set the threshold percentage targets higher for trims than for buys.
- Being a contrarian requires learning to embrace your fears.
- Or simply do a wholesale rebalance on your birthday.

Chapter 16

A Hidden Well of Income

*"What makes the desert beautiful is that somewhere,
it hides a well."*
—Antoine de Saint-Exupéry, *The Little Prince*

Objective:

**Unearthing passive revenues hidden
in plain sight.**

In the desert a drop of water is like gold, never to be wasted. Yet, to the nomad, even more valuable is camel's milk. Herders regularly milk recently pregnant camels for personal consumption, then sell the excess to enterprising nomads who travel great distances to intercept camel herds. Prized for its nutrients and organic purity, the camel's milk is then sold in villages as an alternative to dairy products.

Comparingly, unwary investors may buy and nurture a portfolio of stocks without ever realizing the opportunity to "milk" additional revenues from their core stocks. This opportunity can be implemented on all stocks with an options chain. This chapter will reveal how to regularly reap low-risk income by selling covered calls[1] (CCs). Becoming a more engaged investor requires effort, but the rewards are worth the undertaking. CCs are

---

[1]Ganti, A. (2022). "Covered Call." https://www.investopedia.com/terms/c/coveredcall.asp (Accessed 26 September 2021).

another of the contrarian processes within *The Investing Oasis* framework. They:

1. Generate surplus revenues from core stocks, independent of any dividends.
2. Partially diminish portfolio volatility.

Comment: To learn about CCs or to refresh your knowledge, the Options Clearing Corporation (OCC) has put together a good YouTube video.[2]

Although deploying CCs may seem like joining the Foreign Legion, through a little education and low-risk trial and error, the revenues generated will serve to enrich your journey.

RMP #11: Income and Protection with Covered Calls

While most investors are pleased to earn 1–2% in dividends, they remain blissfully unaware of the additional 2–4% of undiscovered riches sitting right under their saddle. CCs can even be deployed on stocks that don't pay dividends. Imagine owning a home with a basement suite but never renting it out. Each stock in your portfolio is another "fully furnished suite" capable of generating attractive rental income. CCs also act as a buffer to volatility. Their value runs contrary to rising markets. So, when markets devalue, the value of CCs rise.

Sell High, Buy Low

Rather than "Buy low, sell high," selling CC options contracts reverses this adage: "Sell high, buy low." When an investor sells a contract, it represents the right for another investor to purchase the targeted core shares at a set price – the strike price (SP) – by a future date. The buyer of a contract is bullishly speculating that the underlying share price will rise sufficiently to trigger an exercise and receive those shares at the SP. Contrastingly, the seller (you) hopes the contract will fail by the maturity date, thereby keeping the underlying shares and the cash from the contract premium. Selling options contracts is therefore considered a "passive" investment yet receives favorable capital gains tax treatment.

---

[2]"Trading Covered Calls to Generate Income," uploaded by The Options Industry Council (OIC), 31 March 2016. https://www.youtube.com/watch?v=Jd0htvJATz4.

Odds Are in the Seller's Favor

According to the CBOE, on average only 10% of options contracts are ever exercised and another 30–35% regularly expire out-of-the-money worthless.[3] Therefore, selling option contracts is already skewed in the seller's favor. With a little planning, the odds can be further improved. Let's start with the basics.

Covered Calls

A covered call (CC) is the writing (selling) of a contract against shares already held in the core portfolio in exchange for a cash premium. At maturity, if the price of the underlying share remains below the strike price (SP)[4] of a call contract, then the seller of the contract (you) keeps the premium and the shares.

However, at maturity, if the underlying share price has risen above the SP, the shares will be sold out of the portfolio at the SP. The investor keeps the original premium and will receive the cash equivalent to the SP times the number of contracts in exchange for the underlying shares.

Most mid-to large-cap stocks have options chains.

Winning by Winning

Three buffers to improve the odds of success (i.e. keeping both the premiums and the underlying shares) are:

1. **Advantage by Trend** (When to deploy) – Sell CCs after a surge in stock prices either due to a wholesale rise in the general market or with favorable news specific to a stock (i.e. surprise quarterly results, positive earnings projections, or M&A activity).
2. **Advantage by Time** (Duration) – Sell only short-term contracts (from 1 week to 2 months). Short-term contracts reduce the time left for a stock to advance toward the SP.
3. **Advantage by Strike Price** (OTM) – Higher SPs provide room for the underlying shares to rise further before a contract would be exercised.

---

[3]https://www.stockoptionschannel.com/slideshows/seven-myths/most-options-expire-worthless/ (Accessed 19 February 2022).
[4]Fernando, J. (2022). "Strike Price." https://www.investopedia.com/terms/s/strikeprice.asp (Accessed 26 September 2021).

CC Analogy

Buying a Home

Imagine buying a house five years ago for $250,000. It's now estimated at $350,000. One day a speculator knocks at the door and expresses interest in buying your home. They are willing to sign an exclusive contract to buy it. However, the home would only be sold if the market price were to equal or exceed the agreed-upon price on a future specified date. Since you are intrigued by the offer but want to retain ownership, you set the terms:

- An unusually high price ($400,000).
- A very short contract term (1 month).
- A cash premium of $1,000 to be received.

Outcomes: The premium is yours to keep whether the contract is exercised or matures worthless at the end of the month. Remember, the sale only happens if the market price of the house has risen to $400,000+.

The speculator is gambling that the housing market in your area will rise so strongly in 1 month that the agreed price of $400,000 will be a bargain for them. If it did, you would receive $400,000 at the end of the month and be asked to vacate. Would you be sad? Possibly, but you would be paid $50,000 more at the end of the month for the home, plus a cash premium of $1,000.

However, if the market price of the home was $399,000 or less at the end of the month, the contract would terminate worthless. You would keep the house and the premium.

"Rinse and Repeat": Next month another speculator expresses a similar interest. You sell them a 1-month contract but at a strike price of $410,000 (assuming the house price has risen slightly during the month). In exchange, you receive another premium to potentially sell your home in 30 days if the market price rises to $410,000+.

Each month, you sell a new 30-day OTM contract at a home price just high enough ahead of the advancing market price. Over time, these premiums add up.

The Importance of Deltas

Statistical data for options is called the "Greeks."[5] In assessing whether to trade an options contract, there are four Greeks: delta, gamma, theta, and vega. Together, these are used by traders to assess the sensitivity of an

---

[5]Hall, M. (2022). "Using the 'Greeks' to Understand Options." https://www.investopedia.com/trading/using-the-greeks-to-understand-options/ (Accessed 16 May 2022).

option's price to quantifiable factors. In *The Investing Oasis,* only the delta is used to help choose the strike price (SP).

To help pick a SP, find the delta[6] associated with each SP (see example below). This is usually listed conveniently next to the individual SPs of an options chain. An option's delta reflects the degree of sensitivity for change in the SP with any change in the underlying share price. For example, for a SP with a delta of +.20, when the underlying share price rises by $1, the SP is likely to rise by approximately $0.20. In other words, low delta's equal low-price sensitivity and vice versa. Alternatively, the delta could be said to approximate the probability that a SP will be exercised at maturity (e.g. a delta of +.20 suggests a 20% chance of being exercised at maturity). The higher (deeper) the SP, the lower the delta, and, therefore, the less probability of a contract being exercised.

For growth stocks, sell monthly OTM call contracts with an SP at a delta at .20 or less. This delta implies only a modest chance (20% or less) of the call being exercised against the investor at maturity. These contracts are preferred because they generate an acceptable premium but are generally sufficiently outside of the range of an advancing stock for the short duration of the contract.

Covered Call Example: MSFT

Figure 16.1 is the June 19, 2020, options chain for Microsoft as reviewed on May 8, 2020 (42 days until expiry). The current price of MSFT is $184.50. There are many options choices. How to decide?

	CALLS			STRIKE	PUTS			
BID x ASK	VOLUME	OPTN O...	DELTA		BID x ASK	VOLUME	OPTN O...	DELTA
25.40 x 25.60	76	10.6K	0.893	160	1.39 x 1.40	638	15.0K	-0.114
20.95 x 21.15	168	9.50K	0.847	165	1.97 x 1.99	1.77K	11.7K	-0.158
16.80 x 16.95	483	16.7K	0.785	170	2.79 x 2.81	689	9.64K	-0.218
12.95 x 13.10	1.05K	10.9K	0.707	175	3.90 x 3.95	1.15K	8.57K	-0.295
9.50 x 9.60	2.01K	16.4K	0.612	180	5.40 x 5.50	1.72K	4.78K	-0.390
6.55 x 6.60	2.62K	12.1K	0.501	185	7.45 x 7.55	894	6.53K	-0.500
4.15 x 4.20	1.91K	20.2K	0.381	190	10.05 x 10.15	79	2.20K	-0.621
2.42 x 2.44	2.96K	33.9K	0.265	195	13.25 x 13.40	12	719	-0.738
1.30 x 1.32	3.21K	12.8K	0.167	200	17.15 x 17.30	14	135	-0.838
0.37 x 0.38	524	6.82K	0.058	210	25.90 x 26.50		26	-0.948
0.15 x 0.16	493	14.0K	0.024	220	35.95 x 36.45		441	-0.980
0.07 x 0.08	694	14.9K	0.012	230	45.60 x 46.45		431	-0.992

Figure 16.1   MSFT options chain.

---

[6]Chen, J. (2022). "Delta." https://www.investopedia.com/terms/d/delta.asp (Accessed 26 September 2021).

Call contracts are located on the LHS of the central "Strike" column. Ignore the put contracts on the RHS. Highlighted in the delta column are three choices from .265 down to .058, corresponding to the three SPs.

Table 16.1   Call contract choices.

#	Delta	Strike Price Maturity Date	Strike Price	Average Premium (Avg of the Bid/Ask)	Percentage Cushion Before Threat of Exercise (From $184.50)
1	0.265	June 19, 2020	$195.00	$2.43	5.69%
2	0.167	June 19, 2020	$200.00	$1.31	8.40%
3	0.058	June 19, 2020	$210.00	$0.37	13.82%

Table 16.1 outlines these same three choices, their corresponding SP, premiums, and the percentage cushion before threat of being exercised. This buffer reflects the percentage rise for the underlying MSFT shares.

For example, consider option contract #2. By selling one contract maturing June 19, 2020 (= 42 days), at an SP of $200, an investor would receive a premium of $131.00 (= $1.31 × 100) and would have an 8.40% buffer before the call might be exercised. A delta of .167 suggests that there is a 16.7% chance of the MSFT shares rising by 8.4% within the next 42 days.

With the delta less than 20% and a reasonable premium, choice #2 appears attractive. #1 would provide a higher premium but comes with a slightly higher probability to be exercised (26.5%), and #3 would be much less likely to be exercised (5.8%) but would provide a lower premium.

> **Note:** Each option contract equals 100 shares. Only sell a CC contract if you own at least 100 shares of a targeted stock. **If not, do not pursue this activity.** This would be an unnecessary speculative risk.

Covered Call Benefits

When selling OTM CC contracts, take into consideration the three buffers (trend, duration, and price), as noted above. Together, they can significantly reduce the risk of a contract being exercised by maturity. By repeatedly selling monthly or bi-monthly contracts on the shares in a portfolio, the investor could generate up to 12 extra revenues per stock per year.

Q. Why bother repeating this process monthly when an investor could sell just annual CC contracts on options eligible stocks?

Although selling monthly contracts is time consuming, selling a series of one-month contracts actually generates a higher total premium relative to selling singular longer-term contracts. As well, by selling shorter-term contracts, an investor can adjust the strike prices monthly to stay comfortably ahead of the advancing share prices.

Q. But what if the price of the underlying share were to rise above the SP at maturity and force a contract to be exercised?

Non-critical Risk

The actual risk of selling OTM CCs is minimal. It could even be termed "non-critical" risk. This is not because there is no uncertainty but rather because, even if the shares were to be called away, the impact is relatively benign:

- The investor keeps the original premium.
- The value of the underlying core stock will have risen even further into profitability due to the higher SP.
- The investor will receive the cash equivalent equal at the higher SP.
- No margin capacity was used. So, no interest to pay.
- However, when the underlying share price rises above the SP prior to maturity, the position becomes neutralized. Gains in the underlying shares would be offset by accrued losses in the CC. Allow the contracts to mature and be exercised. The shares would be sold from the portfolio and the investor would receive the cash proceeds equivalent to the number of contracts sold × the SP.

To reinstate the underlying shares, there are four possible recourses:

1. Purchase the same shares using a limit order on the open market, but likely at a now-higher price.
2. Sell short-term OTM put contracts (1 week to 1 month) at the SP of the previous call contract. Although this has a low probabiliy of success, it would reinstate the shares if the underlying share price were to fall back below this lower OTM SP by maturity. However, whether the contracts were ever exercised, the investor would keep the premiums. If unsuccessful, an investor could repeatedly sell short-term OTM put contracts until they might eventually be exercised and have those shares reinstated into the portfolio.
3. Sell short-term at-the-money (ATM) put contracts (1 week to 1 month) at the current SP. This would offer a medium probability of success

to reinstate the lost shares if the underlying share price were to remain at (or below) this SP. The payment of a premium helps to offset some of the missed gains.

4. Sell short-term deep in-the-money (ITM) put contracts (1 week to 1 month) at higher prices than the current share price (to generate a higher premium). This tactic would offer a higher probability of success to reinstate the lost shares, plus a premium to help offset some of the missed gains above the previous SP.

Choosing whether to sell OTM, ATM, or ITM contracts to reinstate the lost shares is a function of the trend of the underlying share price. If the rate of price change were low to moderate, then consider selling either OTM or ATM put options for low to moderate premiums. If the share price appreciation were to be strongly positive, then consider selling ITM contracts for the higher premiums.

Covered Call Tactics

Overall, the potential benefits of selling CCs far outweigh the risks. The real skill is to set SPs low enough to garner a decent premium but just high enough (OTM) to stay just beyond the advancing share price by the maturity date. This takes experience. Start with a bigger buffer (higher strike prices = lower deltas).

1. **General notes**
   - Risk tolerance is not relevant in deploying CCs. CCs should only be deployed on core stocks that are already agreeable with the risk tolerance of the investor.
   - CCs can be deployed in margin and retirement accounts.
   - CCs do not affect margin capacity.

2. **Selling contracts**
   - Although contracts can be sold any time over a market cycle, favor selling CCs on stocks that have recently surged or are near their 52-week highs.
   - CCs can also be sold on index funds and ETFs.
   - Always sell fewer contracts than the number of core shares owned (1 contract = 100 shares). For example, if an investor owns 370 shares of ABC, they should sell no more than three contracts (3 × 100 = 300 shares).
   - Choose monthly strike prices with a delta <.20.
   - Only sell contracts on up-market days. This generates higher CC premiums.

- If a core stock's current share price is below its ACB, the minimum CC strike price should still be set equal to or greater than the stock's ACB. This will prevent shares from being exercised away at a capital loss. Unfortunately, if the gap is quite wide, the premiums will be smaller.
- When setting a CC, don't worry if the contract does not sell immediately. Let your trade sit. Only make small price adjustments periodically. Algorithms dominate this arena and tirelessly exploit inefficient pricing.
- Sell only a few CCs per trading session per stock.
- Never deploy CCs immediately after a serious stock decline or a market correction. Let the stock(s) rebound and stabilize before redeploying CCs. If CCs had already been deployed, consider harvesting (buying back at profit) and only redeploy once the shares have recovered.
- When trimming (rebalancing) core stocks, be aware to also adjust any outstanding CCs on those same core stocks.

3. **Be mindful of quarterly corporate earnings season**
- Be aware of earnings announcements dates during each of the four earning seasons. With the approach of an earnings announcement, delay setting CCs until after the announcement and the ensuing market reaction. Blindly setting CCs across an earnings announcement date could result in having a position exercised out of the portfolio if the corporation posts unexpectedly good results and the CC were not set high enough.

4. **Closing out CC contracts (buying back)**
- Upon successfully selling a CC ("sell to open"), immediately set up a "buy-to-close" order for the same number of contracts at only 10–25% of the original premium (e.g. sell one contract for ABC at $2.00 and then set the buy-back to close order at $0.20–0.50). Being proactive allows the CCs to eventually close out without needing to be monitored. Since a call contract could be exercised at any time until expiration, a last-minute favorable corporate event could reinvigorate a nearly worthless contract. Best to close out contracts once gains achieve 75%+.
- For smaller accounts, let CCs expire to avoid the "buy-to-close" commission.
- Upon the maturity of a contract, get into the rhythm of setting new CCs and adjust the strike price appropriately.

5. Commissions

- Commissions are charged for selling and buying contracts. However, closing commissions are waived if a contract is exercised or if it expires naturally.

6. Don't be premium greedy

- Strike prices closer to a share's current price offer higher premiums but come with an increased probability of being exercised.
- Learn by selling higher OTM strike prices (deltas lower than .15) on core stocks with stable growth patterns (e.g. Costco, Dollar General, Visa, Mastercard).

At the Oasis: Chapter 16

- Deploying CCs according to these protocols is a low-risk, contrarian activity.
- The probability of selling CCs successfully can be further improved by:
  - Selling CCs on core stocks with recent price uptrends (near 52-week highs).
  - Selecting higher strike prices to stay ahead of the underlying share's rising price.
  - Choosing 1- to 2-month contracts to minimize the exercise period.
  - Selling contracts on green market days. This nets higher premiums.
- CC income adds to your cash reserve.
- CCs serve to dampen portfolio volatility because the value of a CC varies inversely with the markets.
- Selling CCs does not affect margin capacity, nor is risk tolerance relevant.
- CCs can be sold in any account with optionable shares (margin or retirement).
- CCs are selling risk to speculators. Don't be the greedy one. Set higher strike prices.

"I think I just solved my cash flow problem."

Source: Cartoonstock.

Tier 2 Summary

Tier 2 focused on getting the core portfolio launched, deploying contrarian rebalancing tactics, and introducing covered calls. These decisions can all generate real additional value by lowering your ACBs, increasing your cash reserve, and reducing portfolio volatility.

Together, Tiers 1 and 2 are the "Path."

Tier 3 introduces three additional contrarian tactics. Two might shift your paradigms, while the third will distinctly steer you off the Path, requiring greater vigilance. Only proceed once you feel you have fully understood and adopted the concepts of Tiers 1 and 2.

THE INVESTING OASIS: Tier 3

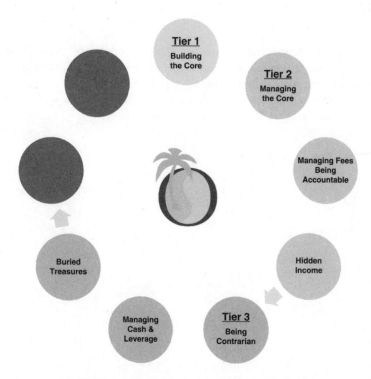

Tier 1
Building
the Core

Tier 2
Managing
the Core

Managing Fees
Being
Accountable

Hidden
Income

Tier 3
Being
Contrarian

Managing
Cash &
Leverage

Buried
Treasures

MISSION#3: To Outperform the Average Professional

	Mission #3
	To Outperform the Average Pro
Tier 1 – Building a Core Growth Portfolio	✓
Tier 2 – Core Management and Income from Covered Calls	✓
Tier 3 – Managing Cash, Debt, and Stealth Growth	✓

Tier 3 increases the investing challenge by introducing several more contrarian techniques:

1. Contrarian cash and debt management
2. Digging for treasures
3. Emotion-free selling

Cash and debt are strategic weapons that deserve to be more effectively deployed. And with ample treasures buried in the capital markets desert, finding and unearthing them requires greater vigilance and the right tools. These contrarian concepts combined with more effective selling should create even more value for intrepid investors.

Chapter 17

Warren B – The Ultimate Contrarian

"Be fearful when others are greedy,
and greedy when others are fearful."
—Warren Buffett

Objective:

Shifting paradigms.

Becoming a Contrarian

When deciding on where to invest, historical returns are a natural starting point. Most investors should instinctively know that the worst-performing investments often harbor the better potential in subsequent periods. Yet, overwhelmingly, investors plunder into last year's best-performing stocks or funds seeking to capitalize on past trends. In behavioral finance this is known as "representation bias": investing in the familiar and comfortable. This chapter focuses on learning to eschew the crowd to embrace our inner contrarian.

Rejecting the Behavior Gap

Warren's maxim in the chapter heading is a time-tested truism. At times of peace and tranquility, our brains function freely. Yet when we are stressed, fear can overwhelm us. All rational thoughts are short-circuited, usually with devastating consequences. So, if Warren's adage is accurate, why is selling into a market upswing and buying on discounts so elusive for most investors?

The essence of panic is to sell assets without regard for their fundamentals or price. And since market corrections happen so unexpectedly, the shock heightens our emotions. In the ensuing fear, our amygdala overtakes the thought processes and steers all mindfulness toward self-preservation. Sell first, ask questions later (buy low, sell lower).

Therefore, turbulent markets coinciding with bad behavior equates to a "double whammy."

> *"The supreme art of war is to subdue the enemy without fighting."*
> —**Sun Tzu,** *The Art of War*

Back to Market Timing

At those critical market moments, even the most prudent investors entertain market timing: the attempt to liquidate a portfolio at the early onset of a market sell-off, followed by a subsequent repurchase at lower prices. What thwarts this fantasy is that typically, most investors are late in realizing that a market rout is underway and then the reinvesting takes place well after the markets have recovered.

Historically, as noted in Chapter 2, the very best market performances are also within days of the worst market sell-offs. "Market timing" is a prolific destroyer of wealth because of our rational mind's need for a clear recovery trend to be established. As noted earlier, the best investment opportunities are embedded in the fog of war. Once the dust settles, it's too late.

As it turns out, there is room for market timing in wealth management; however, it needs to be deployed contrary to the markets: buy low during the panic and sell higher during the calm. When markets are roiling, it's easy enough to see the discounts, yet triply difficult to take action. How to get there?

Technology: A Double-Edged Sword

Easy access to technology renders it all so very easy to act on bad behavior. In times of crisis, we often justify that doing something is better than doing nothing. Sadly, with a few clicks of the keyboard, panicked stock trading is the easiest known voluntary method of wealth transition between complete strangers. Enter the contrarians. One person's fears are appeased by another's capital.

So, despite that all investors should know that market corrections happen with reasonable frequency, most remain indifferent. However, those who do prepare will gain a valuable strategic advantage.

Surprisingly, true contrarians tend to be risk-averse investors. Bargain hunters intuitively understand that every downtick in the markets means less risk and more assurance of an eventual positive outcome, particularly with highly prized quality stocks. They understand that markets have always recovered from every downturn and move on to new record highs. So, buying stocks during a market correction doesn't overtly require courage; it requires preparation to build cash, patience to wait for the market discount, and then faith that the markets will be forever resilient. This wisdom is reinforced when our head, heart, and gut align on such decisions.

Principles and Behaviors of the "Wise One"

To Warren, investing is simple, as he lives life. Managing money was never for the financial rewards. Proof in hand is that he still lives in a home he bought in 1958, drives a 2014 Cadillac XTS, and his favorite meal is still a Big Mac, fries, and a Coke. Instead, he gets the greatest joys from his loving family and bargain hunting.

Famously, he likes to buy excellent companies with superb management teams, preferably at steep discounts, and then hold them forever. He pays no attention to diversification, nor to the principles of portfolio management. Respectfully, Berkshire Hathaway now consists of over 70 broadly diversified companies, rendering it, by default, to be a well-diversified portfolio. It's just that this was achieved without intent or foresight.

Success Follows Character

Warren's success is not because he is lucky or rich. Rather than trying to be smarter than "Mr. Market," he humbly admits that his primary core strategy is to do no wrong. He also believes in being disciplined and being prepared. Although he has unswerving faith in the capital markets and believes in being fully invested, he builds cash until a compelling stock bargain commands his attention. He views the purchase decision as his most significant opportunity to create value for the portfolio.

However, once a stock is bought, he relies on the underlying management team to prove his decision wise. That's why Warren places equal emphasis on knowing the management team, as well as the business model itself. He has famously simply scribbled his due diligence on the back of a napkin for some of his most significant purchases, followed by a handshake. Courage? No need. Wisdom and faith. The quality was evident to him; it was just a matter of price.

In summary, Warren finds investing success because he practices his core beliefs:

- Investing is probabilistic. He ignores the short-term market noise in favor of long-term certainty.
- North American businesses have cultures that breed innovations and are held to high standards of accountability.

- Cash is a strategic weapon to be deployed with deep discretion.
- Buying quality at a discount is his best chance to create portfolio value. The rest is left to "Mr. Market."
- Companies that excel require great leadership. Once the numbers add up, Buffet's investing commitment is confirmed by meeting with the management.
- To build perspective, he reads incessantly and triangulates his views with others (i.e. Charlie Munger).
- He ignores value-destructing temptations, like frequent trading, undue leverage, and speculation. Why bother when he can periodically buy quality companies at distressed prices every 2–3 years.?
- Corrections are inevitable, as are the subsequent recoveries.
- He embraces market turmoil because he sees value where others feel pain.

So, when he implements a trade at the bottom of the market, he's just following his instincts, which happen to be contrary to those of the average investor. Warren knows the value of assets well enough. Even cash earning 0% will eventually be translated into a business-buying opportunity. Warren's three primary strategic advantages turn out to be his discerning character, his alliance with Charlie Munger, and his disciplined use of cash.

A market in turmoil renders him optimistic. Quality stocks have always recovered from sell-offs. As you might surmise, there is no secret formula to his success. He invests using simple principles, trusts his contrarian instincts to find bargains, and holds faith in the markets. While these are simple enough to grasp, our self-doubts make them difficult to practice.

Time in the Markets

It has been calculated that Warren's net worth of $90B is due mostly to compounding.[1] He started when he was 10 and continues to invest into his 90s. Over 99% of his net worth came after his 50th birthday. If he had started investing at 25 and retired at 65 and generated the same 22% annual returns as he did throughout his career, his net worth would have been only a modest $11.7 million.

The rest of us either have too little patience or not enough time.

---

[1]Cardone, G. (2018). "Warren Buffett has made 99.7% of his money after the age of 52." https://medium.com/the-10x-entrepreneur/warren-buffett-has-made-99-7-of-his-money-after-the-age-of-52-71e2ce04c347.

Become a Contrarian

Of course, no one ever knows when or by how much the markets will devalue, yet we do know that a significant "event" occurs, on average, every 20–24 months (see Chapter 3). By adopting even just a few of Warren's practices, an investor could be on much better footing when the next "big one" arrives. Understanding Warren Buffett's style becomes an opportunity to self-reflect on our own beliefs, philosophies, and behaviors.

At the Oasis: Chapter 17

- Learn that the queasiness of fear is the feeling of opportunity.
- Preparation and patience are the foundations of contrarian investing.
- Assess, recalibrate, and reinforce both yourself and your portfolio before the next sell-off.
- Reduce vulnerabilities: low-conviction stocks, weak diversification, speculation, and debt.
- Build cash. It will be your most valuable asset.
- Better decisions occur when our gut, heart, and brain centers align.
- Triangulate your research. Wise men listen more than they speak.
- Investing during a correction doesn't take courage; bargain hunters are notoriously risk averse.
- If you're going to "time the markets," be like Warren and wait for the sell-off.

"The stock market is a device to transfer money from the impatient to the patient."

—Warren Buffett

Chapter 18

Contrarian Cash and Leverage

*"Money is a tool. Used properly, it makes beautiful things.
Used wrongfully, it makes a mess."*
—Bradley Vinson, advocate, speaker, coach, grieving
grandfather

Objective:

Learning to deploy cash and leverage like a capitalist.

Building a cash reserve and having access to debt cannot be over-emphasized. These are the primary wealth-building tools of the capital markets. When lacking, we're vulnerable. In abundance, they should be guarded awaiting compelling opportunities. Their true value is often mis-calculated.

With interest rates near zero, cash accumulation can be difficult to justify. Meanwhile, low-cost debt can entice investors to lever up their portfolios.

Figure 18.1 reveals the skittish behavior of investors as they respond to the behavioral cues of greed and fear. The dark pyramids on the graph highlight the rush of retail cash in and out of the market (MSCI All-World Index) depending upon the prevailing market performance (dark line). If investors were genuinely prescient capitalists, cash flows would be diametrically opposite, not concurrent, with the market perfor-mance trends.

To improve capital market returns, investors might wish to re-evaluate their management of cash and debt reserves.

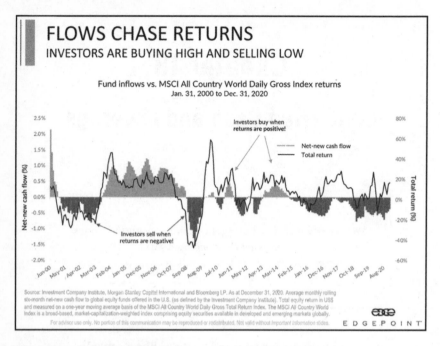

Figure 18.1   Chasing performance.
Source: Reprinted with permission from the EdgePoint Investment Group, Toronto. https://www
.edgepointwealth.com/article/dear-volatility/ (Accessed 16 July 2022).

RMP #12: Four Steps to Effective Cash Management

Traditionally, cash is viewed more as a haven asset serving to buffer against volatility than as a source of wealth creation. A capitalist views cash and debt reserves more as "dry powder" to be deployed opportunistically. Here are four steps toward more effective cash management:

1. Cash by Purpose
2. Generating more Cash
3. Investing Cash
4. Cash Deployment Opportunities

Despite historically low interest rates, more effective cash management can translate into more potent long-term portfolio performance.

1. Cash by purpose

Think of building cash like compressing a coiled spring: the more accrued, the more significant the potential impact. For a reserve to eventually have any meaningful impact on results, it should eventually be grown to 15–25% of a portfolio's value. Cash can be divided into two purposes:

   i. Idle cash – Up to 5% of portfolio AUM: used to periodically rebalance individual stocks.

   ii. Cash reserve – An additional 10–20% of portfolio AUM: built up between corrections in anticipation of the next market pullback.

Accumulating cash should be a mindful activity. For some, like retirees, cash is a finite resource to be managed sparingly. For others, like those with employment, it is a renewable resource. Yet, for all investors, new cash can be accrued through explicit portfolio management tactics.

2. Generating more cash

Aside from depositing surplus personal savings into an investment account, here are six portfolio management techniques to build up your cash reserve:

   i. Periodically trimming advancing stocks (see Chapter 15).
   ii. Dividends and special dividends paid by the core stocks.
   iii. Income paid by short sellers to borrow shares from your portfolio.[1]
   iv. Premiums from selling low-risk monthly covered calls (see Chapter 16).
   v. Premiums from selling put contracts on discounted quality, non-core stocks (see Chapter 19).
   vi. Proceeds earned sporadically from portfolio protection.

Building up reserve cash should be a concerted and consistent activity. The actual amount of cash accumulated normally depends on the length of time between market corrections. However, the real merit of a cash reserve is directly tied to an investor's willingness to deploy it when a compelling market discount eventually prevails. Otherwise, hoarding cash just becomes a drag on performance. In other words, it requires discipline to accumulate cash as well as courage to deploy it opportunistically.

As the economy moves through its cycle, focus on growing your cash but don't let FOMO steal your cash "mojo."

---

[1]This option must be explicitly selected on your trading platform. There are no costs, nor risks to the investor.

Secrets at the Oasis

Raising $USD Cash without FX Fees

In margin accounts, for Canadian investors, $USD can be generated without ever having to exchange $CAD for $USD. Premiums paid on the sale of US put and covered call contracts are paid into your account in $USD.

3. **Investing cash**

Earning interest on idle cash in a zero interest–rate environment is still possible. Since your cash reserve could be sitting for months, consider these choices:

i. A high-yielding brokerage account (we use Interactive Brokers for trading, which pays an industry high yield on idle cash).

ii. A high-yielding cash ETF with these traits:
  - No minimum
  - No lock-up period
  - Daily liquidity
  - Low management expenses (all ETFs will have an MER; the lower, the better)
  - No hidden fees

Trading commissions apply to ETFs, unless using a zero-commission trading platform. The amount of each ETF trade should be large enough to offset the costs.

iii. Selling cash-secured OTM put contracts on core stocks that are not yet fully allocated. This is a low-risk way to generate income on idle cash.

For example, if an investor plans to invest $25,000 into shares of The Trade Desk (TTD), they might start by buying an initial 100 shares @ $81 (= $8,100). While waiting to allocate the remaining $16,900, they could sell two TTD OTM put contracts. Each contract equals 100 shares. One could be sold for one month. The other, for two months. The contracts would generate about $400 to $600 per contract depending upon the strike price and duration. See TTD Example in Figure 14.1.

At maturity, if the TTD shares had risen, at least the investor would have generated some income to compensate for not owning the shares outright. They could then repeatedly sell new short-term OTM put contracts until eventually exercising shares into the portfolio, thereby completing the buy-in process. The cash generated would be a function of an investor's willingness to sell cash-secured put contracts on select stocks.

Investor Caution

SPAC Warning

Some investors park cash in SPACs (special purpose acquisition corporations). Even though a SPAC is a cash-laden corporation, these are highly speculative instruments. Pricing will vary depending upon the latest rumor regarding what a particular SPAC may eventually purchase with their cash hoard.

Investment Tip

DRIP Programs (Dividend Reinvestment Plans)

DRIP programs are dollar cost averaging on autopilot. Where corporations would otherwise pay out dividends to their shareholders, those with DRIP programs will reinvest dividends into additional shares with the following potential advantages:

- **Instant share purchase** on the dividend payment date (no transfer delay).
- **No commissions** charged to buy additional shares.
- **Discounts** to market prices offered by some corporations.
- **Fractional shares** permitted (no rounding issues, nor leftover cash).
- **Objective and perpetual** deployment. No human judgment required.

To invoke a DRIP plan, contact your discount trading platform or broker.
The URL for a current US Stock DRIP list is in the footnotes.[2]
The URL for a current Canadian Stock DRIP list is in the footnotes.[3]

4. **Cash deployment opportunities** (see Chapter 16)

   i. **Deploying cash on devalued individual core stocks**
      Periodically individual core stocks will discount more than the normal cycle gyrations of 15–20% for reasons specific to that stock. Every quarterly corporate report season will bring opportunities when the market is disappointed with top-line revenues, bottom-line profits, or the corporate outlook. But

---

[2]https://www.firstshare.com/subpage-available-companies.aspx (Accessed 26 September 2021).
[3]http://www.dripprimer.ca/canadiandriplist (Accessed 26 September 2021).

before averaging down, whether by DCA or lump sum, confirm that the root cause is not material (see Table 15.1 or 19.1).

ii. **Cash management during a market sell-off**

When a market sell-off affects the whole portfolio, consider:

- Deploying lump sums to render individual stocks back to the portfolio average.
- Deploying specific DCAs to gradually render a stock back to the portfolio average.
- Selling short-term OTM put contracts to conserve on cash and to improve on the discount.

Once the cash reserve has been deployed, the cash accumulation cycle begins anew. In the ensuing recovery, prudence then would be to gradually unwind any excess position(s) profitably. This is an example of good market timing (buy low, sell high).

To not undertake action when presented with an opportunity will banish a cash reserve to being a drag on long-term performance. On the other hand, to deploy cash but not unwind excess positions upon recovery implies a willingness to take higher risks. Being a responsible capitalist requires mindful execution in both directions.

In *The Investing Oasis*, there is room for a prudent investor to coexist with their inner capitalist. But it takes self-awareness and discipline to wear both hats.

Seven Steps to Effective Debt Management

Leverage is another privilege that is not available to every investor. The use of debt requires vigilance and discipline. If not well managed, debt can be hazardous to your wealth and health:

- *Magnifies portfolio volatility.*
- *Increases emotional stress.*
- *Reduces personal risk tolerance.*
- *Can induce capitulation.*
- *Can increase irritability and erode personal health.*

Despite the simplicity of debt, it is also the most potent weapon in an investor's arsenal. An investor should put mindful thought toward when and how to use their debt privilege:

1. When to deploy leverage?
2. How to deploy leverage?
3. What assets to leverage?
4. How much leverage?
5. When and how to unwind leverage?

6. Access to low-cost debt facilities (interest-bearing).
7. Debt facilities without direct borrowing costs.

1. When to Deploy Leverage?

The ideal moment to use leverage would be at a market bottom or within the early days of a recovery. The shock of a downturn and the uncertainty could still be mentally and physically reverberating. Picking a market bottom precisely, though, will be pure luck. Instead, focus on choosing a compelling moment.

> *"Do not fire until you see the whites of their eyes."*
> —American Colonel William Prescott (1726–1795),
> command shouted by the colonel to his American Patriot
> troops at the Battle of Bunker Hill

In 1775, American Patriot Colonel Prescott wanted every shot to count against the British RedCoats' overwhelming advance. This analogy describes well when to deploy precious debt reserves. Although not a matter of life and death, before sending debt into battle, the situation should be compelling. Since borrowing capital has built-in costs, debt should be the last tool deployed.

As gut instincts go, the best time to deploy debt is when one feels most emotionally overwhelmed and sick to the stomach by a collapse in the prevailing markets.

| **Note:** A market correction of up to 20% should never feel emotionally compelling.

When a market correction accelerates into bear market (20–30+%) territory (historically, once every 4.3 years), your inner capitalist instincts should be perked. That's when the "whites of their eyes" will be more visible.

2. How to Deploy Leverage?

In the early stages of a correction (market down by 15–20%), idle cash and the cash reserve should be deployed first. If a bear market (20–30+%) prevails, consider gradually deploying a portion of your debt reserve. But it takes will and courage.

Experienced traders know intuitively when the market is bottoming. However, to time it perfectly would be fortuitous. Instead, the better plan of action is to capture bits and pieces by taking a dollar-cost averaging approach. This would result in buying shares on either side of the eventual market bottom.

Note: As noted in Figure 2.5, the most significant profits are usually gained within the first days or weeks following a market bottom, a time when most investors sit on the sidelines. Perfect timing is not required. But some action is.

3. What Assets to Leverage?

Leveraging should not be confused with investing. Investing cash into individual core stocks is a long-term strategic decision based on substantive selection criteria (see Chapters 8–10). Deployment of the cash reserve should be to deploy DCA or lump sum on discounted core assets.

On the other hand, the use of leverage is a weapon that should be reserved for tactical investing but only in high-quality, severely discounted broad market index ETFs (i.e. SPY [S&P 500], QQQ [Nasdaq], XIU [TSX]) because:

- North American index ETFs are a bet on Western quality and ingenuity.
- North American markets have always been resilient to recover from sell-offs, no matter how severe.
- North American markets have the support of the world's reserve bank (the Fed).
- Index ETFs incur less volatility than do individual stocks, industries, or sectors due to broad diversification.
- Index ETFs are usually low cost.
- Index ETFs are highly liquid and able to be unwound gradually. Individual stocks may experience material matters (see either Table 15.1 or 19.1) and could become temporarily value trapped.

Investor Cautions

Being Debt Smart

- **Never leverage speculative, small-cap, foreign, or commodity stocks or leveraged ETFs.** Combining a risk multiplier (debt) with higher-risk assets can double or triple the trouble.
- **Never deploy leverage during calm markets.** Calm markets are full of deception. Be smart about when to use debt. Wait for compelling circumstances, which should include a market bottom and an initial recovery.
- **For protection**, consider simultaneously setting a stop-loss limit trade order about 10–15% below the index's ACB to limit against a further wholesale decline. As the position rises into profitability, consider changing the stop-loss order to a trailing loss order. This will only be triggered if the position deteriorates back to the trailing limit price but will continue to rise to protect more gains as the position advances.

Comment: These cautions are not to throw cold water on the use of leverage. Instead, it is an encouragement that the most potent weapon in your arsenal should be deployed only in highly compelling circumstances.

4. How Much Leverage?

"Opportunities come infrequently.
When it rains gold, put out the bucket, not the thimble."

—Warren Buffett

As a maxim, Warren suggests taking advantage of the opportunities when they prevail. More realistically, even if your debt facility is much greater, only lever a portfolio up to what can be comfortably repaid within 12 months from personal resources. If a bear market ensues, the debt may have to be repaid from other sources than the leveraged assets.

5. When and How to Unwind Leverage?

Although the average bear market recovery duration is around 15–18 months,[4] the depth of the bear market will strongly influence how the recovery proceeds (i.e. the deeper the sell-off, likely the longer the recovery). As such, plan to unwind this tactical position:

- Plan A – Once the leveraged asset has attained a reasonable profit (investor's personal judgment), consider setting a trailing stop-loss trade order to protect those profits and allow for further gains (perhaps 2–5% behind the prevailing index ETF price).
  However, once the markets have fully recovered, waiting for additional gains may not warrant the borrowing costs.
- Plan B – If markets stagnate and have not recovered within 12 months, consider paying down debt aggressively with other personal cash flows and assets not compromised by the sell-off.

Don't let debt become your master.

---

[4]Before 1985, bear markets had lasted up to 18 months. However, since 1985, unwavering support from the Fed has significantly shortened this cycle. The great COVID-19 bear market of 2020 was routed in only four months.

	USD 25K	USD 300K	USD 1.5M	USD 3.5M
Interactive Brokers	3.08%	2.74%	2.53%	2.41%
E-Trade	9.95%	8.45%	N/A	N/A
Fidelity	9.32%	8.07%	5.50%	5.50%
Schwab	9.32%	8.07%	N/A	N/A
TD Ameritrade	10.50%	9.00%	N/A	N/A

Figure 18.2   USD margin loan rates comparison.

6. Access to Low-Cost Debt Facilities (Interest-Bearing)

Debt is often too easily obtained. However, how we service our obligations ultimately decides whether we keep the privilege. Given that the intended use of debt should be opportunistic and short-term, look for flexible repayment terms at relatively low costs.

    i. **Margin Accounts** (on a discount trading platform) – This is usually the easiest and quickest leverage with access embedded directly into your account. Apply for this margin privilege at the time of account opening. The rate will be variable but check the fine print. Interest rates are often tiered according to the total amount borrowed. Figure 18.2 is an example of a US margin rate comparison provided by Interactive Brokers as at August 2020 (not intended as a promotion).

    ii. **Secured Personal Lines of Credit** (bank) – When secured against the home or other assets, an LOC or HLOC usually offers a competitive rate without rate tiering and equal flexible repayment terms as the best of margin accounts.

7. Debt Facilities without Direct Interest Costs

Leverage for those who don't have access to a debt facility (**see Investor Cautions** below):

- Leveraged index ETFs offer levered exposure to several broad market indices with debt costs built into the management fees (~1.05%).
  - SPXL – 3× leverage of the S&P 500 (broad US market)
  - TQQQ – 3× leverage of the Nasdaq (US technology)

- TNA – 3× leverage of the Russell 2000 (US small-cap)
- HXU – 2× leverage of the S&P/TSX 60 (Canadian blue chip)
- Selling put options contracts on individual stocks or index ETFs creates leverage without incurring direct interest costs and which rewards investors with cash premiums. This concept is outlined in Chapter 19. **For advanced investors only.**

Investor Cautions

Leveraged ETFs–Not recommended but if you must.

- Only invest in broad North American market–leveraged ETFs for the higher quality.
- Avoid industry- or sector-leveraged ETFs due to unnecessary unique risks.
- Avoid buying leveraged ETFs near market tops.
- Leveraged ETFs are prone to extreme volatility and require a high tolerance to uncertainty. Use stop-loss orders. Keep in mind that a 10–15% decline in the broad market would be approximately 30–45% decline in a 3× levered ETF.
- The range of volatility could exceed the average investor's risk tolerance limits, potentially leading to the realization of permanent losses.
- In a declining market, a reduction in the account's equity could render an unnecessary margin call (forced liquidation).

North Star Compass

Leverage Cuts Both Ways

Until you've experienced the pressure of carrying serious debt in a declining market (maxed-out lines of credit, margin calls from a broker, rotating payments between credit cards, etc.), it's hard to describe the overwhelming, emotional, and spirit-crushing negative impact when debt goes wrong.

Investors use leverage because they are convinced of an investment opportunity. As such, positive results are expected. Yet, in an ebbing market, our personal equity is the first to disappear. Compound this with the obligation to repay the borrowed capital plus interest, and suddenly being indebted can put a squeeze on our risk tolerance. When the markets sag, a well-intended levered investment can quickly sour into capitulation. This then realizes those long-feared, avoidable permanent losses. No matter how strong our convictions, with a market dip and the ensuing fear, the use of leverage often self-justifies taking adverse actions.

Continued

This is the double-edged sword of leverage. Either tears of joy or regretful sorrow. There is no in between.

Managing Leverage like a Capitalist:

1. Ensure an investment opportunity is compelling (market discount >25+%).
2. Only borrow what can be repaid within 12 months.
3. Only leverage a broad market ETF (SPY, QQQ, or XIU).
4. Protect your debt-fueled assets by setting stop-loss and/or trailing stop-loss orders.
5. Plan to unwind leverage upon profitability. Remember that leverage is meant to be used tactically and for short periods of time.

North Star Compass

Graduation

For cash and leverage deployment to be successful, it requires:

- The *discipline* to proactively build up a cash reserve and repay outstanding debts.
- The *patience* to await the arrival of a market correction, or beyond.
- The *courage* to deploy your idle cash, cash reserves, and some debt during chaos.
- The *wisdom* to unwind those winning positions post-chaos.

When an investor learns to capably manage these reserves through a market cycle, they will have conquered the ultimate capital markets challenge: *contrarian investing*.

Summary

Reserves of cash and debt are advantages that not all investors have. Too many investors are starved for cash and heavy into margin territory. When such reserves are deployed well, they can render extraordinary results. Cash and debt reserves should only be deployed contrarian to the rhythms of the markets: accumulated in quiet times and deployed in mayhem. If unmanaged, their true potential will remain dormant, at best, and, at worst, could add to the behavior gap. Don't be goaded to deploy cash and debt reserves in an environment of low interest rates. Building a cash reserve and having access to debt facilities will be your most potent strategic advantages. After all, it is usually only 20–24 months on average between significant market events.

At the Oasis: Chapter 18

- Cash and debt are loaded springs. They are the capitalist's most potent tools.
- Practice the multiple ways to raise cash in a portfolio outside of adding in personal savings.
- DRIPs systematically invest through good and bad markets.
- Use cash to buy overly discounted stocks and unwind the excess on recovery.
- Debt is your nuclear weapon. Reserve it for deeply discounted markets. Favor investing the proceeds into a broad-based ETF.

"Gold is the money of Kings.
Silver, the currency of Gentlemen.
Barter is the exchange of Peasants.
Debt, the noose of Slaves."

—Norm Franz,
ordained minister and biblical economist

Chapter 19

Digging for Buried Treasures

Objective:

Generating supplementary passive, risk-adjusted revenues
using stealth leverage.

Warning:

This chapter is discretionary and only suitable for investors with a high risk
tolerance. Writing (selling) put option contracts uses margin capacity to
generate passive income but without the associated interest costs. This can
be termed "stealth" leverage. Individuals should only write put contracts
discerningly and be always mindful of their margin capacity limits.

Who doesn't love a good old-fashioned treasure hunt? The idea of finding
something valuable by searching for clues and using one's intellect to deci-
pher a mystery has universal appeal. This is a desert treasure hunt made for
the DIY investor!

This chapter introduces methodology to reap additional capital growth
by selling put contracts on select, discounted quality non-core stocks. And,
although this leveraging strategy requires margin capacity, there are no
interest costs. Speculators will pay the seller (you) to write these contracts.
Although this endeavor is discretionary, whatever "treasure" is found will
be yours to keep.

Sell High, Buy Low

Even in reverse, this adage still works. Take, for example, a scenario where an investor is optimistic about a recently discounted quality growth stock but is short on cash.

Ordinarily an investor would buy shares on the open market, hold the shares until their target price was achieved, then sell the shares at a profit. That would be "Buy low, sell high." But to conserve their cash, an investor can similarly profit by selling cash-secured[1] put contracts on a desired stock. Then, as the underlying shares rise in value, the deteriorating put contract could be bought back later at a lower price (or just let it mature unexercised). This concept works for four reasons:

1. The extrinsic value[2] (time value) of a put contract naturally deteriorates over time.
2. The intrinsic value[3] of a put contract deteriorates as the underlying share price rises.
3. The long-term trajectory of the stock market is concertedly positive.
4. With time, devalued quality stocks eventually recover their growth trend.

Relative to buying shares with cash at market prices, this is an improved method of buying shares because the seller earns a cash premium by offering to buy shares by a future date at a specific strike price (on terms of their choosing).

Education: Buying a put option[4] gives the owner the right to sell a set number of shares at a set price, called the strike price (SP),[5] by an expiration date. Bearish speculators buy put contracts because they believe

---

[1]"Cash-secured" refers to holding the necessary cash to be able to implement the purchase of shares if the put contract is exercised against the investor. Since most contracts expire worthless, it is only necessary to hold a portion of the necessary cash or have access to margin.

[2]Chen, J. (2022). "Put Option." https://www.investopedia.com/terms/p/putoption.asp (Accessed 26 September 2021).

[3]https://www.investopedia.com/terms/p/putoption.asp (Accessed 26 September 2021).

[4]Mitchell, C. (2022). "How Is a Put Option Exercised?" https://www.investopedia.com/ask/answers/06/putoptionexcercise.asp (Accessed 26 September 2021).

[5]Fernando, J. (2022). "Strike Price." https://www.investopedia.com/terms/s/strikeprice.asp (Accessed 21 February 2022).

that the underlying stock's share price will decline further by the contract maturity date. On the other hand, those who sell put contracts are optimistic about a recovery in the price of the underlying stock. With the historical trend of the stock market being positive, selling put contracts already favors the seller.

Further, according to the CBOE, statistically on average only 10% of options contracts are ever exercised and another 30–35% regularly expire out-of-the-money worthless. This provides a put seller (you) with the opportunity to generate premiums with only a modest chance of having to own the underlying shares. The odds for success can be further improved by controlling the contract terms.

Seller Sets the Terms

Success would be to sell a put contract that does not get exercised. This occurs where the underlying share price rises above the chosen SP by the maturity date. To further improve the odds for success, the seller can control four factors:

- **Quality of Asset** – Target only high-quality stocks not currently held in the core portfolio, but which would diversify well with the current portfolio.
- **Degree of Discount** – Ensure that the targeted stock has recently incurred a significant discount of 25+% for non-material reasons.
- **Strike Price** (SP) – Choose an SP that reflects your degree of optimism for a recovery in the underlying share price: OTM, ATM, or ITM.
- **Duration** – Select a contract duration long enough to allow the underlying share price adequate time to recover and eventually exceed the SP by the maturity date.

Three Possible Outcomes

Scenario #1: At maturity, if the underlying share price has risen above the SP, the contract will be terminated. No further action need be taken. This is the ideal scenario.

Scenario #2: At maturity, if the underlying share price remains below the SP, the contract will be exercised, yet the outcome can still be favorable:

- Adequate cash/margin should be available to buy the contracted number of shares (cash-secured puts).

- The stock was predetermined to be adequate quality and diversification fit for the core portfolio.
- The stock's ACB will be lowered by the amount of the premium. This is a strong reason why selling put contracts should be favored over buying shares with cash.
- Going forward, while the share price remains below the ACB, an investor can sell covered calls to raise more revenues while waiting for a full recovery.
- When the shares eventually rise above their ACB, they can be sold at profit.

Scenario #3: Despite all the precautions to sell put contracts on high-quality stocks, a company may still become materially impaired, causing the share price to decline further. If a stop-loss limit trade order was not set on the put contract to protect against further price deterioration, then consider these choices:

1. **Move on.** Close out (buy back) the put contract(s) at a loss. Review whether any lessons could be learned from the original decision to sell these put contracts.
2. **Still hold faith.** Buy protective put contract(s). See the "Investor Tip: 'Bull Put Spread' Protection" box. This would insure the position against worsening losses.

   Buy an equal number of ATM or OTM put contracts with a similar maturity date as the current outstanding put contracts. If the underlying share price continues to deteriorate, the accelerating loss in the premium of the original put contract(s) sold would be offset by gains in the premiums of the protective put contract(s). If the underlying share price subsequently rises, the original put contract premiums will rise minus the cost of the protective put contracts. With this protective solution, there is still a chance to recover value in this trade.
3. **Do nothing.** Accept that the shares will be exercised into your portfolio. At which time, if there is no material impairment, consider deploying DCA to average down and sell CCs while waiting for the shares to fully recover.

Investor Tip

"Bull Put Spread" Protection

Whether ITM, ATM, or even OTM, selling put contracts has some degree of risk. If the underlying share price deteriorates further, the contracts would likely be exercised against the seller (you) prior to maturity. In the worst-case scenario, if a business were to go bankrupt, you would be obligated to buy the shares at the original SP and therefore absorb the full loss. This is a good reason to stick to high-quality stocks.

An investor can institute insurance when they sell a put contract by simultaneously buying an equal number of lower-priced OTM put contracts with the same maturity date. This is called a bull put spread.[6] The lower the SP, the lower the cost of the premiums.

This decision can be implemented at any time and could bring peace of mind that, once deployed, a position can't deteriorate any further than the lower SP. The downside is that the cost of buying this protection will reduce the eventual net proceeds from the original put sale.

This next section outlines how to find quality non-core stocks and set favorable contract terms. Three examples are provided (OTM, ATM, ITM).

Let the Hunt Begin

There are up to four steps to opportunistically selling put contracts:

#1 – Finding Candidate Stocks
#2 – Strike Price Selection
#3 – Duration Selection
#4 – Protection (discretionary)

Step #1: Finding Candidate Stocks

Periodically, great companies will stumble, becoming front-page news. The greater the concern, the deeper the discount, the greater the opportunity. Every 3 months, during corporate reporting season, there are high-quality stocks that disappoint the market for one reason or another (usually revenues, earnings, or outlook). Companies can also experience a variety of self-made problems, such as product failures, poor marketing campaigns, a failed merger attempt, etc. In mere seconds, the market can punish with

---

[6]Hayes, A. (2021). "Bulls Put Spread." https://www.investopedia.com/terms/b/bullputspread.asp (Accessed 26 September 2021).

10–20% discounts. To be considered a viable candidate against which to sell put contracts, here are four requirements:

1. Confirm a 25–50+% discount from a stock's recent 6-month highs.
2. Confirm that the discount reason is non-material (see Table 19.1).
3. Confirm a stock's quantitative and qualitative metrics (see Chapter 14 checklist).
4. Confirm a stock's diversification merits and portfolio fit (see Chapter 11. Use the correlation matrix[7]).

Scenarios for a Share Price Discount

1. **A wholesale market discount/correction/bear market** (not stock specific). In a general market correction (10–20%), many quality names could become prime candidates. Cherry-pick for the most compelling discounts and best potential fit with the core portfolio. Some may already have been pre-vetted during the original search process but were not chosen for the core portfolio (see Chapter 12).
2. **An industry sell-off** (not stock specific). Suppose a discount affects all stocks within a specific industry (e.g. health care legislation changes due to a change in political parties). Being an industry-wide trauma could be considered a material event requiring time to resolve. Once the industry stabilizes, this could be an opportunity.
3. **Reasons specific to a single stock** (see Table 19.1, which is a repeat of Table 15.1). When a stock loses value, investigate whether the reason is material or non-material.

Table 19.1   Material vs. non-material matters.

Material Risks (Requiring Significant Adjustments)	Non-material Risks (Transient)
• Questionable/bad business practices	• Missed quarterly revenues/poor earnings
• Pending lawsuits	• Weak earnings forecast
• Accounting discrepancies	• Supply and production problems
• Fraud or deceptive practices	• Distribution challenges
• Regulatory changes affecting an industry	• Speculative media comments
• Poor deployment of M&A activity	• Union strikes/lockdowns
• ESG violations (environmental, social, and governance)	• Loss of a significant client
• Unexpected changes of C-suite or management	• Limited lawsuit
• Bankruptcy threats	• Limited natural disaster

[7]https://www.portfoliovisualizer.com/asset-correlations   (Accessed   27 September 2021).

Material Risks

Material reasons should be a deal-breaker. In some way, the company will need to be transformed, likely requiring outside influences and resources (i.e. legal aid, capital, etc.). Material matters managed poorly result in value traps.[8] Yet, even with a material trauma, there still could be life for the business if leadership handles it well. Corporate announcements outside of the regular quarterly reporting season often signal a material event. Triangulate with several sources to research your concerns. Before selling put contracts, wait for the corporation to publicly announce its plan of action to address the deficiencies. If doubts linger, sell and move on.

Non-material Risks

Non-material issues are typically transient and more often associated with operational issues due to the traditional business cycle. While material and non-material matters may equally garner headlines, the latter usually can be resolved in a reasonable time and with only minor corporate adjustments. With confidence in the fundamentals and the management team, only the pace of share price recovery might be in question. Discounted, but otherwise unblemished, companies would be a prime opportunity for selling put contracts.

Steps #2 and #3: Strike Price and Duration Selections

Once a target stock is identified, decide on your level of confidence in a recovery of the underlying share price to align with a strike price and duration (see Table 19.2). The degree of confidence in a share price recovery is equivalent to an investor's risk tolerance.

Table 19.2 Options contract parameters.

Degree of Confidence in a Recovery	Strike Price	Duration	Expected Rewards
Low	OTM (out of the money)	4–8 Months	Lowest premiums
Medium	ATM (at the money)	8–12+ Months	Medium premiums
High	ITM (in the money)	12–18+ Months	Higher premiums

---

[8]Chen, J. (2021). "Value Trap." https://www.investopedia.com/terms/v/valuetrap.asp (Accessed 26 September 2021).

Three PUT Selling Examples (OTM, ATM, ITM)

The following are three real examples of put contract sales performed in the Oasis Growth Fund.

   1. **OTM Put Contracts** (Table 19.3)
      - Sell OTM put contracts when there is confidence in the stock but still expectation for further weakness in the underlying share price.
      - Lower risk; lower premiums.

Table 19.3   OTM example.

	Apple **(Current price = $307)** **(Recent 6-month high = $324)**	
STEPS	**Assessment**	
1	**Current Stock Discount %**	• Only 5% = ($324–$307)/$324
	Confidence Level and Discount Reason(s)	• High. • Issue is not stock specific. Discount due to market pullback. • Pandemic is an external material matter affecting all businesses. • Technology is expected to benefit from work-at-home business culture.
2	**Strike Price Considerations**	• Stock has only discounted partially. OTM contracts can be sold at a lower SP to achieve the full 20% discount. • Seek a strike price at a delta < .25.
3	**Duration Required**	• 4–8 Months
		Calculations / Reasons
Contract Chosen: **Sell OTM Put**	**$260 Dec 2020**	OTM
Delta =	−.247	Should be below −.25 Figure 19.1
Exercise Price Buffer =	15%	= (307–260)/324 The stock could decline to $260 before it would be exercised.
Duration =	7 months	Figure 19.1
Premium Received =	$16.37/contract	Average of Bid / Ask Figure. 19.1
Annualized Rate of Return** =	**10.8%**	= $16.37/$260 × 12/7 months
Breakeven Share Price =	$243.63	= $260 – $16.37 Price below which position becomes unprofitable.

**Returns are annualized by dividing the "premium" per contract by the capital at risk multiplied by 12 months divided by the contract duration. Trading commissions are ignored.

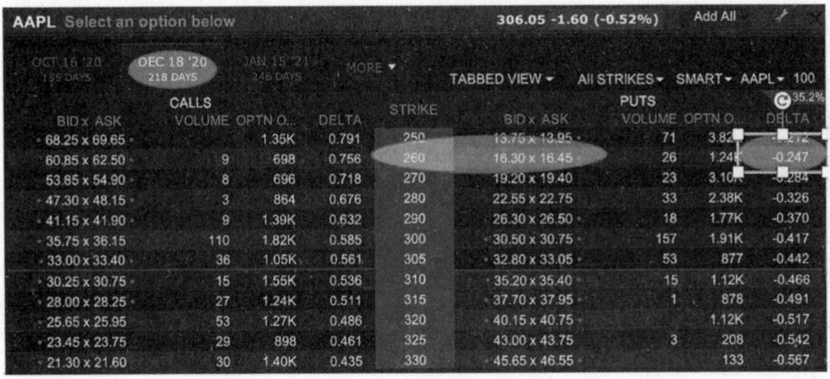

Figure 19.1   Apple options chain as at May 2020.

- For investors with a lower risk tolerance.
- OTM put contracts could also be sold on partially discounted stocks.

Strike Price Considerations: Since an OTM SP is below a stock's current price, this builds in even more room for the underlying stock price to decline before maturity and greatly reduces the risk of a contract being exercised.

If a stock has only partially discounted (i.e. 10%) from its 6-month highs, OTM contracts can then be sold at an even lower SP (10–15% lower) to help achieve the desired 20–25% discount.

Ideally, the put delta should be below –.25. **Note:** Deltas for put contracts are negative.

Contract Duration: Contracts should be at least 4–8 months. Longer durations offer higher premiums and further reduce the probability of a contract being exercised.

Figure 19.1 is the AAPL options chain on May 13, 2020, with the relevant metrics highlighted.

Figure 19.2 is a five-year price history chart for Apple:

- Current price ($307) = Solid line
- OTM put contracts sold ($260) = Dotted line
- Breakeven share price ($243.63) = Dashed line

At maturity (Dec 2020), if Apple shares remain above $260 (dotted line), the contract will be completely successful. Since the breakeven price (dashed line) is reduced to $243.63 (= $260 – 16.37), this contract will be profitable at any price greater than $243.63.

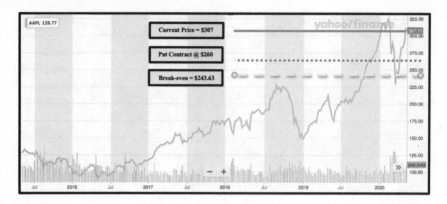

Figure 19.2   Five-year Apple share price history with deployment of options contracts.

2. ATM Put Contracts (Table 19.4)
*   Sell ATM put contracts when a stock's share price has stabilized and the expectation is for a slow and gradual recovery.
*   Medium risk; medium premiums.
*   Investors with a medium risk tolerance.

Strike Price Considerations: An ATM SP is the current stock price. To be successful, the stock's share price at maturity needs only to remain at or above the ATM price. The delta is not relevant.

Contract Duration: Only consider contract terms of 8–12+ months. The higher a stock's beta[9] (>1), the longer the time horizon should be to provide adequate time for the stock to regain its long-term growth pattern.

Figure 19.3 is a screenshot of the PBH.TO options chain with the relevant metrics highlighted.

PBH Select an option below					83.510 +0.320 (+0.38%)		Add All	
JUL 17 '20	OCT 16 '20	**JAN 15 '21**	MORE ▼					
32 DAYS	155 DAYS	**246 DAYS**			TABBED VIEW ▼	All STRIKES ▼ CDE ▼ PBH ▼ 100		
CALLS				STRIKE	**PUTS**		IV: 28.5%	
BID x ASK	VOLUME	OPTN OP...	DELTA		BID x ASK	VOLUME	OPTN OP...	DELTA
8.95 x 11.20			0.650	78	4.95 x 6.70			-0.365
7.75 x 10.05			0.609	80	5.80 x 7.55			-0.405
6.85 x 8.80			0.568	82	6.70 x 8.50			-0.445
5.70 x 7.80			0.527	84	7.60 x 9.50			-0.485
4.80 x 7.05			0.485	86	8.70 x 10.65			-0.526
4.00 x 6.25			0.443	88	9.55 x 11.85			-0.568
3.30 x 5.45			0.399	90	10.85 x 13.15			-0.611
0.20 x 2.25			0.176	105	22.60 x 25.35		2	-0.828
0.05 x 1.90			0.125	110	27.10 x 29.90			-0.878

Figure 19.3   Premium Brands Holdings options chain as at May 2020.

---

[9]Beta is the measure of a stock's degree of volatility relative to the market. For example, a relatively high beta of 1.25 would mean that a stock varies 25% more than the movements in the market.

Table 19.4   ATM example.

STEPS	Premium Brands Holding (Current price = $84.33) (Recent 6-month high = $103)	
		Assessment
	Current Discount %	• **19%** = ($103–$84.33) / $103
1	Confidence Level and Discount Reason(s)	• High • Issue is not stock specific. • External material matter. Pandemic is affecting entire restaurant industry. • People still need to eat.
2	Strike Price considerations	• Stock price has already partially rebounded from worst discount.
3	Duration required	• 12–18 months. • Beta = .94 • Pandemic requires a longer recovery period.

Contract Chosen: Sell ATM Put	$84 Jan 2021	Calculations / Reasons
Delta =	n/a	Not Relevant for ATM Contracts.
Exercise Buffer =	ATM contracts have no buffer.	0 = ($84 – $84.33) / 84
Duration =	8 months	The longest contract available. Figure 19.3
Premium Received =	$8.65/contract	Average of Bid/Ask Figure 19.3
Potential Annualized Rate of Return** =	**15.4%**	= $8.65 / $84 × 12 / 8 months)
Breakeven Share Price =	$75.35	= $84 – $8.65 Price below which position becomes unprofitable.
Downside Buffer =	10.6%	= ($84.33 – $75.35) / $84.33

**Returns are annualized by dividing the "premium" per contract by the capital at risk multiplied by 12 months divided by the contract duration. Trading commissions are ignored.

Figure 19.4 is a five-year price history chart for Premium Brands Holdings (PBH):

- Both current PBH price and the ATM put contract sale price ($84.33) = Solid line.
- Breakeven share price ($75.35 = $84 – $8.65) = Dashed line.

At maturity (January 2021), if the Premium Brands share price remains above $84 (solid line), the contract will be completely successful. Since the breakeven price is reduced to $75.35 (= $84 – 8.65) due to receiving a

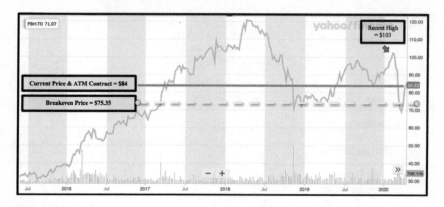

Figure 19.4 Five-year Premium Brands Holdings share price history with deployment of options contracts.

cash premium, any share price greater than $75.35 will render the position profitable (dashed line).

3. **ITM Put Contracts** (Table 19.4)
   - Sell ITM put contracts on higher-beta stocks where the discount is greater than 25%, the share price has stabilized, and there are no material concerns.
   - Higher risk; higher premiums.
   - Only for sophisticated investors with a "high" risk tolerance.

Strike Price Considerations: ITM contracts offer the highest potential rewards but also hold a higher possibility of being exercised against the investor. To be fully successful, the underlying share price needs to rise above the chosen SP by the maturity date. However, even a partial share price recovery could render the position profitable because of the size of the premiums and longer duration.

Choose a strike price between 50% or less of the difference between the stock's most recent 6-month high and the recent low (see Figure 19.6). The depth of ITM contract sold will depend upon an investor's risk tolerance and their level of confidence in the stock to recover. The delta is not relevant.

Contract Duration: An ITM SP requires a 12–18-months-plus contract. Shorter durations could result in unnecessary time pressure.

Table 19.4   Align Technology assessment.

	Align Technology Assessment (Current price = $206) (Recent 6-month high = $298)		
STEPS		**Assessment**	
1	**Stock Discount %**	• 30% = ($298 – $206) / $298	
1	**Confidence Level and Discount Reason(s)**	• High • The dental industry is a stable, growing industry. • Currently affected by global pandemic (temporary office closures). • People still require dental services, although discretionary. • Demand still strong in developing nations.	
2	**Strike Price Considerations**	• Significant share price discount. • Pandemic is an external material matter. However, the business is likely only be temporarily impacted. Dentistry is a perpetual industry.	
3	**Duration Required**	• 12+ months due to the pandemic and the choice for an ITM contract. • Beta = 1.68 (high)	
			Calculations / Reasons
Contract Chosen > Sell ITM Put		$240 Jan 2022	= 50% × ($293 (hi) + 177 (low)]
Delta =		n/a	Not relevant for ITM.
Gain Required to Avoid Exercise =		14%	= (($240 – 206)/$206)
Duration =		20 months	Go as long term as possible for a high-beta stock. (Fig. 19.6)
Premium Received =		$78/contract	Average of Bid/Ask (Fig. 19.6)
Potential Annualized Rate of Return** (if uninsured) =		**19.6%**	(= $78 / $240 × 12/20)
Breakeven Share Price (if uninsured) =		$161	= $240 – $78 Price below which position becomes unprofitable.
Downside Buffer =		21.5%	= (206 – 161) / 206 × 100 Same calculation except in percentage.
4	**Bull Put Spread = Buy OTM (Optional Protection)**	$145	= 70% × $206 (Allows for 30% more decline)
Premium Paid =		$26/contract	Average of Bid/Ask (not provided)
Net Total Premiums Received =		$52/contract	= $78 – $26
Breakeven Share Price (if insured) =		$188	= $240 – $52
Potential Annualized Rate of Return** (if insured) =		**15.1%**	= $52 / $206 × 12/20

**Returns are annualized by dividing the "premium" per contract by the capital at risk multiplied by 12 months divided by the contract duration. Trading commissions are ignored.

Figure 19.5 is a screenshot of the Align options chain with the relevant features highlighted.

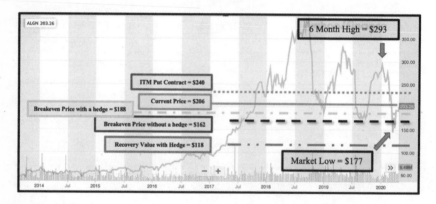

ALGN Select an option below						206.09 +5.11 (+2.54%)	Add All	
OCT 16 '20 155 DAYS	JAN 15 '21 240 DAYS	JAN 21 '22 617 DAYS	MORE ▼		TABBED VIEW ▼	All STRIKES ▼	SMART ▼ ALGN ▼ 100	
CALLS				STRIKE		PUTS		IV 56.6%
BID x ASK	VOLUME	OPTN O...	DELTA		BID x ASK	VOLUME	OPTN O...	DELTA
• 60.50 x 68.50 •		6	0.680	195	• 47.30 x 55.30 •		5	-0.323
• 58.10 x 66.10 •		25	0.666	200	• 50.70 x 57.80 •		337	-0.336
• 53.60 x 61.80 •		17	0.639	210	• 56.00 x 64.10 •		56	-0.364
• 51.00 x 58.30 •		7	0.614	220	• 61.00 x 69.10 •		3	-0.389
• 45.60 x 53.20 •		10	0.589	230	• 67.80 x 76.50 •		12	-0.414
• 41.70 x 49.80 •		27	0.562	240	• 74.10 x 82.60 •		20	-0.442
• 40.00 x 47.20 •		59	0.539	250	• 80.60 x 88.30 •		34	-0.466
• 35.00 x 43.40 •		16	0.514	260	• 87.70 x 95.00 •		5	-0.491
• 33.40 x 41.10 •		9	0.487	270	• 95.00 x 103.00 •		1	-0.519
• 29.30 x 36.20 •		206	0.461	280	• 101.80 x 109.70 •		5	-0.545
• 26.60 x 35.50 •		11	0.439	290	• 108.70 x 117.40 •		2	-0.568
• 25.50 x 33.20 •		152	0.411	300	• 116.50 x 124.50 •			-0.596

Figure 19.5   Align options chain as at May 2020.

Figure 19.6   Five-year Align Technology share price history with deployment of options contracts.

Figure 19.6 is a given-year price history chart for Align Technology:

- ITM put contracts sold ($240) = Dotted line
- Current price ($206) = Solid line
- Breakeven share price with insurance ($188) = Dash-dot line
- Breakeven share price uninsured ($162) = Dash-dash line
- Recovery value if stock falls below the insurance ($118) = Dash-dot-dot-dash line

If the underlying stock price rises above $240 (dotted line) by January 2022, the contract will be completely successful. Since each contract pays a premium of $78, the breakeven price will be $162 (= $240 – $78). Therefore, any price point greater than $162 at maturity renders this position profitable (dashed line).

Selling $240 Align put contracts, less the premium received ($78), renders the entry point of $162 far more attractive than buying the shares on the open market at $206.

Step #4: Protection (Optional) – Where a put contract has been sold and the investor remains wary of further share price weakness, set a stop-loss limit order trade about 15–20% above the current put contract price. (Note: Put contracts rise when the underlying stock price falls.) Alternatively, consider buying a protective put (bull put spread).

- Buy an equal number of OTM put contracts as were originally sold but at a lower SP and the same maturity date.
- By deploying insurance at $145 (arbitrarily chosen) at a cost of $26/contract, the breakeven price now rises to $240 – $78 + $26 = $188 (dash-dot-dash line).
- This insurance will arrest any losses below $118 (= $145 – $26) (dash-dot-dot-dash line).
- If Align Technologies went bankrupt, the maximum loss would then be $43/contract (= – $240 + $78 – $26 + $145).
- Bull put spreads can be also deployed for any of the other examples above. However, usually, selling put contracts should be reserved for the highest-quality stocks to avoid concerns about permanent share price impairment or, worse, bankruptcy.

Comment: Even with the cost of insurance, if the ITM put is eventually successful, the net annualized return would be 15%, as outlined in Table 19.4. Without protection, the absolute rate of return would be approximately 20%.

Clarification

Selling Short-Term ITM Puts as Initiation vs. Selling Longer-Term ITM Puts for Leveraged Returns

Although there are similarities between selling short-term put contracts as described in Chapter 14 to initiate a buy-in for core stocks vs. selling contracts opportunistically on non-core growth stocks (in this chapter), tactically, they have different goals:

- In Chapter 14, selling short-term (1 week up to 1 month) ITM put contracts is used to initiate core stock positions in the Tier 1 portfolio. The premiums earned reduce the ACB of the respective shares more than if those shares were bought at current market prices. The contracts are expected to be exercised against you.
- In this chapter, selling 4–18+-month ITM put contracts on a diversified array of devalued non-core growth stocks is a tactic to generate tax-efficient capital gains, supplementing the growth in the Tier 1 core portfolio. Yet, by deploying the risk reduction methodologies

Continued

as outlined, the probabilities of contracts being exercised and forced into your portfolio are greatly reduced. Essentially, selling ITM put contracts leverages portfolio returns without using your own cash or incurring interest costs, yet generates cash premiums.

The put-selling decision flowchart in Figure 19.7 should help to identify the appropriate type of put to deploy given the opportunity and the investor's level of conviction.

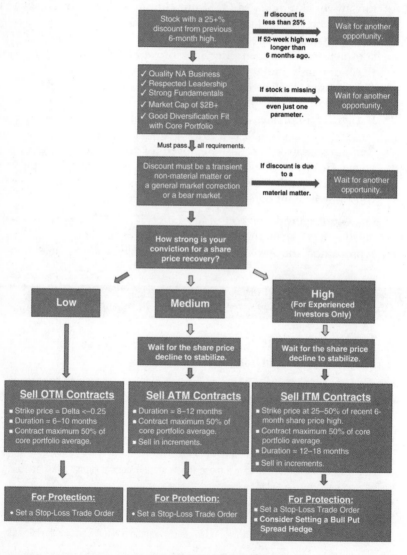

Figure 19.7   Speculative put-selling decision flowchart.

Effective Management of a Portfolio of Puts

Comment: If the user is unfamiliar with options chains, take a look at Google's Top 10 options trading education sites.[10]

Caveat: Selling a put contract is deploying leverage.

1. **Options privileges:**
   - Put contracts can only be sold in margin accounts.
   - Contact your discount trading platform to gain access to margin.
   - Chapter 27 "Tools and Resources" offers discount trading platform choices.

2. **Option premiums:**
   - Higher strike prices (SPs) pay higher premiums.
   - Longer contracts pay higher premiums.
   - Higher-volatility stocks pay higher premiums (e.g. tech stocks).

3. **Sell contracts gradually:**
   - Set high limit orders. Adjust periodically (hourly/daily). Be patient.
   - Sell contracts on a targeted stock over several trading sessions.
   - Sell contracts when the stock is in decline. This generates higher premiums because put contracts rise as a share price falls.
   - If required to go back further than 12 months to find a stock's all-time high, likely this stock has been in correction mode too long and may be verging on becoming a "value" stock. Look elsewhere.
   - Be mindful of corporate reporting dates. Writing contracts on a targeted stock before an earnings report date is an unnecessary risk. Preferably sell put contracts in the days following an adverse market reaction (following bad corporate news).

4. **Sell no more contracts than 50% of the nominal value of the average core stock:**
   - If exercised into the core portfolio, this allows an investor room for DCA.

---

[10]https://www.personalincome.org/options-education-review/ (Accessed 27 September 2021).

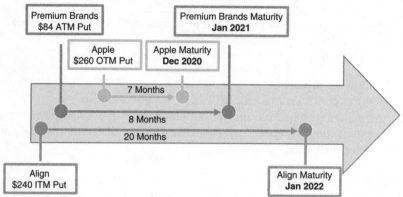

Figure 19.8   Put ladder timeline.

5. **Diversify a portfolio of put contracts by:**
   - Economic sectors/industries/beta. Be mindful to target stocks that would be complementary to the core portfolio diversification.
   - Strike price and duration (see Figure 19.8 for a timeline of the three examples):
     - Sell 50% with one SP and an 8–12+ month maturity date.
     - Sell 50% with a higher SP and a longer maturity date.

6. **For primary protection, set stop-loss trades:**
   - Set stop-loss limit order trades about 15–20% above the current put contract price to protect against adverse share price movements (put contracts rise when the underlying stock price falls). When triggered, it closes out the contract. This is zero-cost protection.
   - For insurance, consider setting up a bull put spread.

7. **Minimize trading commissions:**
   - No trading commissions are charged if a contract is exercised or if the contract expires naturally.

8. **Consider early closure on contracts with gains of 75%+** (an expected return):
   - When a stock price is close to the SP with less than 2 months remaining, consider closing out the contracts. Markets are highly random and could reinvigorate suddenly with bad corporate news.

- Most options contracts are American style and can be exercised at any time before the maturity date. Most index options are European style, which settle in cash at maturity.

X Marks the Spot

Once a discounted quality stock is identified, do your research. Walk through the assessment framework in Figure 19.7. You set the contract terms: OTM, ATM, or ITM, and for how long. The more cautious the terms, likely the better the sleep.

So, while the Tier 1 core stocks are working hard and Tier 2 covered calls are earning a regular low-risk income, now an investor can add in supplementary growth from a diversified portfolio of time-laddered, value-priced put contracts. Welcome to modern-day treasure hunting!

At the Oasis: Chapter 19

- Selling put contracts is discretionary but you decide the level of risk and set all the terms.
- Protect your positions with stop-loss trades.
- Build a diversified, time-laddered portfolio of put contracts gradually:
  - Triangulation (research) ensures stronger conviction for taking on these opportunities.
  - Sell contracts on "red" days. Put contract premiums increase when stocks are declining.
  - The premiums from selling put contracts add to your cash reserve.
  - Selling put contracts is stealth leverage (uses margin capacity but with no interest to pay).
  - Only sell contracts on stocks you are willing to own.
  - Since you're selling risk to speculators, don't be the greedy one!

"Holy Shamoley! It's a Bobby Dazzler!"

—Gary Drayton,
metal detection expert,
Mystery of Oak Island

Chapter 20

Emotion-free Selling

"You're only rational once . . .
before you buy."
—VP, Lehman Brothers

Objective:

Selling stocks constructively.

---

nvesting is meant to be for the long term. However, eventually, most every position held will be questioned. An investor either creates or destroys wealth when they trade. Unfortunately, spontaneous trades more often add to the behavior gap. Triggered by frustration, disappointment, or fear, our guts and amygdala conspire together to demand action.

Selling Protocols

So, let's step back for a minute.

Every stock in the core portfolio should have been researched, filtered up to 16 times, and ultimately determined as worthy of our capital. As such, it should take far more than a price fluctuation to shake our confidence.

Unfortunately, without accountability mechanisms, like an investment policy statement (IPS), a supervisor, a mentor, or the regulator, an investor can be vulnerable to deploying reactive trades.

To limit spontaneous trading decisions, like a pilot doing a pre-flight check prior to take-off, an investor might benefit from reviewing a trading checklist, as was presented in Chapter 14.

Realistically, once our emotions are engaged, no list will ever work. However, the intent is that if reactive trading is subverting performance results, having a list is better than not having a list. With time, it could become second nature to confirm each selling decision. While all trading decisions are specific to the investor, a list is meant to help affirm a selling decision or prompt enough doubts that result in deflecting a decision. Either way, if there is no other accountability mechanism, then a list could help promote becoming a better capital markets actor. Introducing a few professional protocols could favorably nudge your performance results.

The following checklist is designed mindfully from the perspective of an investor willing to be reflective before they click the sell button.

Personal Reasons

1. Is cash required for lifestyle or other financial obligations (i.e. debt repayments)?
2. Have life's circumstances changed that might influence your risk tolerance?
   - Loss of job/disability?
   - Marriage/divorce?
   - New birth/college?
   - Loss of assets/lawsuit?

Any significant loss of revenues, assets, or increased liabilities should prompt a review of your asset mix.

Portfolio Reasons

3. Is this a trim to rebalance a position?
4. Is this sale for harvesting a tax loss?
5. Did the brokerage firm issue a margin call?

Security-Specific Reasons

6. For the stock in question, has a **material event** transpired that should prompt consideration for removal from the portfolio?
   - Leadership changes?
   - Product problems?
   - Legal issues?

- Political interference?
- Unsettling M&A activity?
- A change in the competitive landscape?
7. Did the stock originally meet all the buy-in criteria, or were there originally some compromises?
8. Was this position bought on speculation or leverage?
   - Will selling it help to de-risk the portfolio?
9. Has a superior stock prospect emerged (i.e. higher Sharpe ratio, lower beta, better fundamentals, etc.)?

Notably, this modest list of nine questions does not address share price volatility. If a sell trade is deployed because of performance disappointment, this could be a learning opportunity:

- Was enough due diligence done before the stock was bought?
- If a stock was liquidated due to the degree of volatility, consider running a **correlation coefficient** test on the entire portfolio. This could reveal other stocks with similar high-volatility profiles that could be candidates for removal.
- If a highly volatile stock is to be kept in the core portfolio, consider setting up protection (several ideas are offered further below).
- If a position is sold to make quick profits or sacrificed to avoid short-term losses, this reveals the objectification of a stock. When the reasons for owning a stock are divorced from the fundamentals, they were always going to be vulnerable. Once bitten, twice shy, three times sounds like a habit.

> *"Half of all coin-flippers will win their first toss. Like gambling, none of the winners should expect to profit if they keep playing."*

—Warren Buffett

According to Warren Buffett, stocks should be bought based on their business fundamentals. Portfolio management takes this one step further. Stocks should also be assessed for how well they fit together in the portfolio. Their growth or defensive characteristics can be antagonistic or beneficial in the right combinations.

However, if price changes alone are enough to trigger sell decisions, there is likely room for self-reflection about research methodology or personal risk tolerance limits. Building wealth requires holding conviction to your convictions.

The Essence of Capitulation

Selling against one's better interests is often the culmination of a series of escalating factors eventually leading up to a tipping point. Unfortunately, the price of giving in to our fears is essentially a voluntary transfer of wealth to a complete stranger on their terms. If capitulation is an acceptable selling choice, then an investor owns the behavior gap.

Yet most investors should want to understand the circumstances that led to this vulnerability and then learn how to defuse or buffer their behavior to limit or eliminate capitulation as an option. Every involuntary sell trade is a learning opportunity about how the circumstances failed us, including identifying the point where perceived fear was greater than our will to resist (risk tolerance limit). Periods of stress and crisis, and how we react, are rich learning opportunities. In the real world, capitulation is a final decision. In investing, we get to live another day.

The Benefits of Capitulation

- **It cleans the slate.** If an investor throws in the towel on a position, it should also be one of our best learning opportunities. If the stock(s) did not fit the original selection criteria, there is an opportunity to go back a few steps to reassess which traits in a stock are important enough to reinforce our confidence during the most difficult markets.
- **Make money while you wait.** Even with a significant share price decline, consider keeping the position and selling covered calls to garner extra revenues while waiting for a recovery. If the security does not have an options chain, then perhaps the learning opportunity is to only invest in stocks with options chains.
- **Be the other side of the transaction.** That lowball bid that stole away your stock was likely preset. Algorithms set bait trades and then patiently wait until a capitulation trade is delivered. Once filled, algorithms will quickly set a sell trade at a higher price point. The algorithm makes money on the spread. Why not become the opportunist and set your own lowball trade orders? Then wait.

Testing Your Resolve

Market corrections offer the ultimate test whether an investor has prepared well and whether they have the mental fortitude to be a committed long-term investor. Most investors initiate their long-term decisions when the markets are in favor. As such, performance expectations often ignore the potential degree of volatility that eventually ensues.

Unfortunately, the performance gap is testimony to those who trade into a market correction because either they haven't proactively prepared their portfolio or that their risk tolerance limits have been exceeded.

If unable to resist market timing, an investor should reconsider their asset mix, but only after the ensuing market recovery.

Market timing is destructive to our wealth and corrosive to our confidence. Dedicated investors rarely focus on the short term, except to seize the advantage from those who have lost their patience.

North Star Compass

Anger Management

Five minutes of anger is known to suppress the immune system for up to six hours.[1]

A bad trade can certainly induce a five-minute tirade. The trauma of undulating markets can induce a flood of hormones. It takes about one hour for adrenaline to subside. Realistically, market volatility is likely causing many of us long-term harm, psychologically, physically, and potentially financially, if "Mr. Market" triggers us into action.

"In numerous studies of cancer, the most consistently identified risk factor is the inability to express emotion, particularly the feelings associated with anger," wrote Dr. Gabor Mate in his book *When the Body Says No*. Both "anger–outburst" and "anger–passive" types incur more illnesses (heart attacks, strokes, and autoimmune diseases) and tend to die younger.[2]

Behavioral Adjustment: And what's worse than anger?

Regret that a stock position recovers right after having sold your entire position. While regret can lead to anger, before it gets there, it harbors very insidious, often corrosive thoughts. So, for the sake of your mental and physical health, as well as your portfolio, before pulling the trigger on that next trade, take a deep breath, count to 10, or go for a walk. Emotionally induced trades rarely end well.

Emotion-Free Selling

Proactive Protection

Proactively setting up protection trades such as stop-loss (SL) and trailing stop-loss (TSL) trades orders removes the investor from the front lines.[3]

---

[1]Rein, G. & McCarty, R. (1995). "The Physiological and Psychological Effects of Compassion and Anger." *Journal of Advancement in Medicine*, 8(2), 87–105.

[2]Alistair Moes, A. & Proano, A. (2015). *Lose Your Temper – A Conscious Exploration of Anger*. Vancouver, Canada: Moose Anger Management.

[3]The recommended version of the SL and TSL trades are actually GTC FORTH limit orders. This means that an order remains open (good 'til canceled), that it can be filled after hours (fill outside of regular trading hours), and that once triggered at the stop price, the order becomes a limit order such that a selling price must be above the stated limit price. To ensure getting filled, an investor should set an adequate range between the stop price and the limit price.

They are set with rational forethought during calm markets and serve to protect an investor's invested capital and their gains. This means less stress time monitoring stocks and zero chance for the hypothalamus/amygdala complex to incite spontaneous trades. And once a trade is triggered, don't second guess yourself. Those trades were deployed using rational thoughts. There are no costs to setting up GTC (good 'til canceled) SL or TSL trade orders.

To protect some or all the invested capital, set SL and TSL about 10–15% below the current share price on most of the portfolio. Setting these protective trade orders too tight to the current share prices, though, could be a frustrating experience of being "stopped out" and then scrambling to repurchase the sold shares. In the normal course of a year, growth stocks will vary up to 15–20% without being off their long-term growth trend. A TSL is dynamic and will follow along behind the advancing stock until a sufficient pullback triggers the order. An SL order remains static at the stop price and is triggered only if the share price descends far enough.

The overall intent of setting these proactive defensive trade orders should be to protect against steeper market declines. Ideally, set them with a little breathing room.

An alternative to setting SL and TSL trade orders would be to buy put contracts on core stocks. Since this is insurance, the cost of buying contracts will reduce the overall portfolio performance but will allow an investor to keep the portfolio intact.

Eliminating a Position – ITM Calls

When planning to sell an entire position, rather than selling shares immediately on the open market for cash, consider selling short-term, deep ITM call contracts and get paid a cash premium for getting rid of a painful position. By choosing a strike price that is lower than the underlying share price, the investor could earn a generous premium even though the eventual sale is not guaranteed.

If the underlying share price falls below the strike price by the maturity date, the investor keeps the premium and the shares. They can then sell another short-term ITM call contract. If the underlying shares rise above the SP by the maturity date, the shares are then removed from the portfolio for cash (strike price × number of shares). In all cases, the contract seller (you) keeps the contract premium.

Q: When to cut your losses?

By now, you should know the signs: shortness of breath, queasy stomach, sweaty palms, and heart palpitations. No, it's not a heart attack, we're talking about trader's remorse. You've just bought a position and it's sinking. Your convictions are already being tested. How far do you let it go before abandoning it?

Holding Faith

If you did your homework, the stock price will find a bottom. Luckily, if you just began your buy-in, there should still be multiple additional DCA tranches to deploy. But before continuing with further DCA tranches or a lump-sum purchase, let the share price stabilize and show evidence of a recovery. Research to ensure that nothing material has transpired. Buying quality at a steeper discount should be an even better decision.

Abandoning a Stock

Alternatively, when something material is revealed about a corporation that undermines your confidence and the management's solution seems weak, consider deploying a graduated series of limit sell orders over several trading sessions. If the stock has an options chain, consider selling short-term ITM calls. Try to exit your position gradually. There might still be a recovery. Yet, once a stock is sold, leave it behind. Regret is an unheeded lesson. Grieve by learning how your research could be improved.

Investment Tip (Reminder)

Before deploying any trade (buy or sell), do a cursory review of your portfolio. There may be outstanding open trade orders, including SL or TSL, threshhold limit orders (for rebalancing), CC contracts, or put contracts to consider. To check for current positions and open trade orders, rearrange your portfolio according to "Group by Underlying Securities." This allows an investor to pair up all outstanding holdings and trades grouped by each individual security.

"Markets can remain irrational longer than you can stay solvent."
—John Maynard Keynes (1883–1946),
professor, Kings College, Cambridge, England

At the Oasis: Chapter 20

- Selling a stock should always have purpose, never an excuse.
- Capitulation is the ultimate self-inflicted wound. Learn to insulate yourself.
- Use SLs and TSLs to protect your capital and your gains. Consider buying protective puts.
- Spontaneous trading adds to the behavior gap. We offer a chapter on short-term trading on the password-protected site: www.theinvestingoasis.com.
- Since capitulating to anything brings enlightenment, heed the lessons.

"The broker said the stock was 'poised to move.' Silly me, I thought he meant up."

—Randy Thurman,
CEO of Retirement Investment Advisors, Inc., and author of
*The All-Weather Retirement Portfolio, More Than a
Millionaire,* and *The Worry-Free Retirement Guide to
Finding a Trustworthy Financial Advisor*

Tier 3 Summary

Tier 3 emphasized that while cash and debt are periodically an investor's most potent weapons, a behavioral shift to adopt contrarian tactics could prove equally rewarding. Hunting for alpha treasures off the beaten path requires equal parts vigilance, persistence, and prudence. With experience, the opportunities will become more obvious and the instincts more honed.

When ready to challenge "Mr. Market's" supremacy, Tier 4 will introduce several reliable "storm" indicators, multiple portfolio preparation protocols, and a number of protection strategies.

THE INVESTING OASIS: Tier 4

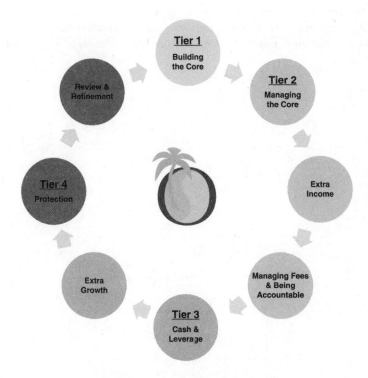

MISSION #4: To Outperform "Mr. Market"

	Mission #4
	To Outperform "Mr. Market"
Tier 1 – Building a Core Growth Portfolio	✓
Tier 2 – Core Management and Income from Covered Calls	✓
Tier 3 – Managing Cash, Debt, and Stealth Growth	✓
Tier 4 – Portfolio Protection	✓

Tier 4 will prepare you and your portfolio to face the worst of "Mr. Market." Peace of mind starts by having a well-balanced, diversified portfolio of quality assets. Yet, when a storm arrives, it can be unsettling even to grizzled veterans. Tier 4 is an opportunity to become one of those rare few who might welcome a periodic purge. Tier 4 offers insights into "storm forecasting," portfolio preparation, and ultimately applying timely protection.

Chapter 21

"Storm" Forecasting

Source: iStock

Objective:

Learning to recognize the signs of impending "bad weather."

With desert sandstorms being a hazard of the camel trade, nomads are highly conscious of Mother Nature's potential to disrupt the best-laid plans. To their keen eyes, the first indications of the pending havoc are sand particles "dancing" at their feet. Winds gradually accelerate until an ominous wall of fury rises up menacingly across the horizon. In minutes, visibility descends to zero and a turbine of wind scatters all that is unattached. In the desert, there are no havens. Conditions can remain dire for hours, days, or even beyond a week. Life-and-death decisions require fast actions to safeguard livestock, the cargo, and themselves. ·

Likewise, market corrections arrive suddenly and may last days, weeks, or months. And without due preparation, they can temporarily render great harm financially and emotionally. Most investors could benefit from learning to read the impending signs and prepare their portfolio, and themselves, accordingly.

If an investor's current situation is devoid of such a plan, three processes over the next three chapters might help to diminish the impact of an impending "storm":

- Learning to Forecast (Assessing the Probabilities) – Chapter 21.
- Prevention, Avoidance, and Preparation (Action) – Chapter 22.
- Setting Up Protection (Action) – Chapter 23.

RMP #13: "Weather" Forecasting

Predictions Are the Uglier Side of Forecasting

Imagine being deep in the desert and looking up at the night sky to see, amongst the millions of twinkling stars, the brightness of the North Star.[1] Over the centuries, it has guided many travelers, particularly when traversing formless deserts.

But for those looking to divine the stock market direction through celestial bodies, AI programs, or otherwise – sorry, but no such method yet exists. And likely for a good reason. The market is comprised of thousands of individual companies performing myriads of value-creating tasks for the benefit of society. The stock market gives them tangible financial value. The bidding process between independent-minded investors defines the market and is meant to be devoid of collusion or fraternity. That's all well and good until, periodically, herd mentality takes over. At which point, seized by primal fears, investors ignore all rational thoughts and act in unison.

---

[1]The North Star (Polaris) is part of the Little Dipper constellation with which the earth's axis is perfectly aligned. As the planet rotates, the North Star remains stable to the naked eye, and therefore has guided mankind through countless journeys.

This is called market mimicry, where the actions of one investor are copied by another, and so on, until it develops into a full-fledged panic. If this lemming-like act of suicide were real, the planet would be purged of millions every 20–24 months.

Was the sell-off predictable? No. But it was probable. The difference is that a prediction implies certainty, while probability encompasses the "likelihood" of an event happening. Many forecasters brag about their clairvoyance skills. Yet if the market were only about numbers, surely, by now, an industry of quants would have figured out how to predict market mayhem. But they haven't. The fly in the camel's eye is that humans are the wild card. Yet we keep blaming the markets for being the unpredictable one.

So, back to those predictions.

Since the launch of the S&P 500 in 1957, the index has averaged 8% annual returns. This includes the worst and the best of markets. While achieving this exact average in any one year is unlikely, the average remains highly probable over the longer term. On the other hand, volatility is highly predictable with 80 pullbacks of 5–10% in 65 years (see Table 21.1). That equals more than one event per year. The more pronounced events, such as market corrections (10–20%) and bear markets (20%+), while less predictable, occur, on average, once every 20–24 months.

Table 21.1 Market mayhem 1946–2020*

	# of Events	Duration (Avg)	Decline (Avg)
Minor Tremors (5–10%)	80	1 Month	7%
Market Corrections (10–20%)	26	4 Months	13.7%
Bear Markets (20+%)	12	14.5 Months	32.5%

*Statistics provided by Goldman Sachs to CNBC (Accessed 27 September 2021).

Sixty-five years from now, these averages likely will have been upheld. But that would be a prediction.

Realistically, it takes years of experience and ultimately gut instinct to make timely decisions in advance of market tumult. Knowing that the market's unpredictability is entirely natural should prompt better preparation. Not out of fear; rather, because panic of the masses is a time of opportunity.

Market Sentiment Indicators

In addition to the Warren Buffett Rule and the CNN Fear & Greed Index previously shared in Chapter 14, below are two more market sentiment indicators. Together, the following four forecasting tools can sensitize investors when to be more mindful about preparing their portfolio for a potential storm ahead (see Chapters 22 and 23). Familiarize yourself with each and bookmark their individual links.

1. **CNN Fear & Greed Index**[2]
2. **The Warren Buffett Rule**[3]
3. **S&P 500 Forward Earnings P/E Ratio** – The JP Morgan Asset Management chart in Figure 21.1 tracks the P/E ratio for the S&P 500 Index over the past 25 years. The P/E ratio reveals the degree of enthusiasm held by investors for stocks. When the ratio

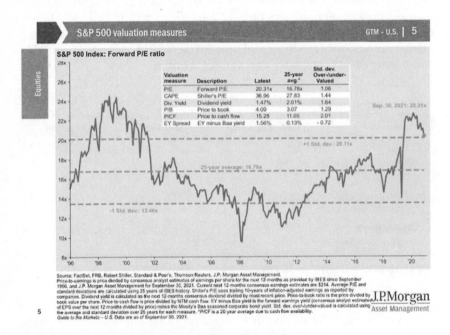

Figure 21.1   S&P 500 Index relative to forward P/E ratio.
Source: https://am.jpmorgan.com/us/en/asset-management/adv/insights/market-insights/guide-to-the-markets/#

---

[2]https://money.cnn.com/data/fear-and-greed/ (Accessed 16 February 2022).

[3]http://www.currentmarketvaluation.com/models/buffett-indicator.php (Accessed 27 September 2021).

rises above 20×, start looking to "round up the camels" (see Chapter 22). The chart provides current readings on other key measures highlighting the market's degree of attractiveness relative to their historical averages. This chart and many others are regularly updated quarterly in the JP Morgan Asset Management "Guide to the Markets."

<u>Comment:</u> In this chart, this P/E ratio is a barometer of general investor sentiment (degree of enthusiasm) toward the earnings of the general stock market.

4. **CBOE Volatility Index**[4]: The VIX reflects the degree of fear in the markets. The higher it goes, the greater the fear. As a reflection of the degree of market pessimism, it works as a contrarian indicator, Figure 21.2 shows several key moments over the past 30 years when stocks went on sale. The best moments to invest would have been when the VIX spiked well above its long-term historical average of 16.

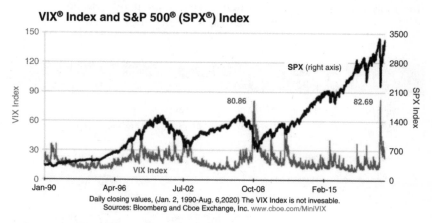

VIX® Index and S&P 500® (SPX®) Index

Daily closing values, (Jan. 2, 1990-Aug. 6,2020) The VIX Index is not invesable.
Sources: Bloomberg and Cboe Exchange, Inc. www.cboe.com/MiniVIX

Figure 21.2   VIX Index vs. S&P 500 since 1990.
Source: https://www.cboe.com/

---

[4]Chen, J. (2022). "What Does the Volatility Index (VIX) Indicate?" https://www.investopedia.com/news/what-does-volatility-index-vix-indicate/ (Accessed 26 September 2021)

The Ultimate Wisdom of the Stock Market

While the stock market is a collection of motivated minds acting independently in rendering their investment decisions, the individual investor is irrelevant. Together, the "wisdom of the crowd" has always prevailed over those who thought they knew better. Historically, a deteriorating stock market has often proven to be an early warning sign of impending economic weakness by 6–9 months, on average, ahead of traditional financial metrics. By the time the economy swoons into a full-blown recession, the stock market will have already begun its rebound. So, as it turns out, the market is a better forecasting tool for the economy than the economy is for predicting the markets. And yet, most market forecasters continue to base their market outlook on economic data. By trying to apply rational thought to predict the market's direction, most often our cognitive faculties fail us.

Instead, the real wisdom about the market is to understand that it is our reaction to uncertainty that most often leads to disappointing outcomes. The market, through all its foibles, just marches on. Although it can be predicted that over 30 years the market will likely have averaged about 8%, it is the short-term noises that overwhelmingly dominate our psyche.

So rather than worrying about it, just be better prepared.

Moral of the Story

If we focus on what might be lost, the glass will be forever half-empty.
Market corrections should be expected but they bring opportunities.
Ignore the rain.
Look for the **RAINBOW.**

Chapter 22 focuses on doing a little pre-storm preparation before the inevitable.

At the Oasis: Chapter 21

- Be discerning about news sources. Most seek to incite our emotions to win loyalty.
- A well-designed portfolio is the first and best line of defense against market tumult.
- Bookmark and learn to read the market "weather vanes."
- Better preparation means portfolio insurance should be discretionary.

"There are two kinds of forecasters: those who don't know, and those who don't know that they don't know."
—John Kenneth Galbraith (1908–2006)

Chapter 22

"Rounding Up the Camels"

*"Predicting rain doesn't count.
Building the Ark does."*
—Warren Buffett

Objective:

Preparing for the next "storm."

Even for the experienced nomad, desert sandstorms are an intense and terrifying ordeal. Imagine an environment of zero visibility where micro-sized sand particles are whipped about by 50–75km-per-hour winds. With the sun blotted for the duration, it could feel like Armageddon.

Such drama is an expected part of plying the ancient trade routes across an expansive, featureless desertscape. From a very early age, though, nomads are taught to read the signs and respect the desert. Before each expedition, they get organized. Only the healthiest of camels are selected, provisions are gathered, and oversized cargoes are cinched up. Each journey begins knowing they may come to face Mother Nature's worst wrath and fury. Their very lives depend on being well prepared. And when the sand particles begin "dancing," they round up the camels.

As go the nomads into the void, so should the investor. The parallels are striking. This chapter will outline preparations, as well as several "post-storm" actions.

RMP #14: Prepping for the "Storm"

As much as most of us dread a correction, they are an essential part of the free market. Healthy ecosystems need to periodically purge the weak. This includes both corporations and investors. Too many unhealthy corporations and business practices can be sustained well after their "expiration dates." Then, in the blink of an eye, the markets convulse. De-risking the market is just a natural part of the process. Even though most investors pray for market stability, volatility is the norm.

Where market uncertainty tends to evoke reactive behavior, the following are proactive steps to preparing your portfolio, and you, for that next downturn.

Revisiting the Asset Mix

Over time, with the long-term positive trend of the stock market, an asset mix will naturally migrate to become more heavily weighted in stocks. Reducing exposure to equities is Risk Management 101. This decision offers the single most potent reduction in volatility. The time to reduce equity exposure is when either the signals suggest a "storm" is approaching or when you can't sleep at night. That is not a flippant comment. This is called "body talk." If our daily lives are being unduly impacted, something needs to change.

So, if the equity allocation is reduced for peace of mind, don't be frustrated if the market moves higher. This was a risk-mitigation decision decided during a sane moment.

Yet, when the correction finally arrives, be brave and be vigilant to gradually push some cash back into equities. Investing takes patience, not perfection. Any purchase of stocks below their adjusted cost base (ACB) should already be a good decision. Yet not feeling compelled to make adjustments before, during, or after suggests an investor has made peace with their asset mix.

North Star Compass

Winning Twice

- If tempted to lower your asset mix during a market correction, hold tight. This is not a suggestion. Although selling into a market correction may temporarily bring emotional relief, it could realize unnecessary permanent losses and invoke the inevitable regrets that come from hasty decisions and delayed reinvesting. Markets have always rebounded. It's just the time and duration that are uncertain.
- Instead, learn that those unsettling feelings in the pit of your stomach are a signal of investing opportunity. If you are feeling them, so too are most other investors. Yet only those who embrace the moment and average down will be better off.
- The time to review and adjust the asset mix is when you no longer feel queasy and your thoughts are rational.

Being brave and acting smart: a double win.

Keys to Moderating Portfolio Volatility

No matter how well a portfolio is designed and managed, growth stocks inherently have higher ranges of volatility. This is where investors need to be honest about their risk tolerance limits. In Chapter 9 "Stock Selection," setting an absolute variance acceptability limit meant possibly sacrificing a higher-performance stock for one with a lower volatility profile.

Figure 22.1 highlights the primary sources of volatility embedded within a portfolio of stocks. The sources are identified as either diversifiable risk (solid boxes), which can be influenced via our stock selections, or non-diversifiable risk (dotted box), which is beyond our control.

Yet even the most prudently designed and diversified growth portfolio will still suffer along with the masses when markets convulse. Below are several additional ways to mitigate portfolio volatility.

Risk Framing

Market corrections are the greatest opportunity to make wealth gains relative to our investing peers. Those who attempt market timing by selling into the panic are failing themselves and, more often, falling further behind. Those who don't panic will do just fine. And those who seize the moment

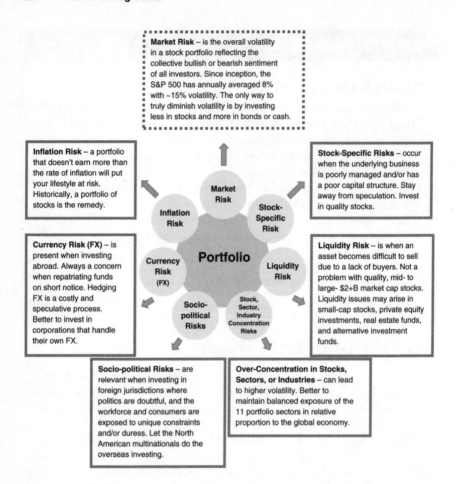

Market Risk – is the overall volatility in a stock portfolio reflecting the collective bullish or bearish sentiment of all investors. Since inception, the S&P 500 has annually averaged 8% with ~15% volatility. The only way to truly diminish volatility is by investing less in stocks and more in bonds or cash.

Inflation Risk – a portfolio that doesn't earn more than the rate of inflation will put your lifestyle at risk. Historically, a portfolio of stocks is the remedy.

Stock-Specific Risks – occur when the underlying business is poorly managed and/or has a poor capital structure. Stay away from speculation. Invest in quality stocks.

Currency Risk (FX) – is present when investing abroad. Always a concern when repatriating funds on short notice. Hedging FX is a costly and speculative process. Better to invest in corporations that handle their own FX.

Liquidity Risk – is when an asset becomes difficult to sell due to a lack of buyers. Not a problem with quality, mid- to large- $2+B market cap stocks. Liquidity issues may arise in small-cap stocks, private equity investments, real estate funds, and alternative investment funds.

Socio-political Risks – are relevant when investing in foreign jurisdictions where politics are doubtful, and the workforce and consumers are exposed to unique constraints and/or duress. Let the North American multinationals do the overseas investing.

Over-Concentration in Stocks, Sectors, or Industries – can lead to higher volatility. Better to maintain balanced exposure of the 11 portfolio sectors in relative proportion to the global economy.

Figure 22.1   Various sources of portfolio volatility.

to average down will make the greatest gains (ignoring the short sellers, who thrive on a "glass half empty" philosophy). Therefore, it's a matter of perspective. The decision to succeed during a market sell-off starts long before the next correction.

Buying devalued stocks during a market correction is like buying distressed real estate. Most of us fantasize about the opportunity to buy high-quality properties at discounts but when all properties are under duress and you have no cash, the situation is irrelevant. Wishful thinking but bad planning. A current market discount (and likely illiquidity) prevents us from extricating our capital from an existing property to make a bid on other discounted properties.

On the other hand, the stock market has three inherent but underappreciated traits:

1. In the short term, the market is highly volatile.
2. In the long term, the market is highly predictable.
3. At all times the market adjusts to create liquidity.

Second-to-second price changes allow us to grow accustomed to some volatility and accept it because the market holds an inherently positive bias (historically, it rises annually 74% of the time). However, during sell-offs, the majority of investors retreat. What may have been a correction of market fundamentals becomes a behavioral stampede. As the crowd capitulates, most stocks suffer, even the very best.

Opportunity knocks.

Mental Preparation

With the stock market going into distress on average every 20–24 months, an investor can plan around this cyclicality more easily than they can for the real estate markets whose cycle can last up to 20 years. Those who can look through the panic to see the opportunity likely already:

1. Trust the resiliency of the markets.
2. Hold conviction in quality investments.
3. Have confidence in their risk management plan.
4. Have prepared their portfolio.

"Rounding Up the Camels"

A diversified portfolio of quality stocks that is being mindfully managed is a solid beginning. Here are another seven proactive measures in preparation for the next upheaval:

1. **Lower the Portfolio's Beta (<1.0)** – A portfolio with a beta greater than 1.0 is likely to react more violently during volatility. Beta figures for individual stocks and the weighted average for the portfolio are available on your trading platform.
   - Trim exposure to high-performance stocks – They may be amongst your favorites but are equally likely to be leaders to the downside.

- Tilt exposure from cyclical sectors (Technology, Commodities, Consumer Discretionary, Industrials, Financials) toward more defensive sectors (Telecom, Health Care, Utilities, Pipelines, Real Estate, Consumer Staples).
- Close out ITM put contracts – Selling put contracts is leverage. Close out positions that are now sitting profitable. The best time to redeploy leverage is during market sell-offs.
- Reduce or eliminate peripheral, non-core assets (e.g. small caps, foreign stocks, IPOs, leveraged ETFs, etc.).

2. **Confirm Diversification:**
   - Ensure non-duplication of the 69 industries.
   - Verify that stock correlations are acceptable – Use the Auto-Correlation Platform to compare and remove correlations higher than +0.6 (which is lower than the usually acceptable +0.8).

3. **Deploy Covered Calls for More Cash** – Sell monthly OTM covered call contracts (or slightly longer since sell-offs can endure for extended periods) to generate income for the portfolio. CCs also help to dampen volatility since the sale of call contracts is pre-selling growth from the portfolio. Ordinarily, the target is to sell deltas of .20 or less. In anticipation of a market correction, consider selling lower strike prices with a higher delta (.35+). This will produce more income.

    However, if there were no ensuing correction and the underlying stock prices continued to rise, CCs with higher deltas (lower strike prices) could now be vulnerable to being exercised. Yet, even if any contracts were to be exercised and the underlying stocks removed from the portfolio, new positions can be reintroduced through any of the methods discussed in Chapter 14 (i.e. lump-sum, DCA, selling put contracts). An inconvenience but not critical.

4. **Raise Cash and Margin/Debt Reserves** – At the top of a market, when the popular stocks are making new daily highs, eliminate all debts and keep building cash. Cash and debt reserves are powerful strategic advantages to hold during market pullbacks. Chapter 18 outlines cash-raising techniques.

5. **Set TSL Orders to Preserve Gains** – To protect some capital gains, set a series of TSL orders at 5% (investor's discretion) intervals totaling up to 25% of a stock's value (investor's discretion). Each TSL order will trail along behind an advancing stock until triggered by a market pullback. If untriggered, when a stock's price rises further, so will TSL orders continue to advance.

- Only set a TSL order once a stock position has been fully invested up to the portfolio average and is profitable. Until then, while still in the allocation process, use DCA to continue lowering a stock's ACB on price weakness.
- Set the TSL trade for perpetuity by selecting "GTC" (good 'til canceled) and selecting "RTH" (fill outside of regular trading hours). This was also mentioned in Chapter 14. Earnings reports and material event announcements are usually made after hours.
- Set a large enough gap between the "stop" and "limit" prices to improve the chance of triggering a trade even if the market suddenly gaps down.

6. **Set SL Orders to Protect Capital** – To protect some of your original capital, set an SL order for as much as 25% of a position (investor's discretion) at a price point above a share's ACB to ensure that at least some of the position will be sold at profit.

    SL and TSL trade orders are potent backstops to protect some of the portfolio's gains and core capital. By proactively setting SL and TSL trade orders, a sudden correction should not require spontaneous trade decisions, and a significant proportion of the core portfolio should be triggered into cash, which should reduce the need for portfolio insurance. The downside is that if SL and TSL trades are set too tight to the current market price, positions may get "stopped out" based on normal volatility rather than a true correction.

7. **Consider Partial Insurance Coverage** (see Chapter 23) – This becomes a discretionary decision if the six risk-reduction measures (above) have been deployed.

By deploying any or all the recommended risk preparation measures, an investor might begin to view a market correction or a bear market more opportunistically. Instead of relying upon gut instinct and market timing, be proactive. By deploying tactics contrarian to the masses, an investor could lessen the overall impact and accelerate their wealth recovery. Table 22.1 identifies the average market recovery periods from the last 74 years. Keep in mind that the greatest market gains are often within days of the worst drawdowns.

Table 22.1   Market mayhem 1946–2020.*

	# of Events	Duration (Avg)	Decline (Avg)	Recovery Time (Avg)
Minor Tremors (5–10%)	80	1 Month	7%	1 Month
Market Corrections (10–20%)	26	4 Months	13.7%	4 Months
Bear Markets (20+%)	12	14.5 Months	32.5%	48 Months

*Statistics provided by Goldman Sachs to CNBC (Accessed 27 September 2021).

Getting Reinvested

Once the "storm" has arrived, the bigger challenges will be deciding when to begin buying stocks, which ones to buy, and using which methods.

When to Buy?

Knowing when a correction has run its course is a judgment based on an ability to interpret human behavior. There are no quantitative fundamentals that can predict the turning point. No investor, no guru, no algorithm has the secret formula. A market bottom is only perfectly known in hindsight.

However, once the market discounts by 20–30+%, the probability of a recovery will have improved dramatically. As identified previously, based on 92 years of data, corrections of 10–20% are twice as frequent as bear markets (20%+). The lemming-like mimicry that triggered the latest stampede will work equally as well during the recovery. As such, reinvesting decisions don't have to be perfect, but they require holding faith that eventually markets will stop sliding and return to a growth trajectory.

A recovery starts when there are fewer sellers and more buyers. Clues that the market may be near a bottom are often contrarian in nature:

- **"Piling on"** – Mainstream media and financial prophets announce that financial Armageddon has arrived with further predictions of never-ending trauma (unemployment skyrocketing, rising bankruptcies, no end in sight, etc.).
- **Multiple stocks hitting 52-week lows** (usually associated with bear markets).

- **Mimicry** – Stocks initially suffer together as investors seek safety. Stand your ground. Equally, the turning point should also be observable when a broad-based recovery takes root across most sectors and indices. This is the rare time when following the crowd has investment merit. But don't be surprised if there are a few "head fakes," where the market appears to have bottomed, only to see a few more days or weeks of weakness. Use the opportunity to buy increments of high-quality stocks well below their recent highs. Don't worry about perfect timing.
- **Depressed core portfolio prices** – When the quality core stocks drop below their ACB prices (breakeven), it is a signal to consider gradually deploying DCA on the more depressed stocks. This will average down the share's ACB. Be persistent during a correction.
- **Follow the contrarians** – By nature, they are bargain hunters. Warren Buffett is known for his prescient calls. There are other notable contrarians,[1] like Michael Lee-Chin, Jim Rogers, and Marc Faber. Check their most recent SEC 10-Q reports.[2] Although filings are well after the fact, they can be relied upon to reveal these bargain hunters' choices. Also, seek out recent media interviews. There are investor sleuths who track the "wise ones" and like to report on their recent investment decisions well before the SEC 10-Q reports are released (see Chapters 8, 14, and 27).
- **Follow the insiders** – Who knows the value of their own corporations better than the management group? History shows that those in the C-suite makes their most significant commitments during sell-offs. Since SEC Form 4 reports are only filed well after the fact, they can be useful to confirm their bottom-picking stock decisions (see Chapters 14 and 27).

Which Stocks to Buy?

Start with your core stocks. Most should have been originally chosen on the merits of their superior business models and long-term promise. A correction has little to do with the worthiness of a particular stock but rather is simply a broad-market price multiple contraction (aka "fear").

---

[1] "Contrarian Investing." Wikipedia, https://en.wikipedia.org/wiki/Contrarian_investing (Accessed 27 September 2021).
[2] U.S. Securities and Exchange Commission. https://www.sec.gov/edgar/searchedgar/companysearch.html (Accessed 27 September 2021).

Before allocating cash, though, differentiate between underweight and underperforming core stocks:

1. **Target underweight stocks.** In an equal-weighted portfolio, these are the stocks that have not yet received their full allocation and are below the portfolio average.

2. **Target underperforming stocks.** These stocks are likely sitting with losses and were already candidates for averaging down via DCA. For the worst performers, research to ensure nothing material has transpired.

Note: If you've grown disillusioned with certain stocks, the time to jettison them from the portfolio is not during a market sell-off. Be patient and sell them on the basis that a rising tide tends to lift all boats. When you've decided to remove a stock from your portfolio, instead of selling them at market prices, consider selling ITM call contracts. This will, at least, generate a little more value from the transaction relative to selling them at current market prices. See Chapter 20.

3. **Consider dream stocks.** If hesitant to invest in certain quality stocks due to excessive valuation metrics, a wholesale market discount is likely the one best opportunity to finally initiate a position. Keep an active watchlist and prioritize a few of them for when the time comes.

Note: Alternatively, if you don't have the cash, consider selling put contracts (see Chapter 19). OTM vs. ATM vs. ITM will depend on your confidence for a recovery and your level of risk tolerance.

Investor Caution

Beware Those Boxing Day Sales!

Think about post-Christmas sales. Before entering a store, a prudent shopper should already know what they want to buy. Yet stores count on customers becoming easily distracted during the crush to buy their overpriced junk.

No matter the bargain basement pricing that a correction brings, it is never a good reason to start introducing lower-quality assets into a portfolio (i.e. IPOs, speculative stocks, foreign stocks, small caps, etc.).

How to Buy during the Market Panic?

This is the one time when "market timing" can be forgiven. With a collapsing market, bad behaviors will be triggered in all directions. Yet, if a disciplined investor is ever going to let their emotions get the better of them, let the emotion be that of "greed" during a correction. It takes guts to buy into a sagging market, but buying quality stocks contrary to the panicking masses has always proven fruitful.

- **Lump sum** – Investing lump sum is usually the better way to buy stocks during a wholesale market discount. However, trying to time a market bottom with a large sum may lead to "buyer's remorse." The bottom may take several weeks to form. Ensure your conviction is solid enough to hold through any further price weakness.
- **DCA** – Alternatively, deploying DCA allows for price-averaging and diminishment of "buyer's remorse." Don't worry that prices continue to fall. Once the market has peeled back by 20+%, the odds are highly favorable that a recovery is closer at hand.
- **Leverage (for experienced investors only)** – If lacking cash, consider selling longer-term put contracts on a broad market ETF. The seller receives a cash premium and pays no interest costs. Be mindful not to exceed your margin capacity.

Storm: Post-Mortem

As in earthquake preparedness, a little pre-planning can save a lot of grief. Imagine living in California perpetually awaiting the "big one" but never seriously preparing for it. Even small market tremors can be valuable learning opportunities.

With an equal-weighted portfolio, it's easier to observe and compare the performance characteristics of individual stocks, side by side, across all 11 sectors. Some stocks may have been more highly correlated than anticipated. Some may have revealed themselves to be hedges. So, post-event is the opportunity to evaluate the entire risk management plan. After all, reducing the impact of a market pullback is the entire reason for having a risk management plan.

Portfolio:
- Was the asset mix appropriate?
- Did the TSL and SL trade orders trigger?
  - If not, should the gap between the "stop" and "limit" prices be larger?

- Likely all stocks suffered. Review those which struggled the most.
  - Did the high-beta stocks recover as expected?
  - Have any positions now become value stocks (remained at a discount)?
  - Did research discover any material issues?
- Was cash deployed to average down on core stocks?
- With the recovery, have the overweight positions now been trimmed back?
- How effective was the diversification?
  - Which sectors performed best/worst?
  - Should the sector weights be revised? (Too much technology?)

Portfolio Leverage:
- Was leverage deployed (broad market ETF)?
- Was it unwound upon recovery?

Portfolio Protection:
- Was some form of protection able to be initiated? (See Chapter 23.)
- Was the portfolio protection able to be unwound at profit?
- Were the outstanding CCs bought back at profit?

Personal:
- Were you as risk tolerant as initially thought?
- Was this a "wake-up call" to adjust the asset mix?
- How would you do things differently?

Like earthquakes, corrections arrive suddenly, wreak havoc and can be outright exhausting. Yet, market selloffs are also the single best opportunity to make financial gains relative to world at large. But it requires pre-planning and some courage to act.

At the bottom of the market, the media noise will be loudest, and your guts will feel their queasiest, yet these are the clear signals of opportunity. Since every market downturn has been followed by a new record upturn, makes corrections a false torment. The sun will shine again.

Once the torrent has passed, an honest self-assessment should help to both strengthen your risk management plan and reinforce your gumption to take action. Being prepared would be the better practice.

The nomad's confidence to withstand nature's ferocity lies in their knowledge, their planning, and the preparations before the storm has arrived. Ultimately, their trust is in the herd.

Plan well, batten down the camels, and when the storm arrives, take shelter. The sun will shine again.

> *"The key to making money in stocks is not to get scared out of them."*
> —Peter Lynch,
> ex-Magellan fund manager,
> Fidelity Investments

At the Oasis: Chapter 22

- A correction is simply the market purging the weak. Don't be one of them.
- Volatility is the constant agitated state of the markets. It's always there. How an investor reacts is a function of their preparation and discipline to stay on course.
- Real risk is losing capital permanently, whether investing in a lousy business, choosing speculative assets, or undisciplined trading. These decisions are in your control.
- Market timing requires four near-perfect decisions. Skip selling. Be a hero and buy more.
- Buying during the mayhem is the best opportunity to build wealth. Follow the insiders.
- Market bottoms are only known in hindsight. The wise invest because they have faith in the markets and understand how panic blinds the masses.
- Prepare for the big one but live for the little things.

Source: https://www.crushthestreet.com/articles/precious-metals/
a-bull-market-and-the-bear-dow-and-sp-500-technical-analysis-part-2

Chapter 23

Portfolio Protection

危机

Danger + Opportunity

Objective:

Profiting from panic.

T he Chinese symbol for "crisis" is a combination of danger and opportunity. It fittingly describes how to approach portfolio protection.

"Within danger, there lie opportunities."

—Confucius

No one knows when the next big "storm" is coming. However, having already reviewed and prepared your portfolio as per Chapter 22 should reduce the impact when it does.

The next step will be to introduce several insurance techniques for those seeking to partially protect the remainder of their portfolio. After all, financial progress can also be measured by losing less than the rest when the "storm" arrives.

Market Corrections/Bear Markets

Every 20–24 months, on average, markets purge weak businesses and vulnerable investors. This is a very necessary part of a healthy market. Unfortunately, diversification alone offers only modest relief since stock prices tend to be highly correlated during such events. Instead, deploying timely portfolio insurance could help to counter a sudden market swoon.

Corrections – Market discounts of 10–20% averaging one every 33 months. They are typically short in duration (usually weeks) and often quickly overcome by the advancing market.

Bear Markets – Discounts upwards of 20% occurring once every 4.3 years on average. They tend to endure 18–36 months as corporations recalibrate their business practices to accommodate prevailing macroeconomic challenges.

Between the two, however, significant market tumult averages once every 20–24 months.

Portfolio Insurance 101

Insurance is the last line of defense in this guide's comprehensive 16-Step Risk Management Plan. Like all insurance products, a fee is to be paid to a third party to absorb a risk over a select period. Setting up effective protection should allow a portfolio to remain relatively intact through the tumult.

The risk/reward profile for protection should be asymmetrical. This means that the probability for profit should well exceed the cost of the insurance. As in home insurance, a homeowner should only expect to pay a modest annual premium for gaining substantial coverage. Equally, if a market pullback does not transpire, the insurance product will expire worthless. Such is the nature of insurance. Yet, to keep a portfolio constantly and fully insured would be too costly, so discretion is required for how much and when to apply it. Several cost reduction methods will be introduced further below.

Overall, since market corrections arrive with little warning, it pays to heed the warning signals. Just as leverage should only be considered seriously at the bottom of a market swoon, so should insurance be taken more seriously at the top of a market when stocks and the market are hitting all-time highs.

RMP #15: Profiting from the Panic

Reasons Not to Hedge

To be fair, there are several reasons not to attempt hedging a portfolio:

- **Already well prepare.** Since market corrections or bear markets are relatively short-lived if the portfolio is well designed and a risk plan is being followed, does it really matter what happens in the short term to the exposed portion of your portfolio?
- **Deploying insurance is reverse market timing.** To profit from market volatility requires investors to proactively initiate a hedge, followed by a timely exit at the height of fear to secure profits. These two decisions require instinct, discipline, and courage.
- **Dr. Jekyll (the short seller) and Dr. Jekyll (the day trader).** Deploying insurance requires an entirely different psyche. Corrections arrive dramatically and last for relatively short periods. This requires the instincts and gumption of both a short seller and a day trader. There is no room for Mr. Hyde in these decisions. Even the most experienced investors have self-doubts during heightened volatility.
- **Costs.** Portfolio insurance has costs and a limited life. If volatility does not materialize, the insurance will lapse. Ongoing costs directly impact portfolio performance. Finding effective, low-cost, enduring insurance is highly unlikely.

> *"More money has been lost trying to protect from corrections than is actually lost in a sell-off."*
>
> —Peter Lynch,
> ex-Magellan Fund manager, Fidelity Investments

- **Potential hedge mismatch.** Even a well-planned and constructed hedge may not perform as expected.
- **Stock markets are resilient.** To collect on home insurance, an owner would expect to suffer a catastrophic financial and personal loss. No one should expect to be fully compensated for their losses or for the tremendous inconvenience.

With stock market sell-offs, however, real losses are only suffered if we lose our composure and sell into the ensuing panic. Historically, all downturns have proven to be just temporary inconveniences. If an investor practices prudent risk management and can be patient during the tumult, they could save on buying insurance.

WISDOM

Which Should You Insure?

A.   Imagine owning a $200,000 Mercedes AMG GT R (Coupe). Pure adrenaline!

B.   Now, think about handling a $200,000 stock portfolio. Not likely as much fun.

Q: Which one needs protection?

When a portfolio is poorly designed and comprised of speculative securities and leverage, insurance should be required. A single market correction could wipe out substantial value. On the other hand, a prudently designed portfolio comprised of quality securities may never require insurance despite incurring an "incident" every 20–24 months. Historically, the markets have always been resilient for those owning quality assets.

Meanwhile, just one accident could render your Mercedes useless. While we are legally required to insure our vehicle, many will "drive" their portfolio like a sports car yet pamper their sports car like it was uninsured.

The Merits of Insurance

Reasons why an investor may consider insuring their portfolio:

- **To protect embedded capital gains** (not wanting to crystallize existing capital gains).
- **To offset the risk of a poorly diversified portfolio** (i.e. overweight in stocks, industries, or sectors).
- **To offset the risk of owning speculative securities** (not wanting to sell high-risk positions).
- **To protect against getting a margin call.**
- **Behavioral reinforcement.** When the markets enter a corrective phase, active investors likely feel compelled to act. However, if they have proactively deployed portfolio protection, an investor's behavior could be calmed from making otherwise unnecessary and, likely, adverse trades knowing they have some degree of protection in place.
- **As a discretionary market timing opportunity.** Unlike with a home, portfolio insurance is a capitalist opportunity to gain from both insurance restitution and a rebound rally in your portfolio.

Insurance Decisions

Since portfolio insurance is discretionary, each investor will have different ideas about what type, how much, and when to apply insurance.

| **Note:** The terms "insurance," "hedging," and "protection" are used synonymously.

How Much Insurance Is Enough?

Since applying portfolio protection is an expensive proposition, the goal should be to find ways to reduce risk rather than attempt to eliminate it.

> *"An ounce of prevention is worth a pound of cure."*
> —Benjamin Franklin (1706–1790),
> Founding Father of the United States of America
> (Ben Franklin coined this phrase in 1736 to remind the
> citizens of Philadelphia to remain vigilant about fire
> awareness and prevention.)

Investors heeding Ben Franklin's advice should already have their diversification and protection strategies in place. As the market sells off, preset defensive TSL and SL orders should have been triggered and covered calls should have turned profitable. In combination with any initial cash reserves, up to 20–50% of the portfolio could now be liquid at the early stage of a market pullback. For the remaining equity exposure, it is a personal decision just how much coverage to apply. Trying to hedge the remaining equity would be too costly, as would trying to protect your portfolio for extended periods.

Since the cost of protection is directly deductible from a portfolio's total performance, target the annual cost of protection at 1%, or less, of a portfolio's total value. Since the duration and amounts of insurance can vary dramatically over the course of a year, it is more feasible to suggest an insurance budget than to try to identify an amount of coverage. Once again, since markets have always recovered and insurance is entirely discretionary, target lower-cost solutions.

Hedging Cost Reductions

There are already several real ways to reduce the costs of protection:

- Reduce the amount of equity exposure in the portfolio through more stringent, preset SL and TSL trade orders.
- Hedge only a portion of the remaining equity exposure (15–25% – investor's choice). Less coverage equals less cost.
- Introduce a deductible on the hedge. Since ordinary market volatility frequently ranges up to 10–15% each year, set the deductible

at 15%. This would mean targeting to protect more against a potential bear market (beyond 20%) than trying to protect against ordinary volatility. This deductible is the same as for car or home insurance policies. The higher the deductible, the lower the premiums. An example will be provided below.

- Subsidize protection costs by selling off higher unnecessary coverage. After all, markets only ever sell off so far before stabilizing and then staging a recovery. An example will be provided below.
- When protection can be unwound profitably, the 1% insurance budget starts fresh.

When Best to Deploy a Hedge?

How good are you at predicting corrections? Since a significant market event happens on average every 20–24 months, the probability of a setback increases the longer the stock market advances without having incurred a substantive correction.

For example, the longest bull market in history (March 2009 to March 2020) ended with the fastest bear market in history (–33.8% in four weeks). However, if an investor had begun deploying portfolio insurance 24 months after the end of the global financial crisis (March 2011), they would have spent a modest fortune waiting nine years for the next significant pullback (March 2020). Deploying protection too soon can be as equally costly as deploying too late (expensive premiums). The forecasting tools in Chapter 21 can help to build awareness of when to begin establishing protection even if just gradually. But the timing ultimately comes down to gut judgment.

Being a Contrarian

For the average investor, the best time to deploy insurance is when markets are bumping along near record highs and yet while volatility remains calm. This is likely the time a portfolio would be most vulnerable. However, protection may also be considered at any stage of the market if an investor is vulnerable due to idiosyncratic portfolio construction (high leverage, holding speculative securities, imbalanced positions, low margin capacity, etc.). The solutions in Table 23.1 are intended to counter undesirable volatility incurred at the latter stage of the economic cycle.

Four Hedging Solutions

At the best of times, it is difficult to know when the markets will go into correction mode. Although there are many hedging tools available, Table 23.1 presents two short-term solutions and two medium-term solutions. Since there are trade-offs with each one, protection solutions can be tailored by the investor. Hedges involving leveraged ETFs have not been considered.

All the better if protection can be set up in advance, but if the market roils and catches you off guard, the first two solutions can be quickly deployed.

Table 23.1 Temporary and structured insurance solutions.

Temporary Solutions		Duration	Process	Impact Ratio	Cost	Cost Offsets
1	Shorting the Market	Days	• Buy the SPDN ETF to offset a falling S&P 500	1 × Market	MER of the ETF	None
2	Buying Short-Term Volatility	Days	• Buy the VXX ETN to gain from rising volatility	Multiplied Response	MER of the ETN	None
Structured Solutions						
3	Bear Put Spread	Weeks/ Months	• Buy protective puts on the SPY ETF • Sell OTM puts (cost recovery)	1 × Market (but Capped Returns)	Net Cost of Premiums	One
4	VIX Call Spread Collar ("Fence")	Months	• Buy OTM calls • Sell deep OTM calls (cost recovery) • Sell deep OTM puts (cost recovery)	Multiplied Response (but Capped Returns)	Net Cost of Premiums	Two

1. Shorting the Market

If caught in a market sell-off, portfolio protection can be quickly established by buying units in the Daily S&P 500 Bear ETF (SPDN), an inverse ETF offered by Direxion. An investor would be shorting the market (1×). This provides immediate protection; however, returns are symmetrical. When the market begins to rebound, an investor could be exposed to unlimited losses as the market rises.

After buying the SPDN, to prevent unlimited losses, place a trailing stop-loss order (TSL) a few percentage points below the buy-in price (5–10%). As the ETF (exchange-traded fund) price rises (note that a "bear" ETF moves inversely to the direction of the market), this TSL will follow the ETF higher until triggered on a price pullback. During market tumult, the market (and this ETF) will move quickly. This TSL should lock in profitability but would keep rising if the market continues to sell off.

Pros
- Highly liquid.
- Easily deployed.
- Moves symmetrically but inversely with the S&P 500 Index (one to one).
- Low cost (MER + trading commissions)
- Behaviorally, for an optimistic investor, it is easier to buy protection than to sell an asset to achieve protection.

Cons
- Only provides protection equal to 1× the market.
- Unlimited loss potential when the S&P 500 Index recovers. Use stop-loss orders to prevent runaway losses.
- Due to product design challenges, a position should not be held overnight. This product requires daily timing in and out.

2. Buying Short-Term Volatility

An alternative to selling the market short, portfolio protection can also be quickly established by buying units in the iPath S&P 500 VIX Short-Term Futures ETN (VXX). The appeal is the multiplied response to volatility. For example, during the Great COVID Crisis in March 2020, while the S&P 500 Index declined by 32%, the VXX rose 400%. Once the position is opened, set a TSL sell order 20% below the trading price (due to high volatility) to lock in gains as it rises and to prevent unlimited losses when volatility calms.

Pros
- Highly liquid.
- Easily deployed.
- Expect a substantial multiplier effect when volatility spikes.
- May exhibit a positive response even if volatility is due to a suddenly rising market.
- Low cost (MER + trading commissions).

Cons
- Unlimited loss potential when volatility settles down. Use stop-loss orders to prevent runaway losses.

- This product requires timing in and out. A position in the VXX ETN should not be held open for more than a few days due to a constant deterioration in the underlying futures contracts. The VXX ETN declines on average by 54% each year.

3. Bear Put Spread (BPS)

Even if a sell-off has begun, a bear put spread could provide immediate coverage. Protection can be instituted by buying ATM put contracts on the SPY ETF. A cost offset can then be deployed by simultaneously selling the same number of OTM SPY ETF put contracts with the same maturity date. The premiums received will partially offset the cost of buying the protective puts.

Since the SPY ETF replicates the S&P 500 Index, as the stock market declines, an ATM put contract should rise "dollar for dollar" against the market decline. However, selling lower-priced OTM put contracts for the premiums will constrain profitability. Once the SPY ETF reaches the value of the lower-priced put contract, there will be no further hedging value to be gained. An investor should then unwind this bear put spread. Mission accomplished.

To further lower the cost of protection, an investor could buy OTM SPY protective puts. Since protection would only commence at a lower price point, this would be termed the "deductible." The lower the OTM, the lower the cost of the premium. Cost-offset put contracts would also have a lower strike price and therefore would generate an even lower cost-offset premium.

To deploy a "Fence", four decisions are required:

   i. Choosing the Duration
  ii. Choosing the Number of Contracts
 iii. Choosing the Strike Price for the Protective Put Contract (ATM or OTM)
  iv. Choosing the Strike Price for the Cost-Offset OTM Put Contract

i. Choosing the Duration   The length of a contract depends on whether the market sell-off is likely to be short, medium, or longer term. The BPS can be set up for most any time frame. However, usually investors are concerned about the near term, so installing protection for several weeks up to a month would be reasonable. Both contracts (protection and cost offset) should have the same maturity dates. For this example, the contracts will have a duration of 29 days.

ii. Choosing the Number of Contracts   Since insurance protection is discretionary, unless there is some mitigating purpose, don't try to insure more than 25% of the value of your equity positions in the portfolio. Target to keep the cost of coverage below 1% of the total value of your portfolio.

$$\text{\# of SPY contracts required} = \frac{\text{Amount of portfolio to be insured}}{(\text{ATM SPY price}) \times (\text{delta of the ATM SPY}) \times 100}$$

To determine the number of contracts required, divide the desired amount of coverage by the current price of the ATM SPY contract times the delta of that contract times 100 (each contract represents 100 shares). The delta of the SPY contract represents the sensitivity of the change in the SPY price to a change in the actual SPY ETF. As the market sells off, the SPY put contract price should rise by the degree of delta. The following example should provide clarity.

Example:
Value of portfolio = $200,000
Amount of protection desired = $50,000 (= 25% × $200,000)
ATM SPY = $385
ATM SPY delta = .48 (ignore the negative sign with put contracts) = $385

$$\text{\# of SPY contracts} = \frac{\$50,000}{\$385 \times 48 \times 100} = 2.70 \text{ contracts (round up to 3)}$$

iii. Choosing the Strike Price for the Protective Put Contract (ATM or OTM)
Buying ATM SPY Put contracts offers immediate portfolio protection. However, an investor could reduce their costs by buying a slightly OTM SPY Put contract. This would be similar to introducing a deductible on your home insurance. This would effectively reduce the premium to be paid.

iv. Choosing the Strike Price of a Cost-Offset OTM Put Contract   The difference in strike price between buying the ATM put contract (for protection) and selling the OTM contract (as a cost offset) reflects how much of a market pullback an investor desires to cover. In our example, if we desire to insure for a correction of up to 10%, the offset SPY put contract should be 10% further OTM. With the protective SPY strike price at $385, the cost offset SPY strike price would be $348 (90% of $385).

Net Results (no deductible):

- Premium to buy ATM August 17, 2022 (29 days) $385 SPY puts = $9.60/contract
- Premium to sell OTM August 17, 2022 (29 days) $348 SPY puts = $1.40/contract

Cost of hedge = 3 contracts @$9.60/contract = $2,880
Cost offset = 3 contracts @ $1.40/contract = $420
Net cost = $2,460

To insure $50,000 of portfolio value against a 10% market decline for 29 days using a bear put spread would cost the investor $2,460. This is 1.23% of the value of a $200,000 portfolio.

If the market sells off by more than 10%, the investor should unwind the two positions (protective put and the cost offset put) because the maximum gain will have been achieved. Consider setting the offset at differing degrees of discounts (20%, 30%) to see how much the offset premium changes. However, with rising markets, the rise in the value of the portfolio should more than compensate for lost insurance costs. Short-term insurance always runs the risk of poor timing. For more enduring insurance coverage, consider setting up a VIX call spread collar, also known as a "fence."

Notes:

- To further conserve on insurance costs, choose an OTM SPY strike price and an even lower cost offset SPY strike price. This is building in a deductible. In exchange for absorbing more of a discount before the insurance coverage kicks in, the cost of coverage will be reduced relative to immediate coverage using an ATM SPY strike price.
- Portfolio Armor[1] is a business that uses proprietary algorithms to discover the most economical put contracts. For investors with larger portfolios, their service could be valuable. A subscription is required.

4. VIX Call Spread Collar (Fence)

The VIX Index reveals the state of fear in the general market. The highly volatile VIX is a hedge favored by professionals due to its strong negative correlation with the S&P 500.

A "fence" provides protection while mitigating costs and can be set up to create protection over an enduring period (a ladder series presented further below). It is best deployed during calm markets and particularly near market tops.

Don't let the name dissuade you. Although setting up a fence involves multiple steps, the logic is straightforward and should appeal to conservative, risk-conscious investors. When volatility strikes, for a little bit of coverage, the results from this protection can be outsized.

The following data points for the VIX Index from Figure 23.1 form the basis of the fence hedging strategy:

18   Long-term VIX average (dotted line)
10   Lowest range of volatility[2]
10–15 Reflects relative market calm

---

[1]https://portfolioarmor.com/how-it-works-hedged-portfolios.
[2]According to data provided from the CBOE on the Macroption website: https://www.macroption.com/vix-all-time-low/#close.

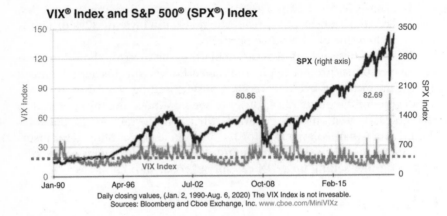

Figure 23.1   VIX Index vs. S&P 500 Index.
Source: Bloomberg and CBOE Exchange, Inc.

20–30   Represents most common range of volatility
30–40   Signals a potential market correction
40+   Signals a potential bear market

Setting Up a VIX Call Spread Collar (Fence)
1. **Buy VIX call contracts** – Primary protection. The negative correlation of the VIX with the S&P 500 and the outsized reaction to volatility offer potent insurance for a portfolio. As the market calms, premiums for VIX contracts decline. Consider deploying the first phase of this protection when the VIX falls below 16.
   • **Maturity Date Choice** (duration of coverage): As in any insurance, the longer the term, the higher the cost. Also, the longer the maturity date, the less effective will be the protection against near-term volatility. Consider 1–3 months ahead.
   • **Strike Price Choice:** An OTM strike price is like the deductible of an insurance plan. Protection is not usually profitable until the VIX rises above the call strike price. The choice of a strike price therefore will depend on how much of a discount an investor is willing to absorb before netting profits. Although higher strike prices are cheaper, if the bar is set too high, it reduces the probability of success (if the VIX does not rise up and beyond the chosen strike price). Since markets naturally gyrate 10–15% annually, consider a strike price 15–20% above the current VIX price (i.e. VIX of 19–22). The idea is to install insurance to cover against a future major correction and not to worry about lesser degrees of volatility.

Table 23.2 offers an example how to calculate an appropriate number of VIX contracts to create a partial or a full hedge.

Once protection is purchased, the portfolio is now partially protected. However, the following two steps will help offset some of the cost of this protection.

2. **Cost Offset #1 – Selling deep OTM puts**[3] (between VIX 9 to 13) – Premiums earned from this sale will offset some of the cost of buying the OTM VIX calls for protection. Use the same maturity date as the original protection.

   During turbulence, as markets fall and the VIX rises, the value of these VIX put contracts will decline. In the limited time until maturity (1–3 months), if volatility remains stable or even increases, these put contracts would expire worthless.

   Higher offset premiums could even be generated by selling put strike prices closer to the current VIX spot (current) price. However, this increases the chance that a calming market might render these strike prices to be ITM (in the money). If so, then this cost would be included in assessing the overall cost of your risk management plan. Historically, the VIX rarely falls under 10; therefore, VIX contracts sold below 13 are more likely to expire unexercised, particularly during periods of heightened volatility.

3. **Cost Offset #2 – Sell deeper**[4] **OTM calls** – By selling OTM VIX call contracts that are higher (deeper) than the OTM VIX call protection contracts (as outlined in step 1, above), the premiums received help to further offset the cost of the original protection. Since the VIX rarely peaks above 30 and even less frequently above 40, it follows that paying for protection above 30 would not be good value for the few times that it might be profitable. Therefore, consider selling the deeper OTM contracts at 5–10 VIX points higher than the long OTM VIX calls with the same maturity date. This cost-offset tactic does not introduce any additional risks. However, when volatility strikes, the potential gains will be limited to the net spread between the long and the short strike prices.

   A wider spread between the long and short VIX calls will increase the reward potential when volatility strikes. However, this will reduce the overall subsidy. On the other hand, a narrower spread will reduce the total cost of protection due to the higher offset premium but will also reduce the potential rewards generated when volatility spikes.

   Over the longer term, receiving premiums for selling off the gain potential above VIX 30 should be considered more valuable as a cost offset than the concern about missing out on the upside of a rare jump in the VIX above 30.

---

[3]Deep OTM puts refer to contracts at lower strike prices than the current (spot) VIX price.

[4]Deeper, in this context, refers to contracts sold at higher strike prices than those of the long VIX calls protection.

Secrets at the Oasis

Self-Funding Protection

Once the OTM VIX call contracts have been bought for protection and OTM put contracts have been sold as the first cost offset, you're protected but not quite finished. An investor now has a discretionary decision when to sell the second cost offset deeper OTM VIX call options.

While buying the base protection is best done when the VIX is falling (markets are rising), the best time to sell offsetting OTM VIX calls is when the VIX is rising (markets falling). This is because the premiums for these OTM VIX calls will be rising and becoming more valuable. By owning OTM VIX calls, the portfolio is protected, yet by delaying the sale of the deeper VIX call contracts, the investor stands to receive higher premiums, and possibly high enough to cover the cost of the original protection.

Since spikes in the VIX can be very brief, selling deeper OTM VIX calls usually needs to be done quickly. When the offset premiums generated equal or exceed the cost of the premiums spent on protection, the insurance becomes self-funding.

The caveat is that if volatility remains subdued up to the maturity date, there may never be a chance to sell higher VIX calls to offset the original VIX call protection. As such, the cost of this round of protection would be unsubsidized.

4. **Laddering** – Rather than invoking all protection in a single month, consider setting up a series (ladder) of smaller equal monthly fences. As each fence matures, they can be rolled over to a longer maturity. This creates enduring, low-cost coverage for as long as appropriate.
5. **Realization of Gains** – If volatility remains relatively dormant, the nearest term portion of the ladder may simply expire. This is a cost of insurance. However, when volatility spikes above the strike price of the deeper short VIX calls, a fence will have reached its maximum gain and should be unwound. The maximum gain will be the spread difference between the long and short strike prices of the vertical call contracts less the net costs of setup.
6. **Reinstating Coverage** – Once gains have been realized on your hedge, reinstate coverage only after the VIX calms again back below 18. This could take weeks or months because market-based fear does not dissipate easily.

Example:
Setting Up a VIX Call Spread Collar (Fence)
(Adjust the numbers to suit any size of portfolio.)

Scenario:
- A $200,000 portfolio of 30 North American stocks.
- The portfolio beta[5] is 1.
- The VIX is relatively calm (16), and the markets are hitting record highs.
- Plan to hedge 15% ($30,000) of the portfolio.
- Deductible of 20%. (Market must fall by more than 20% before the fence becomes profitable.)

Setup:
- Date: August 31, 2021.
- The S&P 500 Index is 4534.
- The VIX is 16. A 20% insurance deductible would be the VIX at 19 (=16 × 120%)
  - i.   Buy Oct 19 VIX calls with a strike price of $20, priced @ $5.00.
  - ii. Sell Oct 19 VIX puts with a strike price of $13, priced @ $0.50.
  - iii. Sell Oct 19 VIX calls with a strike price of $25 priced @ $2.25.

Q: How many VIX calls are required to provide $30,000 of coverage? (See Table 23.2.)

Historically, a 10% drop in the S&P 500 produces an approximate 40–50% rise in the VIX. Higher volatility tends to cause even more pronounced spikes in the VIX. High liquidity and the multiplier effect are two strong reasons why professionals prefer to use the VIX for hedging. Table 23.2 is an example of setting up a VIX call spread collar (a fence).

---

[5]A portfolio with a beta of 1 suggests that its volatility profile is similar to the market (S&P 500). This allows protection to be set up on a one-to-one basis.

Table 23.2 Setting up a VIX call spread collar (fence).

		Data/Formulae	15% Hedge
A	Total Portfolio		$200,000
B	% Portfolio to Be Hedged	15%	$ 30,000
C	Expected VIX Rise	40%	
D	VIX Contract Value Required	B/(1 + C) =	$ 21,429
E	Strike Price of Protection (Long Calls)	$20	
F	Options Contract Multiplier	100	
G	**# Call Contracts Required** (rounded up)	D/(E × F) =	**11**
H	**$ Expected Recovery**	B–D =	**$8,571**
I	**% Recovery of Expected Total Loss**	H/D × 100 =	**40%**
	Calculation of Total Cost of Hedge		
J	Cost of 11 Long OTM VIX 20 Calls	$5.00/contract × G × F	– $ 5,500
K	Offset Premiums from 11 Short OTM VIX 13 Puts	$0.50/contract × G × F	$ 550
L	Offset Premiums from 11 Short OTM VIX 25 Calls	$2.25/contract × G × F	$ 2,475
M	**$ Net Cost of Hedge**	J + K + L =	**$ 2,475**
	% Net Cost of Hedge	M/A × 100=	**1.25%**

Note: Hedging can be increased incrementally. For example, to hedge 30% of the portfolio would simply require double the number of contracts of a 15% hedge.

Pros
- VIX contracts are highly liquid.
- Offers a strong negative correlation to a portfolio of NA growth stocks.
- Can be set up piecemeal during periods of calm.
- Can be set up to cover an enduring period (1–3 months) and can be rolled over on maturity.
- The fence has an asymmetric reward/risk profile. When triggered, the potential profits should far outweigh the net cost of the setup.
- Deploying all legs of the fence provides a cost-effective hedge.
- Using discretion to delay the sale of the second cost offset during a period of heightened volatility could help to neutralize the total hedging costs.

Cons
- Call contracts can expire worthless if the markets remain calm.
- Selling OTM VIX calls will cap the total profit potential to the net difference between the short and long OTM VIX calls.

- If the market were to be unusually calm, resulting in the VIX falling below the OTM put strike price, the contract would be settled in cash at maturity. This would increase the overall cost of protection.
- Don't attempt to set up a protective fence during active market corrections. The spike in VIX option prices will be cost-prohibitive. Instead, consider either of the short-term protection methods, #1 or #2, above.

Profiting from Panic

As is true of any market timing tactic, hedging a portfolio requires gut judgment, courage, and two sets of decisions to render success.

Once a hedge turns profitable, place a TSL order to protect some of the gains until it reaches maximum profit (when the VIX rises up to the strike price of the short OTM VIX call). When triggered, unwind all associated cost-offset positions.

By the time markets have recovered, your portfolio protection should have been unwound at profit. Equally, hopefully much of your cash reserve should also have been deployed to rebalance your core portfolio. These activities are coincidental and require the same gut instincts and courage to implement. Yet it takes time in the markets and personal gumption to win the day. However, if you feel you missed this market timing opportunity, not to worry. The markets have always recovered from history's traumas. So, setting up portfolio protection should be purely a discretionary decision and a function of portfolio construction specific to the individual.

A Risk Management Plan

Having a plan may seem irrelevant when everything is going well. But just wait until it isn't. On average, "Mr. Market" likes to remind us about every 20–24 months. By embracing the 16-Step Risk Management Plan, both your portfolio and you will be better prepared to handle the market tumult. The pyramid in Figure 23.2 reflects the progressive role each layer plays in helping to protect your wealth. As identified in the adaption of Morgan Housel's investor hierarchy in Chapter 1, success of the whole is requisite on mastering each step before tackling the next level.

During times of turmoil, those who are better prepared and are willing to step forward when all others run away stand to make the greatest gains.

> *"In many ways, the stock market is like the weather; if you don't like the current conditions, all you have to do is wait a while."*
>
> —Lou Simpson,
> ex-CIO, Geico Insurance (1979–2010)

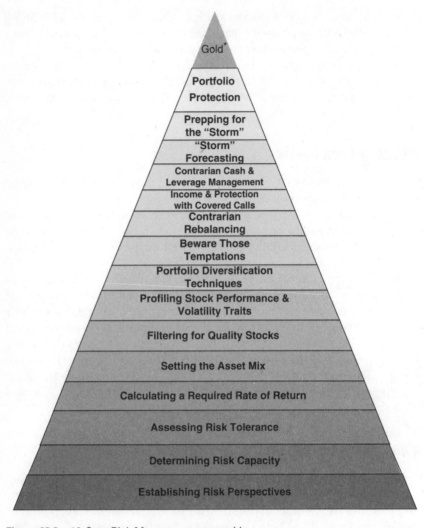

Figure 23.2 16-Step Risk Management pyramid.
*Yin of Gold - Available at the companion site: www.theinvestingoasis.com.

At the Oasis: Chapter 23

- Portfolio insurance is the final, but discretionary, step in the plan.
- Minimize the need for insurance. Start by "rounding up the camels."
- Portfolio insurance is "market timing" in reverse. It requires the skill sets of both a day trader and a short seller. Practice with small positions.
- Install insurance during market calm, particularly when markets are near record highs.
- Minimize the cost of your protection:
  - Insure less of the portfolio.
  - Plan on a deductible.
  - Spread insurance over several months.
  - Sell off unnecessary portions of the insurance.
  - Wait for volatility to increase before securing higher offsetting premiums.
- Don't fear corrections. Be prepared and embrace them. Losing less is still making progress.

"Winter is coming!"
> —motto of the House of Stark, *Game of Thrones*

Tier 4 Summary

By now, volatility should be understood to be the market's ordinary state of being. Stability is the exception. With the introduction of "storm watch" indicators, a preparation checklist, and protection tools, there should be no excuse to be caught by surprise. The longer the period of uninterrupted growth, the more significant the potential impact. Being better prepared also means being emotionally ready to embrace market tumult as an opportunity to get ahead.

While risk mitigation and portfolio insurance are practiced regularly in the professional domain, liquidating any or all of a portfolio of quality stocks should never be necessary. The upside of holding on or, better yet, averaging down through volatility far outweighs those permanent scars created when trying to time in and out of the markets.

Insurance is ordinarily bought to protect something of value. Yet, since the markets are uniquely resilient, invoking insurance is discretionary. After all, it's not like having to replace a stolen car or having a house destroyed by fire. Given time, a quality growth portfolio will survive even the worst downturns.

However, if still desired, portfolio insurance is a contrarian market timing decision to be applied just in time and harvested amid the panic. It requires courage, discipline, and being proactive. The good news is that if deployed well, it can create value. If done poorly, the loss should be contained to just the cost of the insurance. Experiment in small ways until you find a preferred method.

No matter the destination, nor the route taken,
the greatest journey is within.

Chapter 24

Putting It All Together

"Investing is simple,
but not easy."
—Warren Buffett

North Star Compass

- The investment process is a marathon, not a game of juggling hot stones.
- Protocols and accountability give professionals an edge.
- Portfolio management methods and contrarian practices hold a significant edge over tactical trading.
- Saying "No" more often can create value. Wealth grows faster with less trading.
- Permanent losses and mistakes are educational gold mines. Study them. They are a reflection of ourselves.
- Preparing for volatility can turn fear into opportunity.
- Markets are self-healing. With quality assets, mistakes will eventually be remedied.
- Care for your "camels" and they will take care of you.

Congratulations! Getting to this point means you've made a real commitment to managing your wealth and to self-improvement. Adopting even just some of *The Investing Oasis* concepts should bode well for the journey ahead.

Over the last century, despite famines, wars, natural calamities, and disease, returns of the S&P 500 have been positive 54% of all trading days and 74% across all the years.[1] That means that just staying invested should be a

---

[1]Fisher Investments (2018). "Historical Frequency of Positive Stock Returns." https://www.fisher401k.com/sites/default/files/2018-03/Historical_Frequency_of_Positive_Stock_Returns_K03171V.pdf.

rewarding experience. That's the good news. The more significant challenge is to remain on the path despite a constant barrage of disturbances, distractions, and doubts.

"All In"

The behavior gap has long been the nemesis of retail investors. Yet by recalibrating your path and deploying better capital market behaviors, the path forward should look more promising.

As outlined in Table 24.1, *The Investing Oasis* is a four-tiered blueprint outlining the myriad ways to create real investing value; half of what an investor needs to beat "Mr. Market" can be found in these tools and processes.

- **The Foundation** – Affirms the positive principles and behaviors required to win more consistently.
- **Tier 1** (Beta) – Outlines that a well-designed portfolio, comprised of quality stocks, should appreciate along with the long-term positive bias of the markets.
  - 16 progressive selection filters help to reveal quality stocks.
  - An intelligently designed core simplifies portfolio monitoring and management.
- **Tier 2** (Alpha) – Introduces contrarian threshold rebalancing and a low-risk revenue stream by selling CCs.
- **Tier 3** (Alpha) – Offers investors discretion to leverage returns by selling opportunistic cash-secured puts.
- **Tier 4** – A 16-Step Risk Management Plan tempers portfolio volatility while also providing protection tools to partially offset market sell-offs.

Value-Creating Processes

- **Smart Beta** – Better core performance through improved portfolio management processes.
- **Alpha** – Methods to introduce potential incremental excess returns.
- **Risk Reductions** – Diminishment of portfolio volatility and reduction of permanent losses.
- **Cost Savings** – Processes encourage retention of the DIY cost advantage.
- **Time Savings** – Processes designed to minimize the time spent monitoring and managing.

Table 24.1   Four tiers of value creation.

Value-Creating Processes					
Activities	**Smart Beta**	**Alpha**	**Risk Reductions**	**Cost Savings**	**Time Savings**
Pick a Mission (Tiers 1–4)					
Tier 1					
Buying Quality Stocks	✓		✓ Reduces risk of permanent losses.		✓ Less time required to monitor.
Research Triangulation (Confirmation with outside sources)			✓ Improves conviction to hold stocks through sell-offs.		
Degrees of Diversification	✓		✓		
Equal-Weighted Portfolio		✓ Concentrated positions increase performance	✘ Concentrated positions could increase volatility.		✓
Tier 2					
Purposeful Rebalancing		✓ Setting threshold targets reinforces contrarian "Buy low, sell high."	✓ Reduces portfolio volatility by reallocating capital from leaders to laggards.	✓ Trading with purpose reduces commissions.	✓
Covered Calls		✓ Introduces supplementary low-risk revenues.	✓ Contrarian revenues reduce volatility.		✘ Requires periodic management.
Tier 3					
Selling Put Contracts on Discounted Stocks		✓ Introduces the potential for additional risk-adjusted growth.	✘ Leverage may increase volatility.		
Tier 4					
Portfolio Protection		✓ Purpose of protection is to generate contrarian returns.	✓	✘ Insurance has ongoing costs but may also be recouped.	

Better Capital Markets Behavior

The other half of value creation is learning to improve our capital markets behavior. Getting "psyched up" is never a problem. But getting "psyched out" is. Improved behavior can render real value in managing a portfolio. *The Investing Oasis* is also purposefully designed to either quell the impact of "Mr. Market" on our trading decisions or to gracefully steer us around spontaneous behaviors.

> *"The difference between successful people and really successful people is that really successful people say 'No' to almost everything."*
> —Warren Buffett

Learning to resist trading temptations is an understated value-added behavior. As the ultimate contrarian, Warren only buys once, discerningly. And when satisfied, he later buys the rest. He avoids trading, relying instead on the corporate leadership teams and the market to do their compounding magic.

Like Warren, we believe in buying quality assets at reasonable valuations. But we also view the emotional ebbs and flows of the market as tangible opportunities to deploy contrarian tactics:

- Buying quality growth core stocks on market weakness (see Chapter 14).
- Rebalancing core stocks on threshold targets (see Chapter 15).
- Selling and harvesting gains from covered calls (see Chapter 16).
- Selling and harvesting gains from cash-secured puts on discounted quality, non-core stocks (see Chapter 19).
- Deploying cash and debt opportunistically during market weakness (see Chapter 18).
- Setting and harvesting gains from portfolio protection (see Chapter 23).

The faith is that, although the market shall remain forever uncertain, it will also continue to represent the unrelenting progress of humankind. We invest in the best and trust that tactically countering human behavior will provide the rest.

> *"The most contrarian thing of all is not to oppose the crowd but to think for yourself."*
> —Peter Thiel,
> co-founder of PayPal, Palantir Technologies, and
> The Founders Fund

Risk Management

In active management, equally important as performance enhancement is building a solid defense. Every stock decision should address both its performance expectations as well how it may impact a portfolio's risk profile. Nomads would never venture into the heart of the desert without planning their route and porting the tools necessary to protect themselves. Equally, an investor should have a road map, the right tools, and a behavioral compass to steward their wealth safely across unfamiliar and expectedly unsettling investment terrains.

The nine concentric rings in Figure 24.1 accentuate how *The Investing Oasis* addresses risk management in escalating priorities. Of course, investors could choose to deploy some, several, or none of the risk mitigation processes. However, the benefits of designing a risk management plan are most noticeable only during difficult times. But, by then, it would be too late. Being proactive can create tangible value.

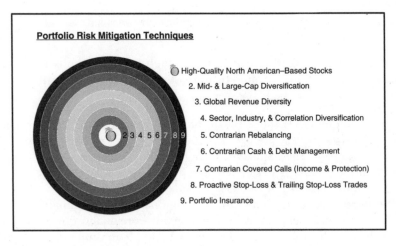

Portfolio Risk Mitigation Techniques

1. High-Quality North American–Based Stocks
2. Mid- & Large-Cap Diversification
3. Global Revenue Diversity
4. Sector, Industry, & Correlation Diversification
5. Contrarian Rebalancing
6. Contrarian Cash & Debt Management
7. Contrarian Covered Calls (Income & Protection)
8. Proactive Stop-Loss & Trailing Stop-Loss Trades
9. Portfolio Insurance

Figure 24.1 Risk mitigation techniques.

Capital Markets Expectations

The all-important caveat is that past performance cannot be used as an indication of future performance. As such, the type of returns and volatility being projected in Figure 24.2, are not generated from the past performance of the Oasis Growth Fund. Instead, all figures are derived from the

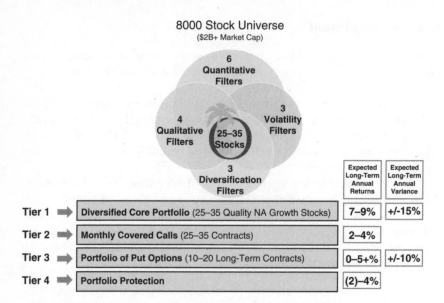

Figure 24.2   *The Investing Oasis* expected portfolio performance overview.

historical averages of the S&P 500. Although investor results may never match the projections, it would be unreasonable to argue against the long-term averages. Here is our breakdown:

- Through nearly 100 years, the S&P 500 average annual performance is approximately 6% growth plus 2% dividends with a range of volatility of +/– 15%. Since the OGF portfolio is comprised of quality US and Canadian stocks, the projection is a similar average annual reward/risk profile of 7–9%, +/– 15%.
- By selling CCs each month, an additional 2–4% is attainable.
- Periodically selling put contracts on non-core quality growth stocks is less predictable but could generate up to 5% in supplementary portfolio gains. However, the range of volatility (– 10%) is expectedly lower than the core portfolio due to the already discounted share prices when the contracts are sold.
- Returns from portfolio insurance are even more uncertain. The amount of insurance will differ per investor, as will an investor's ability to deploy and harvest the positions. Equally, the returns on any

insurance deployment require higher than usual volatility. As such, during periods of calm, the insurance is a cost center. This could sometimes last for extended periods. Overall, though, an investor should never expect to lose any more than the premiums for their insurance.

However, when all is woven together, the results from a portfolio managed as per *The Investing Oasis* should be directly competitive with "Mr. Market."

Final Final

The secrets to success are now in your hands. *The Investing Oasis* has revealed a multitude of tools, techniques, and behaviors that, together, can vastly improve the investing experience. Embracing the process and acting mindfully can be applied universally to investing and to our world at large. The processes and wisdom of *The Investing Oasis* should be timeless resources. There are even further unpublished chapters available at a password-protected website: www.theinvestingoasis.com.

Yet, while trekking into the capital markets desert will forever be unpredictable, volatility is only the enemy of those who did not plan well. In this domain of perpetual uncertainty, follow in the footsteps of the experienced nomads: Create a plan, care for your camels, and keep faith in the markets. Great treasures await the patient contrarian.

Hopefully this journey of enrichment will be greater than just building financial wealth. Every challenge offers the opportunity for self-discovery. Mindfulness is required to protect our precious planet. Safe travels.

> *"Success is the journey, not the destination."*
> —Samuel Langhorne Clemens (Mark Twain)
> (1835–1910), American writer, humorist,
> entrepreneur, publisher, and lecturer

FEEDBACK TO THE AUTHOR[2]

---

[2]Jay.mason@fieldhousecap.com.

Wisdom from the Dunes

1. **Take the journey.** If an investor can withstand the short-term stumbles, the long term is highly predictable. We grow faster having to make critical decisions with scarce resources.
2. **Set reasonable financial objectives and respect your risk tolerance.** In the markets, humans are the wild card. Risk management only works if the investor stays disciplined.
3. **Consult all three brains.** As in all life's decisions, before acting, listen, analyze, and feel.
4. **DCAs and DRIPs represent both trust in corporate leadership and faith in the markets.** The markets rise more than they fall. Choosing quality assets makes it easier.
5. **Act contrarian.** Be the patient warrior. Trim on green. Buy the dip.
6. **Practice restraint.** Be a decade trader, not a day trader.
7. **Don't let temptations lead you astray.** The path of quality offers the least heartache.
8. **Deploy multiple degrees of diversification.** Together, they will steady the path.
9. **Rebalancing** is the foundation of being a contrarian. Stick with threshold targets.
10. **Don't let the "tax tail wag the camel."** Rebalancing is more important. Paying taxes is a sign of success.
11. **"Honor thy convictions."** They will be assaulted daily. Bend only for material reasons.
12. **Once sold, move on.** Regret is a learning opportunity. Heed the lesson. Then let it go.
13. **Leverage sparingly.** Wait for the flag of surrender.
14. **Always be building cash and debt reserves.** Death, taxes, and market corrections are all guaranteed. Keep some powder dry.
15. **Perfect decisions are a fantasy.** Without mistakes, we aren't learning.
16. **The markets tempt and taunt.** Less trading and saying "No" more often create value.
17. **Stay informed.** The entire world is more accessible than ever.
18. **Keep your Advisor.** Complex matters deserve a second opinion. Find an Advisor who supports your DIY journey.
19. **Practice good lifestyle habits.** Find a balance. Incorporate good eating, exercise, and healthy spiritual practices. Forgiveness is a surprising source of strength.
20. **Be mindful and attentive in everything you do.** Little things matter.

Chapter 25

The Next-Gen Financial System

"We're here to put a dent into the universe.
Otherwise, why else even be here?"
—Steve Jobs (1955–2011)

Objective:

A glimpse into the future financial system.

"[The metaverse is defined as] a collective virtual shared space, created by the convergence of virtually enhanced physical reality and physically persistent virtual space, including the sum of all virtual worlds, augmented reality, and the Internet."

—Wikipedia

The Metaverse

With a global pandemic reshaping our lives and forcing millions to remain socially distant, the needs of many have been interrupted but so have the solutions. Enter the metaverse[1]: introduced by Neal Stephenson in his 1992 novel *Snow Crash*, a 3D world converging virtual technology with the limitless internet, the gaming community, and cryptocurrencies. In other words, a technophobe's worst nightmare.

---

[1]Baszucki, D. (2021). "The Metaverse Is Coming: A 3D Virtual World Where Millions Meet Online Will Becoming Our Key Social Hub." https://www.wired.co.uk/article/metaverse (Accessed 27 September 2021).

As our world shrinks, the metaverse will become the socializing hub for the masses and workplace for virtual entrepreneurs. Whether working, shopping, learning, playing, or just hanging out, this online, persistent virtual world will be the place where all humankind will be able to interact and transact. "Persistence" refers to the concept that whether anyone is there to experience it, digital assets in the metaverse will continue to exist and evolve, much like the real world.

Where brick-and-mortar storefronts once dominated our shopping experience, tomorrow's retail and entertainment consumption will be happening increasingly online in a virtual world of augmented reality. What used to be the exclusive domain of online gamers, the metaverse is expanding to incorporate broader 3D experiences, including concerts, movies, videos, and commerce. Speaking of which, in 2020, 30 million raving fans participated in an online concert by Lil Nas X on the Roblox platform. This speaks to the power of adoption for a virtual world. The metaverse infrastructure is developing at light speed.

The metaverse has long been the domain of Roblox and Minecraft, near-limitless gaming platforms, enticing their young audience members to actively program in new digital realities. Roblox has even added a voice chat feature, creating an ether world dominated by preteens – what could go wrong?

The rest of us might eventually create an online avatar to coexist, in real time, with our physical world. Meanwhile, Matterport is co-opting users to map out their real-world business space to be an accurate and immersive twin within the metaverse. Eventually, every square inch will be leasable. Over at Epic Games (developer of runaway gaming success "Fortnight"), they are on a mission to create metahuman avatars to match that hidden alter ego we all so dearly desire to reveal every Halloween. And what about the "big boyz"?

Meanwhile, Microsoft, Google, and ~~Facebook~~, er . . . Meta also recognize the opportunity and are planning to spend billions to help shape the metaverse arena. Microsoft envisions enabling computing to be embedded into the real world as much as indoctrinating the real world into computing. As an entry point, Microsoft plans to introduce the metaverse both into its Xbox gaming console and its video-conferencing service, called "Teams." With billions of subscribers, both Meta and Microsoft will accelerate the metaverse adoption for the mainstream.

Further, Nvidia, the chip-making behemoth, has been fast-tracking its own "Omniverse," a virtual world of digital cars, cities, and people intended for businesses to simulate the building of futuristic products and structures in the real world. Why not work out the bugs in the safety of artificial environments before attempting to manufacture them for real?

If it's not yet obvious, the metaverse is spawning a gold rush mentality. Seoul has announced imminent intentions to roll out a "contactless" metaverse public service platform. Equally, Barbados, a crypto-friendly country, has bought virtual land in Decentraland, a subdivision within the metaverse, and is preparing to launch the world's first virtual embassy.

Every Fortune 500 company is expected to follow suit in announcing their commitment to develop a niche within the metaverse. With the pre-teens already holding a user experience advantage, expect the average age of tomorrow's metaverse CEOs to be the youngest cohort in history.

Seamlessly, pieces of the virtual world will become semi-permanent in the physical world and vice versa. Commerce will be conducted in both. Virtual assets will be able to be transported between communities within the metaverse community and will retain real value across both worlds. Finally, the era of cryptocurrencies should come into its prime. Thousands of previously dormant digital tokens and thousands more to be created will gain functionality. The value created in the metaverse will gradually begin to intercept with our present financial system. Eventually, it won't matter in which dimension we thrive.

Blockchain Technology

Blockchain is the beating heart of distributive technology. With encryption technology and protocols effectively replacing third-party intermediaries, blockchain is appropriately identified as a "trustless environment." Transparency of all transactions ensures the ability to confirm transactions by all. Blockchain will become the foundation wherever ownership tracking and chain of procedures may invite conflict and/or criminal activities. All relevant information can be embedded into every transaction for all users to see and audit without requiring costly, time-consuming third-party affirmation. Among all sectors, the financial industry will be most affected, to the good.

DeFi Technology

Distributive technology based on blockchain is increasingly disrupting the current financial system offering expedited transactions, cost efficiencies, and transparencies. The current patchwork of legacy systems used by the world's financial services firms was never designed to anticipate today's digital world. To complicate matters, regulators have compensated by deploying Band-Aid solutions rather than deploying wholesale modernization. The dominance of the elite financial firms (Goldman Sachs, JP Morgan, Citicorp, etc.) is now being challenged. Financial services can now be performed from decentralized locations at odd hours on any given day. DeFi = decentralized finance. Cost efficiencies of distributive technology are placing unrelenting pressure on concentrations of the elite financial firms in high-rent districts in major cities (New York, London, Hong Kong, Tokyo, et al.). Remotely located data centers and cloud-based solutions will hold more relevance in providing financial services to the masses. With smartphones able to fulfill most individuals' financial needs, consolidations and change will be coming to the financial industry in tidal waves. It is a sign of the times that distributive technology is being harnessed for the benefit of smaller investors globally. The face of financial services firms is quickly evolving, and the pace will only continue to accelerate.

Modernizing Markets

Where it currently takes T+2 days to verify and transfer assets between buyers and sellers, blockchain will bring time and cost efficiencies to all global stock markets. Every investor will eventually be recognized by their digital ID to allow for domestic regulators to follow global transactions and maintain AML[2] and KYC[3] integrity. Transactions will be instantaneous and cost-effective while eliminating human errors and costly back-office functions.

Digitization and decentralization of the financial system will enable fair and equal access for all participants within the metaverse. Here are just a few examples of this potential:

- **Democratizing Initial Public Offerings (IPOs)** – Eventually, IPOs could be floated on the market through processes like a Dutch auction. The market decides the opening bid price, rather than the brokers, and most investors would have equal access to participate. This approach would reduce control from the brokerage firms who traditionally orchestrate most IPOs.
- **Democratizing Capital Raising** – Large, medium, and even small-sized private businesses will be able to cost-effectively raise capital in the markets. Products like SPACs[4] and AIFs[5] are already beginning to democratize access to the world of late-stage funding for private businesses of all sizes. Even now, private firms may also opt for direct listings[6] to cut out the expensive IPO listing process.

---

[2]Anti-money laundering.
[3]Know Your Client – used by regulators to hold Financial Advisors accountable to ensure that investment recommendations are appropriate for their clients.
[4]Special purpose acquisition corporations.
[5]Alternative investment funds.
[6]Private businesses that float their shares on an exchange in lieu of listing as an IPO.

- **Democratizing Monolithic Offerings** – Large-scale securities ordinarily issued by macro entities to high net worth clients (e.g. sovereign wealth bonds, a minimum investment of $500K+, or ownership in large-scale commercial buildings or development projects). Previously the sheer size of assets precluded retail investors from participating due to the associated prohibitive costs. With distributive technology, these can now be partitioned cost-effectively into smaller units for broader distribution.
- **Fractional Share Ownership** – Progressive brokerage platforms now offer ownership in fractional shares, allowing small investors to own publicly listed securities that were otherwise indivisible (BRK.A, BKNG, AMZN, etc.). The concept of fractional ownership will only continue to expand to encompass unique opportunities. For example, credit card users could soon be enabled to invest their cashback savings directly into fractional shares of their favorite companies.
- **Simplification of Cash Transactions** – International money transfers have been forever inefficient and expensive. The banking legacy systems were never designed for the speed and reach of the digital age. Today, money circumnavigates the globe in nanoseconds. Next-generation payment technology (Nuvei, Square, PayPal, etc.) is now successfully usurping the archaic and cumbersome controls favored by the established banks.
- **Universal Regulations** – Although sovereign regulatory bodies continue to be five steps behind, distributive technology will raise and unify global standards, reducing international trade hurdles and forcing contract laws to modernize and synchronize. At the heart of the metaverse, "trustless" blockchain technology should greatly benefit law-abiding citizens globally.

Digital Coins/Cryptocurrencies

Likely most of the thousands of digital currencies still seem opaque. Their exact use has yet to be determined despite the fact that they offer transactional fungibility, efficiency, and cost-effectiveness. Leadership, though, will need to come from corporations to openly accept cryptocurrencies for commercial transactions. In 2018, the estimated cost of printing and managing fiat currencies worldwide was $35B.[7] Managing the fiat money supply is clearly enormously wasteful and cumbersome.

---

[7]https://www.coindesk.com/markets/2014/07/05/under-the-microscope-the-real-costs-of-a-dollar/

Bitcoin

The veteran that launched it all on January 9, 2009, Bitcoin is continuing to make inroads. With the world's financial system being stretched to its limits by undisciplined government borrowing, a borderless currency with a hard cap of 21 million units holds universal appeal. The last coin is expected to be issued around 2140. Wide-scale acceptance would mean that politicians and central bankers at the helm of the global financial system may no longer be able to hold absolute control.

Gradually, investment firms, retail corporations and now countries (El Salvador) are joining throngs of ardent Bitcoin supporters as legal tender in anticipation that the world's financial system will eventually be co-opted into the digital realm. The ability to transact anywhere in the world, for anything, at any time without requiring an exchange rate or the imposition of taxation is becoming a genuine threat to most sovereign states.

Stablecoins and CBDCs

The next step toward digital coin legitimacy was confirmed by the Office of the Comptroller of the Currency (OCC) on January 4, 2021. The OCC supervises all federally licensed domestic and foreign banks in the United States. In a move to thwart private coinage (Bitcoin, Ethereum, et al.), the OCC announced that federally chartered banks can now use Stablecoins for payment activities. A Stablecoin refers to any digital currency whose value is backed by a hard asset or a basket of assets, such as exchange-traded commodities, fiat currencies, or even a basket of other cryptocurrencies. Another Stablecoin version soon to be in our midst will be issued by central banks around the world, called the "central bank digital currency" (CBDC). This will be a digital token issued by any sovereign state stabilized by that nation's right to impose taxation and control that nation's interest rates.

Globally, central banks and regulators are scrambling to introduce CBDCs to defend their sovereign rights to issue and manage their respective domestic currencies, which allows them to retain control over taxation of their citizens.

CBDCs introduce cost and time efficiencies because there will be no physical currencies to issue, to circulate, nor to retire. Equally, governments and national security agencies will be able to monitor and trace all individual transactions more easily. In this regard, China is out front with the "digital yuan." A country that invented paper currency during the seventh century is quickly paring down the use of fiat currency. China is seeking to take the global first-mover advantage relative to western nations by deploying their CBDC at the 2022 Beijing Winter Olympics. US corporations, like Starbucks, MacDonald's, and Subway have been among the many willing participants in China's drive for a cashless society.

CBDC compliance is another mechanism by which China seeks to enforce absolute control over its populace. As such, the Communist Party of China (CPC) has also announced that all crypto mining and the use of cryptocurrencies will be illegal; in particular, Bitcoin.

Globally, CBDCs will also provide governments with an ability to roll out and manage targeted economic policies. Transactions in a digitized economy will no longer be private.

Along with China, a host of additional countries, including Russia, Iran, and Venezuela, are deeply motivated to develop an alternative to the $USD as the global reserve currency. They hope that the digital currency revolution will help them circumvent the numerous crippling sanctions imposed by the US and its allies.

BitGold

Among the thousands of digital offerings, BitGold is perhaps one of the most interesting. The company backs all BitGold purchases with 10-gram gold cubes. Investors can also load up a digital card and spend their gold as they would use a debit card aligned with their bank account.

NFTs

For years, print media held dominance over the advertising world. Nearly insurmountable barriers created scarce supply and, therefore, pricing power over unlimited advertising demand. Then along came the internet and companies like Google and Meta who offered unlimited supply opportunity for advertisers. The scarcity advantage long held by print media was no longer a barrier.

Now enter NFT assets. On May 3, 2014, Kevin McCoy introduced the world's first digital art NFT, "Quantum," auctioned for $6M. A non-fungible token (NFT) is a cryptographic asset on the blockchain with unique identification codes, metadata, and value. Unlike cryptocurrency units which offer equivalency, each NFT is an authentic original. This is creating scarcity once again. Each is singular, provable, and, for select NFT assets, able to retain value. Like any worthy asset, NFTs introduce bid/ask spreads for digital asset collectors.

The digital evolution of NFTs now allows artists, creators, and owners to confirm the authenticity of their assets and monetize their value. Historically, the distribution of art involved a convoluted hierarchy, for which provenance of even the most valuable of assets could not be 100% guaranteed. Today, through NFTs, art can be shared with admirers globally or sold exclusively with the click of a few keystrokes, effectively cutting out the costly middlemen.

The creative use of NFTs will continue to expand as programmers and artists alike discover new pathways of expression and opportunity. For example, the first full-length NFT movie *Zero Contact* featuring Anthony Hopkins was live-streamed on Vuele, the first direct-to-consumer NFT viewing platform inside the metaverse. Such is the power of blockchain to remove barriers of distribution and confirm ownership rights.

Distributive Autonomous Organizations (DAOs)

An unexpected outcome of the burgeoning democratic ways of the digital generation is the creation of DAOs. These are crypto investors banding together to render greater financial clout than any of them individually could deploy. The digital age now allows the ownership of large assets to be fractured into much smaller units and shared between masses of like-minded owners. Think of this as investors who are defining their own mutual funds. DAOs are similar to the SPAC concept where investors speculatively buy shares in a publicly traded company created for the purpose of eventually acquiring or merging with an existing company. DAOs, on the other hand, first determine their target asset, then raise the capital to be able to do their bidding. An example of this was ConstitutionDAO, a group of crypto warriors who got together to bid on a rare first printing of the US Constitution in a private auction. Ultimately, they didn't win the bidding war (sold for $43.2M) but they did introduce another format by which fintech innovations are going to help democratize the future of finance.

Borderless, Frictionless, Timeless, and Fairer

There is no going back. All corners of the globe are benefiting from the fintech revolution. Creation, distribution, and ownership of digital assets, particularly all matters financial, will be rendered trustworthy, delivered faster, cheaper, available to all 24/7 and without the discriminations and privileges practiced by the guardians of the status quo. Democratization of the financial system? What's not to like!

2030

No matter the future you might envision, do yourself three favors:

1. Listen to a podcast introduction of the metaverse by Mathew Ball.[8]
2. Pick up *2030* by Mauro F. Guillén.[9] He paints a sobering, insightful picture of the trends that could shape our lives over the coming decade, let alone decades. He titled it *2030* because the world is reinventing itself so quickly that 10 years is within reach of our imaginations, while being still being tantalizingly just at the outskirts of reality.
3. For those without programming skills, sign up for a metaverse education at either Unity Software[10] or the Roblox websites.[11] With a multidimensional virtual world soon to reshape our analog lives, this is where tomorrow's leaders are currently learning and building their skills.

The future is now.

> *"Happiness is only real when shared."*
> —Christopher McCandless,
> in *Into the Wild*

---

[8]"Multicoin Summit: A Walk Through the Metaverse with Matthew Ball," Youtube, uploaded by Multicoin Capital, December 2021, https://www.youtube.com/watch?v=M7bG6f9BjgA (Accessed 11 January 2022).

[9]Guillén, M. (2020). *2030: How Today's Biggest Trends Will Collide and Reshape the Future of Everything.* New York: St. Martin's Publishing Group. http://www.mauroguillen.com/2030-book/ (Accessed 21 November 2021).

[10]https://store.unity.com/?_ga=2.248723394.439114255.1641082495-1882514600.1641082495#plans-individual.

[11]https://education.roblox.com/en-us/ (Accessed 13 December 2021).

Chapter 26

A Case for Active Management

Source: Shutterstock

The OASIS Growth Fund

Launched in 2016, the Oasis Growth Fund (OGF) is an actively managed, diversified North American equity hedge fund[1] designed to be performance competitive with all core North American and global equity funds. As a pure growth fund, the OGF deploys a wide variety of value-creating tools and techniques as outlined through the preceding 25 chapters. We also designed our business and service models along the same philosophies. All facets are mindful that the client's better interests are integral to our success.

Whether AI, EV, 3D, 5G, AR/VR, ESG, blockchain, or the penultimate metaverse, innovations and progress are taking place across every facet of our lives. The future is exciting, and the OGF's purpose is to capture the growth of companies that are reshaping the world.

---

[1] A trust series fund empowered by Fieldhouse Capital Management based in Yaletown, Vancouver, Canada.

The Oasis Vision

To provide one of the most compelling value propositions amongst all core equity investment funds based in North America.

Investment Objective

To generate annual total performance in excess of 8% (net of fees).

Value-Creating Processes

Comprehensive Portfolio Design:
- **16 stock selection filters** – Ensures ownership in visionary businesses with global reach, surplus revenues, and shareholder-friendly practices.
- **Mix of mid- to large-cap stocks** – Offers operational flexibility and M&A potential.
- **Equal-weighted portfolio** – With ongoing industry convergence, all industries are growing. Vastly improves portfolio management effectiveness.
- **16-step risk management plan** – Multiple layers of risk mitigation techniques to dampen volatility and mitigate market sell-offs.

Comprehensive Portfolio Management Processes:
- **QARP trading discipline** – Trades either improve performance, diminish volatility, or remove undue risks. Buy at reasonable discount.
- **Contrarian rebalancing on threshold targets** – Buy on red. Sell on green.
- **Contrarian cash and debt management** – Discipline to build cash for market pullbacks and hold debt for compelling opportunities.
- **Regular contrarian revenues** – Extensive use of OTM CCs.
- **Opportunistic growth** – Selective sale of cash-secured puts on quality, discounted, non-core stocks.

Fee Model:
- The OGF annual management fee is 0.5%.
- An incentive bonus of 15% is applied if the OGF annual performance exceeds the hurdle rate of 8%. A high-water mark applies to ensure that a performance bonus is paid out only when the fund achieves real growth.

Important Information for Investors

The Oasis Growth Fund is available by Offering Memorandum as the Fieldhouse Pro Funds Trust Series Class O. With a risk profile of medium to high, the OGF may not be suitable for all investors. Professional advice is recommended to determine whether the OGF fits with your investment objectives and within your risk tolerance. For further information, please contact jay@theinvestingoasis.com.

Chapter 27

Tools and Resources

"The definition of a poor man is someone who cannot grasp that the choices he makes today will affect his life tomorrow."
—unknown

Objective:

Rendering better decisions by triangulation.

Investing Education

If you are new to investing, consider undertaking either of the preparatory programs that all North American investment industry professionals are required to complete: the US Series 7 exam[1] or the Canadian Securities Course.[2] Both are at-home study programs with site-specific examinations.

The pinnacle of investment studies is the CFA Charter.[3] This program requires completion of three comprehensive examinations and 4,000 hours of work experience over 36 months to receive the charter.

Since options are used to create value in several chapters of *The Investing Oasis*, some education may be warranted. The Options Clearing Corporation (OCC) offers a short YouTube video on deploying CCs, as well as a video deploying cash-covered puts.

---

[1] https://www.finra.org/registration-exams-ce/qualification-exams/series7.
[2] https://www.csi.ca/student/en_ca/courses/csi/csc_enrol.xhtml?gclid=Cj0KCQjw5s3cBRCAARIsAB8ZjU0GP6i076QYbHdbPzKjV0s2b26tNmDVbvsQiYmY-EYc4qZjTqFr43saAnCrEALw_wcB (Accessed 26 September 2021).
[3] https://www.cfainstitute.org/en/programs/cfa (Accessed 26 September 2021).

For less academic learning, nothing beats listening to podcasts. A URL in the footnotes identifies the top investment education podcasts.[4]

A list of the studies, books, and authors mentioned in *The Investing Oasis* is also provided at the end of this chapter.

All sites and services are the personal selection of the author. No benefits have been promised, negotiated, nor received, from any individuals or businesses mentioned in *The Investing Oasis*. Access to and/or use of any site or resource is the responsibility of the reader.**

Resource Triangulation

Very much like using cell towers to accurately pinpoint a mobile phone location, better decisions happen when using multiple independent sources. The Venn diagram in Figure 27.1 outlines the concept of how deploying different sources of research should lead to better investing decisions. When independent sources arrive at the same conclusion, an investment decision should hold higher conviction for the investor.

Equally, too much data, leading to analysis paralysis, can be as detrimental as too little. Once a trusted data source has been found, then focus on select pieces of high-gain data to form your decisions. To make it easier, below is a list of resources in which we have confidence, most of which have been mentioned in *The Investing Oasis*. The actual URL sites are listed by category in the subsequent pages.

Figure 27.1   Investing tools and resources.

---

[4]https://blog.feedspot.com/investment_podcasts/ (Accessed 26 September 2021).

Research Categories

The following resources are divided into eight categories to better facilitate your research, including several consolidated review sites and the corresponding URLs for all sites. Some sites are complimentary, while others may require subscriptions.

Stock Screener Sites Research platforms to find candidate stocks (see Chapters 8–10):
- www.Zacks.com – https://www.zacks.com/screening/stock-screener
- www.TheGlobeandMail.com – https://www.theglobeandmail.com/investing/markets/stocks/screener/
- www.SeekingAlpha.com
- Review of US Stock Screeners – https://www.investopedia.com/best-stock-screeners-5120586
- Review of Canadian Stock Screeners – https://dividendearner.com/best-stock-screener/#BarchartScreener

Stock Analytic Sites Research platforms to help assess and compare stocks:
- www.StockReportsPlus.com (complimentary to subscribers of TheGlobeandMail.com)
- www.StockCalc.com (complimentary to subscribers of GlobeandMail.com)
- Review of Stock Analytic Sites – https://www.moneycrashers.com/best-stock-market-investment-news-analysis-research-sites/

Corporate Reporting Sites Regulatory sites where publicly listed businesses report their latest financial data:
- US Corporations – https://www.sec.gov/edgar.shtmlw.sec.gov/edgar.shtml
- CAN Corporations – SEDAR: https://www.sedar.com/homepage_en.htm
- Berkshire Hathaway Annual Reports – (Always worth the time) https://www.berkshirehathaway.com/reports.html

Professional Stock-Picking Sites Sites sharing professional stock recommendations:
- www.BNNBloomberg.ca
- www.Stockchase.com (subscription)

Sites sharing the portfolios of investing luminaries:
- www.GuruFocus.com
- www.TipRanks.com
- Top Hedge Funds (periodical by Seeking Alpha) – https://seekingalpha.com/article/4390111-top-buys-from-best-money-managers-q3-2020?utm_medium=email&utm_source=seeking_alpha&mail_subject=must-read-top-buys-from-the-best-money-managers-q3-2020&utm_campaign=nl-must-read&utm_content=link-0

Social Investing Sites   Platforms where independent investors discuss stock-picking preferences:
- www.Stockhouse.com
- www.SeekingAlpha.com
- www.SprinkleTrade.com
- www.StockTwits.com
- Review of Social Investing Sites - https://thecollegeinvestor.com/21341/best-social-networks-investors/
- www.Glassdoor.com – 2022 List of the Top 20 Best Companies to Work for and Invest In – https://austinhankwitz.substack.com/p/case-study-glassdoors-best-places?utm_source=url

YouTube Influencers
- Review of 20 YouTube Investing Vloggers – https://blog.feedspot.com/investment_youtube_channels/
- The Swedish Investor – https://www.youtube.com/channel/UCAe AB8ABXGoGMbXuYPmiu2A
- The Magic of Finance – https://www.youtube.com/channel/UCGy 7SkBjcIAgTiwkXEtPnYg
- Modern Value Investing – https://www.youtube.com/channel/UCr TTBSUr0zhPU56UQljag5A
- Ticker Symbol: YOU – https://www.youtube.com/channel/UC7kCe Z53sli_9XwuQeFxLqw
- Patrick Boyle – https://www.youtube.com/c/PatrickBoyleOnFinance

Special Reports
- Review of Options Education Sites – https://www.investopedia.com/best-options-trading-courses-5120500
- How to Track Insider Trading (Just For Dummies) – https://www.dummies.com/article/business-careers-money/personal-finance/investing/investment-vehicles/stocks/track-insider-trading-221004
- NA Short Sale Reports – https://www.marketbeat.com/short-interest/
- US Insider Trading Reports – https://www.secform4.com
- Canadian Insider Trading – https://undervaluedequity.com/insider-trading-canada-3-free-resources-for-tracking-the-change-in-canadian-insider-ownership/

News and Media
- www.Benzinga.com
- www.Bloomberg.com
- www.BNNBloomberg.ca
- www.Reuters.com
- www.TheGlobeandMail.com
- Review of Financial News Sites – https://www.investopedia.com/articles/markets/111315/top-6-apps-financial-news.asp

Three Thoughts about Second Opinions

- **A second opinion is always a good idea,** particularly when you are the second opinion. Private investment newsletters and mainstream financial media, like CNBC and BNN, continually offer quick and easy investment ideas. Experts regularly make confident recommendations. If a professional's insights and style resonate, it's a good starting point. Likely, they've already done significant research. But now you become the "second opinion." Due diligence should still be required.
- **In whom to trust?** Whether it's your family, friends, coworkers, or professional analysts, following too many sources will lead to confusion. Narrow it down to the few that resonate and engage you in critical thinking. Joining social investing sites can also improve trading acumen but beware the hype without accountability.
- **Loud rarely means better.** If you haven't already noticed, blogs, social media influencers, and sites that peddle their influence are not actually speaking to you. They are speaking to your wallet. Content providers have learned from "rag-mags" how to garner a loyal following through dramatic headlines and clickbait articles. Your loyalty becomes their product. Critical thinking is required to stay in the "sane lane."

Discount Trading Platforms

You likely already have a trading platform. However, there are now many feature differences that may offer pause for thought. While commission-free trades are now commonplace, be aware that these platforms lease out their trade executions to market-making firms, called "payment for order flows" (PFOFs). Market makers intervene between your trade and the best trade execution possible on the open market. As well, commission-free trades may only be offered on a portion of their trades. Options and futures securities may be excluded. According to Investopedia, US brokerage firms that use PFOF services are: Robinhood, E-Trade, Ally Financial, Webull, Tradestation, The Vanguard Group, Charles Schwab Corporation, and TD Ameritrade. Brokers that do not receive payments for order flow include Interactive Brokers, Merrill Edge, and Fidelity Investments.

Overall, though, the greater danger with commission-free trading is an increased temptation to trade more than necessary.

Reviews of Multiple Discount Trading Platforms

- **Top US Platforms:** https://www.stockbrokers.com/guides/online-stock-brokers
- **Top Canadian Platforms:** https://www.theglobeandmail.com/investing/markets/inside-the-market/article-the-2021-globe-and-mail-online-brokerage-ranking-whos-best-for/#final
- **Commission-free Trading in Canada:**
  - Wealthsimple – https://www.wealthsimple.com/en-ca/
  - National Bank – https://nbdb.ca/invest/brokerage.html

At the Oasis

The OGF Trading Platform

The Oasis Growth Fund uses the **Interactive Brokers** platform.[5] It is well suited for both professional and retail investors with an exceptional suite of services, including:

- Access to global stocks, bonds, options, futures, currencies, funds.
- Deploys a "mid-price" algorithm[5] to gain best available price execution.
- An exceptional, comprehensive portfolio analytics platform.
- Minute-to-minute performance calculations and customized benchmarks.
- Complimentary news feeds from a variety of financial media sources.
- The ability for investors to set and trade according to personal ESG standards.
- Fractional share trading for smaller investors to buy partial shares.
- The lowest commission structure in the industry.
- The lowest margin costs in the industry.
- The ability to earn extra income by lending shares to short sellers.

Note: Interactive Brokers does not deploy PFOFs on their platform. All quotes are from the open market.

---

[5] https://www.interactivebrokers.com/en/home.php.

Well of the Wise: References, Studies, Books, and Authors

Table 27.1   Referenced studies, books, and authors.

Title	Author(s)	Chapter
The Art of War	General Sun Tzu	Intro
The Intelligent Investor	Benjamin Graham	Intro
In Pursuit of the Perfect Portfolio	Andrew W. Lo, PhD, and Stephen R. Foerster, PhD	Intro
The Psychology of Money	Morgan Housel	Intro, 1
The Clean Money Revolution: Reinventing Power, Purpose, and Capitalism	Joel Solomon	Intro
Behavioral Finance: The Second Generation	Meir Statman, PhD	1
Big Mistakes: The Best Investors and their Worst Investments	Michael Batnick, CFA	2
The Behavior of Individual Investors	Brad B. Barber, PhD	2
The Talent Code	Daniel Coyle	2
The Hippies Were Right: It's All About the Vibrations, Man!	Tam Hunt	2
Life, the Truth, and Being Free	Steve Maraboli, PhD	2
Freakonomics	Stephen Levitt, PhD / Stephen J. Dubner	3
Thinking, Fast and Slow	Daniel Kahneman, PhD	2, 5
"The Capitalism Distribution: Fat Tails in Action"	Meb Faber	7
A Random Walk Down Wall Street	Burton Malkiel, PhD	8
2018 Sustainable Finance Innovation Forum	Goldman Sachs	10
The Art of Thinking Clearly	Rolf Dobelli	15
Trading is Hazardous to Your Wealth	Brad B. Barber, PhD, and Terrance Odean, PhD	17
Guide to the Markets – Quarterly Report	J.P. Morgan	24
Wisdom of the Crowds	James Surowiecki, Journalist	29
2030	Dean Mauro F. Guillen, PhD	29
Into the Wild	Jon Krakauer	30

Portfolio Time Management

Figure 27.2 is a pie chart outlining how an investor could expect to allocate their time managing all four tiers of a portfolio. Realistically, once the core portfolio (Tier 1) is set up, it should require minimal vigilance. Rebalancing can be managed with proactive trades.

CCs (Tier 2) likely will require the bulk of your time, as each contract is relatively short term.

In Tier 3, since put contracts are to be deployed opportunistically and usually for longer terms, greater time spent will be remaining vigilant during the four corporate earnings seasons.

Although portfolio protection will be a constant concern, Tier 4 time management should be minimal, at least until the markets begin to roil. A well-designed portfolio will make time management all that much more effective, leaving you with more family and pet time!

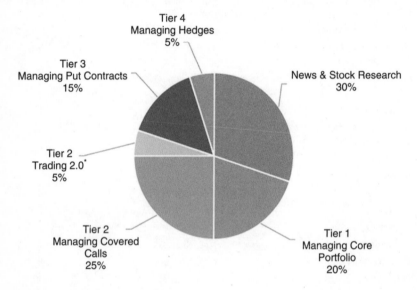

Figure 27.2 Portfolio time management.
*Trading 2.0 is higher-frequency trading with guardrails available at www .theinvestingoasis.com.

About the Website

T hank you for purchasing this book.

You may access the following additional **complementary chapters** provided for your use by visiting: www.wiley.com\go\mason\theinvestingoasis
(Password: Mason123)

- **The Case for a Planner/Advisor**
  - A Professional Backstop
  - Planner versus Advisor
  - Performing an Annual Assessment
  - Hiring a Planner and (or) an Advisor
  - Changing a Planner or an Advisor
  - Going DIY
- **Fees and Accountability**
  - Turnover Ratios
  - Calculating your Personal Turnover Ratio
  - Better Trading Practices
  - Behavioral Trading Buffers
  - Measuring your Value Proposition
- **Day Trading 2.0**
  - Capitalism 101
  - Core Management vs Day Trading
  - Dr. Jekyll and Mr. Hyde
  - An Old Game but with Guidelines
- **It's All About the Sell**
  - Selling Protocols
  - The Essence of Capitulation
  - Anger Management
  - Short Selling is Oversold

- **The Yin of Gold**
  - Gold as an Investment
  - Gold as a Hedge
  - Gold for Diversification
  - Gold as Protection
  - Gold as the Reserve Currency
  - Buying Gold at 20-30% Discount

Index

Page numbers followed by *f* and *t* refer to figures and tables, respectively.